Keys To A Sacred Place
By: J. Solomon Wise

Keys To A Sacred Place
Copyright © 2024 by J. Solomon Wise

ISBN: 979-8894790336 (sc)
ISBN: 979-8894790343 (e)

The Reading Glass Books
1-888-420-3050
www.readingglassbooks.com
fulfillment@readingglassbooks.com

Contents

Dedication:

This book is dedicated to Ethel Lee, my Mama. Without her, I would not be here. More importantly, without her lifelong, living example of many of the principles, laws, precepts and active daily examples of the proper way to walk in Christ's model example, I would not have acquired the insight, wisdom, and understanding to even be the vessel through whom God has poured these humble perspectives and insights! Ethel Lee was truly an awesome and profound example of a "Christ realized" individual and through her daily example, she touched the lives of the entire community we lived in and beyond! She did not pick up her spiritual walk on Sunday morning and put it down on Sunday evening. She lived her spiritual walk every day for all to see and be blessed from, just as Christ did! Her greater works were truly realized through her life!

It is my sincere hope that I have captured, in a fundamental and clear way, all of the lessons you have taught me Mama. It is also my most fervent and sincere prayer that I have also applied and lived these valuable spiritual principles, laws, precepts and examples in a manner that you are pleased and proud of! I hope I am "doing you proud" Mama because I clearly know I have no excuse not to understand all the wondrous things you taught me about living a life that is "Christ realized" and reflective of God in and through me! I promised you I would do everything I could to remind others of you in how I lived my life. When I made that promise, I eventually realized that the things I did that reflected you also reflected the spirit of God in you! I realize I have a way to go yet, but I promise I will continue to stay the course till the end. One of your most famous Biblical paraphrases to me was: "The race is not to the swift, nor strong, but to the one that perseveres till the end." (See Hebrews, Chapter 12, verse 1 for reference). So I am in this till the end! I LOVE YOU MAMA, today, tomorrow, and always!

Since man and woman's original "fall from grace", (Genesis Chapter 3, verse 17), we have all been on a quest to get back to the place of perfect, divine, complete communion and fellowship with God, our maker and progenitor. What man and woman have failed to realize and discover, in all of the eons and millenniums since that original breach of trust, is the pathway to that higher hallowed and sacred ground to God which they seek. Thus, in the lack of awareness and direction, they are infinitely away from God's all consuming, all loving, all powerful presence. There is an initial longing and thirst that man and woman have never quenched since this initial loss. Interestingly enough, God has never left, nor forsaken man and woman even from the very beginning; and have always been in the midst with an ever present, all gracious, caring love. So while man and woman have been infinitely away from that original place of perfection, they have also been infinitely close. God has never forsaken His most cherished creation. While God, from His omniscient perspective, can clearly recognize all things, man and woman have a viewpoint that is miniscule through which to get back to Him. In the recesses of our spirits and souls, each of us relate back to that original place of perfect, divine communion with God because God has never let man and woman forget that fateful moment of transgression. God planted that longing and thirst for a purpose. That initial longing and thirst is our saving grace. It is through that longing that, like a lost child seeks his Mother in a crowded room, we have the strength, passion, and motivation to strive for that which we have lost. God is and has always been a God of Love, Grace and Mercy. He knew from the inception of His creations the course, pattern, and history of His children from beginning to end. He has, and will always provide a means for finding that sacred place that man and woman lost in the very beginning. Countless examples throughout the annals of recorded history, and religious texts from every culture in the world, point to this truism and fact. The intent of the world's great prophets, sages, priest and priestesses, spiritual disciples, ministers, preachers, wise men and women, philosophers, artists, spiritual scholars and geniuses resonates with evidence. Those who are open-minded and inquisitive enough to seek Him, will see and understand, as they live this wondrous journey called life, that God has always left the keys to find that sacred place to Him.

There is a sacred temple wherein God resides. One of the many, many problems man and woman have faced since the dawn of that first breach from God, has been to identify simple, clear keys to understand how to access the temple. Christ stated in the Holy Scriptures in the book of Mark, Chapter 10, verse 15; "I tell you the truth, anyone who will not receive the kingdom of God like a little child will never enter it." Christ was referring to the confusion so-called great religious teachers and leaders of His times had created in understanding the pathway to God, (refer to Matthew, Chapter 23, verse 13). Christ issued warnings to the Pharisees for teaching laws of their times in such a complicated manner that the people could not find the spirit of God within their definition. Christ called them hypocrites because they were denying their people simple, clear direction for finding that sacred place where they could commune with God. Just as this was true then, it is even truer today in our world of information and technology overload. There are keys that we can use to find and understand the place where the temple exists. Once we understand where the temple exists, we can then begin to locate the place within the temple where perfect communion with God is possible. This book has one sole purpose in mind: "to provide simple, clear keys to God for each of you in your daily walk." I will use the Holy Bible as my primary reference because it is the tool from which most of my learning, meditations, and teachings have come. When I received understanding that my ministry was to write this and other works, the Lord laid on my heart that much of the confusion in reaching Him has come from not having simple clarity and truth of the Holy Word. He said to me, "The same way the world has been deceived through My Word, YOU shall be used to provide truth and guidance so my people can follow it with clarity." I do not claim to be a great man of the world; just a humble man with a willing spirit, heart, and mind for God to use for His greater good. I do not profess to have all of the answers as one lowly man of God and am constantly seeking more answers myself; however, I do profess a willingness and passion to seek and understand that which God has laid on my spirit for the benefit of those open-spirited enough to receive it. I do not accept, nor claim any of the credit for what anyone may get from my writings. All credit and things work for the greater good of God and to Him I give all Honor, Glory, and Praises!

The only thing I hope to claim is that which I wanted since I was a young boy: to be of benefit to my people. I determined as a child, after a discussion with my oldest brother and mentor, that my life's purpose was to leave something behind to benefit my people. As I grew into manhood, God told me one day, as I was reflecting back on my purpose, "You shall leave something behind to benefit your people my son, because your people are My people." So I ask that you read this humble text with an open spirit, heart, and mind. Meditate and process what has been channeled through this lowly person. As you do, do not be afraid to look inside yourself and listen for that soft, inner voice within. The Holy Spirit is a soft, quiet inner presence with a Profound, Omniscient insight. That inner presence and insight is unique and specific to everyone. Embrace the thoughts and leadings of this work that delight your heart and spirit. Do not trouble with the text that has no meaning for you because it probably was not meant for you, but someone else. The Word never returns void but always accomplishes the purpose for which it was intended. As stated in Isaiah, Chapter 55, verses 10 and 11, "So is my word that goes out from my mouth; it will not return empty."

Above all, let this humble work help you find the keys to that sacred place within each of you! As you do, you will realize that the sacred temple wherein God resides is within you. It is your responsibility to build that temple through applying the keys you so that it is perpetually sacred and worthy of God's constant communion. As you do, you will do the greater works Christ spoke of for those who follow after Him: "I tell you the truth, anyone who has faith in me will do what I have been doing. He will do even greater things than these, because I am going to the Father" (see John, Chapter 14, verse 12). May you have Godspeed, peace, wisdom, understanding, knowledge, and grace in your journey to your Sacred Place!

The Beginning

Chapter 1

All of this wondrous mystery we call "life" has a beginning. To begin towards the path of clarity, I have been led to start with one of our biggest misconceptions today. My oldest brother, one of my closest and most cherished spiritual mentors, led me to write about this misconception to you. We think of ourselves as a body with a spirit; however, we are not. We are a Spirit with a body! The Holy Bible has a number of references to this simple truth. Genesis Chapter 1, verse 1, Genesis Chapter 1, verse 26, 1st Corinthians, Chapter 6, verse 19, are several clear references. In Genesis, Chapter 1, verse 1, God is referred to as a "Spirit" that hovers over the face of the deep. Later in Genesis Chapter 1, verse 26, God states, "Let us make man in our own image." If God is a "Spirit" hovering over the face of the deep and states He is making "man" in His image, then God is also referring to making man a "Spirit" like Him. Let me ask a question. Have you ever lost a very close family member or friend to death? If so, what died? When my beloved, special, cherished Mama passed away, I pondered the mystery of her death for a long time. In my pondering, I realized when she passed away that all of her physical components were in tact. So, I asked in my meditations what was gone that she was no longer present. I finally realized that the "Spirit" of my Mama was what lived in her body and was now gone home to the Lord. After God decided to make man and woman, shaping them from clay, He blew His breath into them. This divine breath or "Spirit" is the essence of what gives us life and makes us who we are. When we die, our bodies eventually return to dust from whence it came. Hence, the old saying "Ashes to ashes, dust to dust" used ritually during funerals is accurate and true.

I hope you are now asking a question. Why is being a "spirit" with a body so important? It is important because until you recognize that, you may view life and it's pursuits as one to please just the body while totally overlooking the need to pursue and fulfill your spiritual needs and longings. Here's a simple analogy for you to consider. A car has all of the outwardly visible features: shiny new paint, doors, windows, tires, plush leather interior, deluxe sound system, and sporty new rims. However, the engine, which is not outwardly visible and beneath the hood, is what makes the car run and provide transportation. You cannot drive a car without taking care of the engine's needs. The engine, which is not visible unless the hood is opened, needs oil and gas to run. Without the engine running, the car cannot move. Once the engine is destroyed, the car's shiny appearance, doors, windows, tires, plush leather interior, deluxe sound system and sporty rims will not function. Some people take care of the outward appearance of their cars by waxing it, cleaning the interior, shining the tires, buying the sportiest rims, and best sound system that money can buy. However, they fail to keep the oil changed, or use good gasoline, and keep the engine serviced regularly. Their cars look great but have very limited function and life. Those that do all of the exterior maintenance as well as service their engine and keep it in perfect working order, have cars that last a lifetime. Granted, this is an oversimplified analogy of the spirit and the body of humans, but we must change our perspective of being a body with a spirit and realize we are far more: a spirit that is "kindred and part of" the essence of God, with a body. Then we must start looking at life from "within-without, not from without-within." As we seek to evaluate life from "within-without," we seek to understand our inner spiritual engine that drives our physical body and car. That begins us toward the journey to the sacred temple wherein the original source, God, resides.

There is an old saying I often heard in church as a child: "Man is born into the flesh and dies in the spirit." Once we have a clearer understanding of being a spirit in a body, that saying makes more sense. You see, before a child is born into this world, it is a part of God's spiritual realm. When God ordains and blesses a new birth, this child enters into a world as flesh having left the spirit realm where God is. Maybe that's why babies cry because they have to leave the presence of God. As adults, we do not fully know the minds of newborn babies. However, we do know that they are first conscious and aware of their physical needs: hunger, to be close to their parents, sleep, and be changed when they are wet. These physical needs are dominant during the formative stages of a baby's development into childhood. We are just dead to the awareness of ourselves spiritually because our physical needs are dominant during the early formative years of life. Thus, this old saying of being dead in the spirit is really just a metaphor because we are not literally dead in the spirit. Instead we are simply not focused on our spiritual essence as infants in the need to be nurtured physically. However, even when we are reborn into this physical world, we still become spirits in a body. Mama always told me babies and animals know good people and can see angels. I know this is a wise old saying, like many others we hear. Yet, many wise old sayings that have been passed down to us have sound spiritual founding and context. These old sayings have resulted from years of experience and analysis of life's issues. As babies and young children, they are more naturally open to their spiritual intuitions because they are closer to when they were purely spiritual before they were born into flesh. Babies recognizing good people and angels, is just a sign of the spiritual intuitiveness they are still naturally close to.

The path to God is a journey that progresses in steps and stages. Sometimes we take baby steps. At others, we take great leaps as we progress. At this point, these insights are in the infancy stage. All of this is important because as you mature from adolescence into adulthood, it is imperative that you start to acknowledge, recognize, and nurture the spirit within. The earlier you do this the better because you will grow stronger, fuller, faster, and more complete quicker. As long as you live and breathe on this earth, it is never too late to seek spiritual nourishment. Christ said, "Ask and it will be given unto you, seek and you will find, knock and the door will be opened unto you" (Matthew, Chapter 7, verse 7). In closing this insight, I'll pose one last question for your consideration. Are you seeking to know the spirit in you, or satisfying who you are physically?

Man and Woman in God's Image:

Once we are aware that we are a spirit in a body, then we can seek other initial understandings of how our Father and Creator, God, Yahweh, Allah, Jehovah, or any other supreme name you consider Him, made us in His image. Before I discuss these other understandings, I do want to take a moment to address, for the purpose of this work, God's name. The ancient Hebrew text that the Bible was originally written in used the primary name of Yahweh with various attributes attached to that name. The Islamic faith calls Him Allah the Benevolent. Other denominations have called Him Jehovah as well as other names. My comment to these differences is a question. How do you name Him that is ALL! Clearly, no one name, title, label, attribute, or characteristic can clearly define Him. He is All, EVERYTHING. God said to Moses in the book of Exodus, Chapter 3, verse 14, "I am that I am." No man or woman, culture, religious denomination, nation, or country has a name that truly identifies ALL He is. So, don't let your name for Him cause you to judge or alienate you from others. Instead of judging them based on what they call Him, get to know what they stand for in their understanding of Him. Seek to understand their principles and spiritual walks. Also be aware that the essence of WHO He is lies in how YOU display Him in your own life. I had to make this point because all too often, we judge and seek not to understand others because they use different names. Yet, God Himself said He is all, made all, and created all cultures, denominations, dialects, and languages. It is time we clearly seek to understand each other by the content of our spiritual walks, principles, and commitments. Not by the names we call Him. Also, get to know Him so intimately that you have a special name for Him. My special, intimate name for him is Father. I call Him Father during some of my most intimate prayers and discussions with Him. For the sake of this work, I will most often refer to Him as God because that is the name most recognized in my language, English. I recognize and acknowledge all names used in reverence, true commitment, and love to Him.

We are made in God's image from a three-dimensional perspective. We are three-dimensional because we have a mind, a spirit, and a body. This correlates to our Father and creator because He is also three-dimensional; God the Father, (Yahweh) is the mind, the Holy Spirit, (Eloheim), is the spirit, and Jesus Christ, (Yashuah), represents the body. From a spiritual perspective, we often get this confused when thinking about the Trinity. However, it is not so complicated to understand the Holy Trinity when we realize that our mind, body, and spirit are separate and different parts of who we are and serve different purposes to make us a whole person. The same is true of God, Christ, and the Holy Spirit being separate and different parts with different purposes, yet one whole God. Just as you cannot separate your mind, spirit, and body as a part of your whole self; there is also no separation of the whole aspect of God, the Holy Spirit, and Christ. Consider this: man and woman are the only creatures on this earth that God made in His image with a mind, spirit, and body, three-dimensionally, that correlates with His Mind, Spirit, and Body. This is far more significant than we realize because no other creature was set apart and made so special on the earth. Once we realize we are a spirit in a body and then to seek to grow and nurture that spirit and acknowledge who, and Whose we are, we begin to become more Christ-like. Just as Christ sacrificed His body for our saving grace, we begin the process of sacrificing our carnal bodies once we acknowledge the need to conform our spirits to the Holy Trinity. Thus our carnal bodies become the sacrifice for kindred ness with God the Father, the Holy Spirit, and Christ.

We also begin to transform the mind through the nourishing of the spirit. Then we are on our way to locating the sacred place within to restore communion with God that we so desperately seek! This transformation of the mind is what the Apostle Paul was referring to in the book of Romans, Chapter 12, verse 2 when he stated, "Be ye not conformed but be ye transformed by the renewing of your mind and spirit." We cannot begin the process of transformation without first recognizing we are a spirit with a body. Once we acknowledge that, we then seek to accept Whose, (God's children), we are and

5

after Whom, (Christ), we will pattern ourselves. Through this desire, our carnal bodies and minds can be transformed by God, the Holy Spirit, and Christ because we open ourselves up to every dimension, (spirit, mind, and body), to be transformed. Through this initial step of willingness, we begin to search for the keys to our sacred place. This is just the beginning, but a very important beginning. Now, our spirits are open to hear that quiet, inner voice of the Holy Spirit as it speaks to our hearts and minds about the choices and decisions we make every day in life. First Corinthians, Chapter 1, verses 10 through 12 state, "God reveals to us through His Spirit and the Spirit searches all things." When that inner, quiet, Holy Spirit voice speaks to you about life's decisions and choices, is it true that the Holy Spirit has sought understanding on your behalf about those decisions and choices? Yes, He has!

Spiritual Nourishment

In life some things are far more natural than others. Physical nourishment comes naturally because we begin the process of physical nourishment before we do anything else. As infants, our parents begin to nurture us, first physically, then mentally, immediately upon our birth. It is important to understand physical nourishment of the body and mind. Our physical body will not sustain itself without receiving certain dietary staples. It is also essential to exercise and get proper rest along with proper eating habits. The mind begins to be shaped and formed at infancy as well. The development of the body and brain depends largely on proper nutrition, stimulation, and nourishment. As infants, we begin to learn how to talk, reason, understand our surroundings, and communicate with our family members. These early mental exercises shape and mold our mental capacity as we are given the proper nutrition and stimulation by our parents so our brains are properly developed. Since it is now apparent that we are spirit, mind, and body that leads to the following question; how do we nourish the spirit?

Since man and woman fell from grace in the beginning, where they were perfectly and fully nourished in all ways because they had direct communion with God; looking at this age-old question from their perspective provides valuable insight. We once had complete awareness of the spirit equal to our awareness of our physical existence. We also had complete access to spiritual nourishment. The means of nourishment of the spirit changed forever once Adam and Eve lost that intimate, direct fellowship with God through their fall from grace. When they fell from grace, their physical natures became more natural and dominant. It is not by chance then, that man and woman, throughout the ages, have found physical and mental needs and focus as their natural order while their inner spiritual needs lay buried and hidden in a sacred location waiting to be discovered.

Allow me to paint a quick picture for you and ask you to visualize it. Can you visualize being the original man and woman, Adam and Eve, in the Garden of Eden where you were conceived? You are in a place of the most awesome natural beauty, color, and wonder the world has ever and will ever know again. Not only are the physical surroundings tremendously beautiful in every way, this place is also perfect in every environmental way for you to sustain perfect physical conditioning. Every edible thing you need to sustain perfect health is there for you because God said in Genesis, Chapter 2, verse 16, "man could eat of any fruit in the garden for nourishment except the Tree of Knowledge of Good and Evil." Every mental need is provided as well because you have authority and dominion over all life; animals, creatures, plants, flowers, and land. You exercise your mind in ruling your paradise. Since every conceivable physical and mental need is already addressed, your dominant focus is your spiritual fellowship and communion with God! The Bible clearly states that God came down and communed with Adam and Eve directly because He delighted in man and woman above all of His creation. If every possible physical and mental need were addressed, can you see why you would not have to focus on anything except spiritual nourishment?

The rest of the story of Adam and Eve is clear. They ate of the forbidden fruit in the midst of the Garden of Eden and fell from God's grace. What has not been clear is this: in falling from God's grace, man and woman lost direct spiritual fellowship with God.

7

When we did, we lost our spiritual focus and physical wants, desires, and needs became dominant. God saw Adam and Eve choose "that which is physical" in eating of the forbidden fruit, over spiritual communion with Him. So He charged woman with physical pain during labor, (see Genesis, Chapter 3, Verse 16). He charged man with physical labor to sustain his physical needs, (see Genesis Chapter 3, Verse 17). In making these charges, God knew man and woman would have to deal with physical and mental needs as their dominant focus. Knowing that there was still a spirit within man and woman, God still left a means for them to reach Him through seeking spiritual nourishment.

We are reminded and charged to seek spiritual nourishment in a number of places throughout our great philosophical and spiritual texts around the world. In the Holy Bible in the book of Deuteronomy, Chapter 8, Verse 3 we are told, "Man shall not live by bread alone but by every word that proceeded out of the mouth of God." Christ also made reference to man's need for spiritual sustenance when Satan tempted Him by stating, "It is written: man does not live by bread alone but on every word that comes from the mouth of God," (Matthew, Chapter 4, Verse 4). So while God oriented us towards meeting physical and mental demands after that original fall from grace, He still intends for us to have nourishment of the spirit and renewed communion with Him. Let's get to the heart of the matter, nourishing the spirit. Now that we are aware that we are a "spirit in a body," we can seek to find nourishment.

It may sound simple, but awareness of the spirit is the first step. Just as your stomach growls or you get a headache when you are hungry, you must first have awareness of your spirit to know that your spirit hungers for sustenance. Your physical body and mind do not give you the strong warnings of the need to nourish the spirit that it provides for physical and mental hunger. Spiritual hunger is far more subtle than any physical cravings you may have. One thing I find very curious is how God is all-powerful yet His presence, through the Holy Spirit, comes as a soft, meek whisper. If man were God with all of that power, he would make sure his spiritual hunger was expressed so loudly that it would obliterate any other types of hunger! From the very beginning, God gave man and woman the freedom to choose. That is partly why He comes as a quiet whisper. That way, God does not impose His voice over the voice of your own thoughts. It is because of His great love for us that God did not make man and woman follow after instinctive behavior as animals do, but gave us the ability to reason and choose. If you were all-powerful and all-knowing, as God is, why would you need to shout or express with tremendous force? After all, He knows He has all power and authority and waits for us to realize it without having to prove anything to us. When we reach that self-awareness, we willingly seek after spiritual nourishment and no other form of nourishment can replace it.

Where do we start to feed the spirit? We start by analyzing our spiritual environment. Your spiritual environment is initially developed, defined, and dictated by your parents. The parents provide their children all physical, mental, and spiritual development in their early years. Parents clothe, feed, shelter, and educate their children. They also generally have some form of religious worship they teach their children. This is, was, and has always been true the world over since man and woman's original separation from God. Because the world is so diverse in languages and cultures, men and women have had difficulty recognizing within other cultures their spiritual environment and simple truths. Our limited view of our culture's spiritual environment and truths as the only way is a topic I will address later on. Our first chance to receive food for our spirits is established by our parents before we have a chance to seek it on our own. Other family members, friends, our local community, and society at large also influence our spiritual environment. In today's world, the community at large is larger and far more influential than it has been in many, many generations because views are communicated globally far more quickly than ever before.

I am not sure at what stage in a child's life he begins to reason, but I am sure it is at a very early age. One thing I am fairly certain of is he begins, just as we have been oriented to do as adults, by reasoning after physical needs. A baby cries for affection from its mother when he is hungry for food. Even though babies are not aware of it, they are reasoning. They begin to use their minds naturally because they quickly realize that every time they cry, they get attention and nourishment from their mother. Therefore, your initial spiritual environment, religious affiliation, religious habits, spiritual principles and morals, and how these principles and morals are accepted by the world around you, are already in place by the time you begin to reason with, and seek to understand it. Since it is already established, your first step towards spiritual nourishment is to analyze and understand the spiritual environment that is already in place. Just as the baby learns to reason and understand how to get affection and nourishment, you must analyze and understand your spiritual environment in order to find what nourishes your spirit. Why is analysis so important? It is important because your spiritual needs, while very similar to your pre-established spiritual environment are still different, unique and specific to you. There are often many things present that are essential. There are also many things that are non-essential. You must be about eliminating the non-essential things from your spiritual diet and supplementing your spiritual diet with those very essential things you need for nourishment. A good analogy for comparison is your physical dietary needs, because they change from infancy to adolescence, and often change again from adolescence to adulthood. The same thing is true with your spiritual dietary needs. The initial pre-established spiritual environment is your foundation. Once you understand the foundation and are ready to build upon it, it is your responsibility to begin adding and taking away the things that serve your unique, specific needs.

How do you analyze your spiritual environment? Analysis begins with observation. In order to understand, we must observe. As children, we are told that the fire is hot. We are then offered the chance to see it heat and burn. Once we observe it burn, then we realize it is hot. Whatever religious affiliations, habits, principles, and morals you are given in your spiritual environment, observe them to see if they are consistent and true in the actions enforced in daily life decisions and choices. Consistent and true habits, principles, and morals should always produce consistent and true decisions and choices. The Holy Spirit told me this during my meditations on spiritual laws and principles: "The laws work the same every time." What that means is God's divine spiritual laws, principles, morals, and precepts work, HAVE ALWAYS worked, and WILL ALWAYS work infinitely through all of time! It is not God's divine laws that change. It is our consistent application of them, that changes! Think of it this way. In mathematics, an equation will only be correct when the proper variables are plugged into it. One plus one was, is, and always will be two. Once you begin to analyze your spiritual environment, you will begin to see the truths within it. One thing about truth is that we are blessed, as young children, with the ability to recognize it. Children are brutally honest about what they see and observe. In observing your spiritual environment, be open and child-like to seeking and seeing the truth behind the habits, practices, morals, principles, and actions that result from them. Once you observe, you begin to understand, reason, and ask questions about what you observe. Then, you are beginning to seek. Seeking is a good thing! Seeking delights the spirit because once you begin seeking, you open your mind and body to hearing the Holy Spirit. In opening up, you position yourself to hear and receive. As you observe, ask, and reason, you also have the chance to see the outcome of the actions behind what you are observing. Your spiritual environment should be measured through its actions. The book of Hebrews, Chapter 4, Verse 12 states, "For the word of God is living and active, sharper than a two-edged sword, it penetrates even to dividing soul and spirit, joints and marrow; it judges the thoughts and attitudes of the heart." In continuing to observe, ask, and reason, you begin to understand the message, (words), behind your pre-established spiritual environment. Once you understand these words, doctrines, principles, morals, and precepts, you can then measure the consistency of truth behind them through the outcome of the actions and decisions that result from applying them. The words, doctrines, principles, morals, and precepts of your spiritual environment are the expression of your faith. As the Holy Bible says in James, Chapter 2, Verse 26, "As the body without the spirit is dead, so faith without works is dead."

How do you know what to add and what to eliminate from your diet? The process of adding to and eliminating things from our spiritual diet relies heavily on analysis, introspection, observation, and application. Once you have begun to seek, ask, observe, and understand the principles and actions of your spiritual environment, you have the foundation upon which to practice application. For example, a key part of good physical health, whether eating or conditioning, relies on application. We try different foods or exercise regimens until we find the ones that are best for us. You must try, as the old saying goes, "practicing what is preached" in order to know if it works. In most cultures all over the world, there is a version of what we call the Ten Commandments. For example, in the ancient Kemetian, (Egyptian) culture, they had what was called The 47 Negative Confessions. In order to accept these commandments as part of your faith, you must apply them. You apply them daily by doing the acts and deeds that support their principles. If you believe in honoring your father and mother, then you must not do any act or deed contrary to honoring them. You must be respectful patient, supportive, and obedient to their requests. Application is a means by which we increase our spiritual understanding, and we grow and develop as we increase our understanding.

Just as you apply and try as you observe and analyze, you must also learn what not to apply. It is just as important to know what not to do as it is to know what to do. If things in your spiritual environment do not pass the test of truth in your spirit, or through the outcome of the actions once you have tried them, do not add them to your spiritual diet. The holier-than-thou attitudes of the Pharisees Christ spoke of are a good example of an attitude not to add to your spiritual environment. We have all met or know people who are always criticizing everybody's spiritual walk and finding fault in everyone else except them or their own family. Observation, analysis, and seeking, provides insight and understanding which does bring about judgements. However, the judgement should be from "within-without," (about you). There's that phrase, "within-without" surfacing again. I'll explain it. Judging should be a process of self-analysis. You should be about judging your thoughts, actions, deeds, feelings, strengths, and weaknesses as you attempt to nourish yourself spiritually. Christ makes reference to self analysis in the Holy scriptures in the book of John, Chapter 8, Verse 7, "If any one of you is without sin, let him be the first to stone her" in reference to the Pharisee's judgement to stone a woman caught committing adultery. Christ was not condoning adultery. He was merely challenging the Jewish leaders not to judge too harshly one who had sinned because all sin and fall short of God's laws, precepts, and principles. No one stoned the woman because they had to search their own sins and realized they were not sinless. You will find that if we seek to judge ourselves from within-without, we will incline ourselves to the soft, inner voice of the Holy Spirit and find continued guidance, understanding, conviction, and direction for ongoing nourishment and development. Through this inner guidance of the Holy Spirit, we learn what to add and remove from our spiritual diet. There is a very important question you must ask. Can you look within, or would you rather look at the actions, faults, and challenges of others instead?

Self-awareness, self-understanding, and self actualization are important for continued development, growth, and added sustenance to your spiritual nourishment. Self-awareness, self-understanding, and self-actualization only come through looking at, analyzing and understanding YOU! Although the main focus of this work is geared towards what is most mis-understood and neglected, (the spirit), I must emphasize that each aspect of our person, spirit, mind, and body, are co-dependent upon the other. You must be about seeking, analyzing, and understanding in every dimension, (spirit, mind, and body). However, you now understand and accept that you are a spirit in a body with a mind. You now understand that getting back to that hallowed and sacred place where fellowship and communion with God is possible. You will have to re-orient yourself to let the spirit become the dominant part of your being again as it was in the very beginning when God created Adam and Eve. We can now move from beginnings toward foundation.

Now is a good time to tie a few things together by providing some helpful recaps. I call these recaps my "Simple Truisms".

Chapter 1 – Beginning Truisms:

You are a spirit in a body, not a body with a spirit. Start thinking about life within-without, (from your inner spirit and not just based on physicals desires, wants, and needs.

Since you are born into a physically dominant body, your natural inclinations will be more physical than spiritual until you realize the need to seek spiritual nourishment. Once you realize the need to nurture your inner spirit, you will need to commit your life to being spiritual by accepting a relationship with the Holy Trinity, (God the Father, the Holy Spirit, and Christ) in the way God has been revealed to you.

You are made in God's image as spirit, mind, and body, (with the Holy Spirit representing the spirit, God representing the mind, and Christ representing the body). Your spirit, mind, and body make you a whole, three-dimensional person, and each part of you has a purpose. Each part of the Holy Trinity, God, the Holy Spirit, and Christ is a part of the whole, and has a purpose as well.

Once you have made that commitment, you begin the process of transforming into a more Christ-like person because the Holy Spirit starts to counsel and speak to your spirit about life's challenges and choices.

It is not by chance that man and woman are physically dominant because Adam and Eve chose physical over spiritual in their original fall from grace. After that decision their existence depended on physical labor and mental development to sustain them. However, God did not remove His presence, nor man and woman's spirit through which to reconnect to Him.

Just as the body begins to develop physically and mentally, it also begins to develop spiritually through our pre-established spiritual environment. This development is not dominant because we are oriented towards physical and mental development first.

While the body has very strong, dominant physical signals, spiritual signals are much more subtle. It is very easy to overlook them, not be aware of them, or have them suppressed and buried beneath physically strong signals.

Your initial spiritual environment, (religious affiliations, culture, principles, morals, precepts, words, and faith), are pre-established by your parents, family, surrounding community, and society at large. It is the beginning of spiritual nurturing and nourishment.

In order to receive spiritual nourishment, you first have to realize your spirit is a part of you, along with your mind and body. Then you can begin to seek out what will nourish that part of you.

You must analyze your pre-established spiritual environment. This analysis is done through observing, asking, and comparing the principles, morals, precepts, words, and actions applied to demonstrate them. You are looking for the truth behind them and truth is naturally recognized at an early age.

From observation and analysis, come growth, development, and understanding. As you grow, develop, and understand, you begin to shape and mold your spiritual diet and foundation. Shaping and molding your diet involves adding and removing things from your diet that improve growth and maturity.

You add things for your spiritual nourishment by trying to apply the principles, morals, precepts, and words to your day to day actions and works. It is just as important to analyze what not to add as well.

Seeking and acquiring spiritual nourishment is a within-without process. It begins by self analysis of your thoughts, actions, deeds, strengths, and weaknesses. It also allows you to incline your spirit to the Holy Spirit, Who provides guidance, conviction, counseling, direction, and understanding. Now you begin to hear and listen to that small, quiet, inner voice of the Holy Spirit.

Judge your own actions, thoughts, and deeds, not the actions, thoughts, and deeds of others. As you do, you will find that your actions will minister or guide others toward their own judgment and analysis of their actions. Then, you are on your way to sustaining, feeding, developing, and orienting your life back towards the spirit in you and the sacred place within where God resides.

Chapter 1 "The Beginning" Workbook

It is my hope that you have already gained some insight and clarity into better understanding YOU. These simple questions in the workbook section are designed to further that understanding

Question 1:
How does being a spirit with a body change your view of life as opposed to thinking that you are a body with a spirit?
Thoughts, Insights, and Reflections:

Question 1-Thoughts, Insights, and Reflections

Question(s) 2:
Once you become spiritually realized and aware, how do you seek nurturing? What can you draw from your life's experiences to this point to help you identify what that nurturing consists of? What can you draw from your spiritual environment to assist in this process?
Thoughts, Insights, and Reflections:

Question(s) 2-Thoughts, Insights, and Reflections

Question(s) 3:

Can you truly focus on, through introspection your own self-development, awareness, understanding, and actualization? Can you also use your continued insights, understandings, knowledge, and wisdom to have the compassion to give to others whom you meet along the way to your spiritual reorientation? How?

Thoughts, Insights, and Reflections:

Question(s) 3-Thoughts, Insights, and Reflections

Question 4:
What other personal perspectives and understandings have you gained from this chapter?
Thoughts, Insights, and Reflections:

Question 4-Thoughts, Insights and Reflections

Foundation and Fundamentals

Chapter 2

I know I have thrown a lot of information at you and I pray it has provided the clarity, enlightenment, insight, understanding, and guidance it was intended to. Moreover, I hope it is simple and clear. If it has any degree of profoundness in it, I give all credit to the Father who has chosen this humble person through whom to deliver and express the thoughts, directions, and meditations. I also hope you see my profoundness as a reflection, or confirmation, of God working through me; and also a response to some of the simple day-to-day ponderings you have had as you seek to understand this mystery we call life. I have found, in my daily spiritual walk that one of God's greatest blessings is allowing me to realize and receive divine revelations as I grow. In reaching those understandings and revelations, I usually realize how simply profound they are afterwards. They are one of God's many signatures and ways He differentiates Himself from man and woman. It is my hope that you agree and find some divine revelations of your own that will enhance your growth as well throughout this work. I ask of you one thing as you read this book: think and process what you read. As you think and process, seek to open your mind to new perspectives as you encounter a divine revelation you were not aware of. God's divine revelations have a way of changing perspectives and bringing a much fuller broader, complete meaning as you open up to them. These divine revelations are the hidden keys to that sacred place you are seeking. In time, you will mature enough to use them appropriately to have access to the Sacred Temple where God patiently waits to renew his intimate relationship with YOU. The Sacred Temple is always there, but just like a mathematical equation is incorrect when the wrong formula is used, His Sacred Temple is inaccessible until the proper keys are maturely, reverently, and consistently used.

It is time to add foundation and fundamentals to your beginning point. I shall start by telling you who God sees you as and ask you to really think about it. It is my hope in telling you that you will accept the awesome responsibility of becoming and being, to the best and fullest of your capacity, what He sees you as. As the Holy Scriptures say in the book of Proverbs, Chapter 5, verse 2, "To whom much is given, much is required." It is also my hope that you will realize just how tremendously "much" you have been given when you understand how God has defined you. If you do, you will take your own personal requirements and charge seriously with a new passion, dedication, and commitment. It is difficult to confine how God defines us to one definition. There are many, many ways He sees and defines us. However, in relation to providing one of the keys needed in accessing your sacred place, a spiritual definition is the most critical one to provide. God defines you in the Holy Bible in the book of 1st Peter, Chapter 2, verse 8, "But you are a chosen people, a royal priesthood, a holy nation, a people belonging to God, that you may declare the praises of Him who called you out of darkness into His wonderful light." God sees you as "a chosen people, a royal priesthood." If each of you are priests and priestesses, then how should you define yourself, your life, and purpose? As you think, meditate, pray, and process the following foundation and fundamentals for continued spiritual progression, think of how you can apply them to, "the you," God has defined.

The foundations and fundamentals are basic spiritual principles. A good way to think of them is that they are the cornerstones of the new spiritual environment you are building. Now that you have had a perspective shift from seeing yourself as a body with a spirit to a spirit that's in a body, you have already begun to seek proper nourishment for your spirit as well. By now, you have examined your pre-established spiritual environment, (or at least you are beginning to examine it). Through your ongoing observations and analysis, you have added certain existing staples to your diet that were already established, and eliminated others that were of no value to your specific development. Now you are ready to add a solid foundation of principles to the spiritual environment you have.

1st Principle: "Our Lives Are A Ministry"

I was led to share with you how God defines you from a spiritual perspective for a reason. If He sees us as chosen, set apart, and a royal priesthood, what does that mean in terms of our roles as we experience this awesome event called "life"? One of our common misconceptions is that only ordained, educated, trained Pastors, Preachers, Ministers, or whatever other labels you use to describe church leaders, are the only ones who minister to the world. I am not taking anything away from the significant role these leaders have because God has given them a special calling, purpose, and mission. However, I do want you to realize that if you are earnestly seeking to walk a spiritual walk and are committed to being a Christ-like example to others, then whether you realize it or not, your life is also a ministry. Your actions, reactions, expressions, behaviors, spiritual platform, (what you say and how you define your spiritual beliefs), are all under observation by everyone you meet in your day to day life. Whether you choose to minister, or choose not to, the outcome is still the same. Often by not choosing to minister, we make or fail to make the impressions on others for the sake of who we are, and (WHO"S we are, God's) that we desire. Others will know you based on your action, or inaction, and take an impression away either way. Christ explained it in the Bible using an analogy about fruit trees in the book of Mathew, Chapter 7, verse 17 when he stated, "In the same way, every good tree bears good fruit but every bad tree bears bad fruit. Ask yourself the following questions. Are others taking away a good impression, (good fruit), or bad impression, (bad fruit), from their interactions with you? Are the impressions they take away the one, (be it good or bad), that you stand for and want them to have? However, it gets deeper than that. Once you acknowledge you are a spirit in a body, accept and seek a spiritual relationship with God, the Holy Spirit, and Christ, take the responsibility to seek after spiritual knowledge, growth, nourishment, maturation, and works; then you are set apart as God said. In being set apart, all that you do is set apart from a world around you that is still physically oriented. Being set apart, you are now more Christ-like because you are a three-dimensional, (spirit, mind, and body) person operating in a world that is one dimensional, (physically oriented). Have you ever wondered why you seem peculiar to others when you are seeking to walk a spiritual walk? That is why! As we become three-dimensional, our spirits, under communion, guidance, and connection with God, Christ, and the Holy Spirit, begin to transform our minds and bodies. We are becoming re-oriented to a spiritually dominant, instead of a physically dominant person. If you are no longer dominated by your physical urges and desires, but in a world that is dominated by physical urges and desires, then it is no wonder that you are peculiar to the world!

Now that you realize your life is a ministry, how will you change the way you view the choices you make and the actions you take in dealing with others? Hopefully, you will realize just how critically important it is to espouse, stand firm, act on, and react to others in a manner that reflects clearly what you stand for spiritually. You will also view your own life from, (here comes that phrase again), within-without. You will always think on, meditate on, and listen for the conscious and voice of the Holy Spirit when living your daily life to guide you toward the proper direction for continued growth, understanding, and wisdom to make sure you minister to others in a responsible way. You do not have to be perfect for your ministry to be of benefit and blessing to others. If that were true, why did so many great people throughout the recorded history of time, and in the Bible, have human flaws? One of the Bible's greatest figures, David, was described as having God's heart. He was well loved by God. He achieved great, great things and is credited with writing Psalms, one of the most inspirational works of the Bible. David is also credited as being the ancestor through whom Christ was later born. Solomon is another excellent example. He was considered one of he wisest men to ever live. He was also one of the richest. However, both Solomon and David loved women outside of their spiritual faith. Even though they had to account personally for their flaws, they were both still very instrumental in benefiting their people of their times through their ministries. Don't be deceived into thinking you are not good enough to help others as you seek to understand your own personal battles. In fact, you will discover that your own battles are needed to help you relate to and empathize with others seeking to overcome the same challenges in their lives. Or, God allows you to serve as a mentor or example to others going through the same battle by their observation of your actions and decisions in overcoming your struggles. You can also nourish and uplift others through providing insight, guidance, testimonials of your own personal experiences, and support as they face personal challenges and battles they are fighting that you have already overcome. You do not have to be perfect. You just have to be willing and open to being of use! You must also have the desire to give of yourself that which you have to benefit those in need. The key of ministry opens the door into your sacred place. It also returns to you what you need to continue getting you closer to the sacred temple because you are giving others what they need. It is a cycle that is continual and perpetual.

Principle 2: "We Must Re-Orient Ourselves From Physical Consciousness To Spiritual Consciousness"

In Chapter 1, I spent time presenting the ties between Adam and Eve's original fall from grace and how man and woman became more physically focused. It is now time to dig deeper so you better understand the struggles of this journey called life that results as we seek spiritual nourishment, growth, and maturity.

With the dawning of your new spiritual awakening comes rebellion! Think of it this way. If you starve the body of food, it rebels by breaking down your organs and tissues to nourish it. As it does, it pushes you towards self destruction until you provide food. By comparison, a world that is dominated by satisfying physical wants, desires, and cravings, rebels when we seek to orient ourselves toward spiritual wants, desires, and needs. In the Bible in the book of 1st John, Chapter 2, verse 16, it is stated: "For everything in the world, the cravings of sinful man, the lusts of the eyes and the boasting of what he has and does—comes not from the Father, but from the world." Before we even begin to concern ourselves with worldly rebellion, we must begin fighting our own internal rebellions of our bodies and minds. Since we are born naturally oriented towards a physically dominant focus, we grow comfortable and accustomed to meeting our physical wants, desires, and cravings. At some point, we also govern our mental processes around those physically dominant needs as well. Now, our bodies and minds work to fulfill our physical cravings for food, shelter, clothing, material possessions, sex, etc… Isn't it interesting that our world centers everything on satisfying our physical needs? The most dominant themes for reaching us through televisions, radio, and printed ads are sex, money, or material gain. These same worldly themes have been around as a challenge for man and woman since that fateful fall from grace and will always be present.

Therefore the first battle of rebellion starts within us. We must start there because until we begin to conquer those inner physical rebellions, there is no way we can fight the larger war around us in the world. If a person develops a physical dependence on alcohol and realizes it is a problem, he must start by fighting the chemical dependence within him to overcome his physical dependence. Fighting this chemical dependence begins in his own home environment. He may remove the alcohol from his home, change his diet to exclude drinks with meals, and stop having parties with alcohol at his home. The inner battle is just beginning. Because there is a chemical dependence, the body and mind react to that dependence. The physical body will go through a number of changes. It begins to experience shakes, loss of appetite, delusions, mood swings, and strong cravings for alcohol. Mentally, the person also begins to have nightmares, see illusions, and rationalize that it is okay to cut down on the drinking instead of stopping altogether. The world around him is an even larger battle zone because advertisements, movies, sporting events, business social events, and social events hosted by friends and family members all glorify the joy, fun, and excitement of drinking. The worldly rebellion is thus more enticing, glamorized, continually present, and subtle. It wears on you unconsciously because it is ever present to remind you all of the good things you are missing out on in a fun way. Just because we grow, seek, and long for spiritual nourishment as we mature, it does not mean we will not have physical and mental battles along the way. Yet, as with all warfare, if we understand the enemy, the enemy's strategy and attack plan, we can devise our own counter measures, tactics, and strategies to overcome and succeed. Plan to confront and face your inner rebellions. Also, realize that those rebellions are forged around physical wants and desires, (material possessions, basic physical desires for sex, food, pleasure, and social recreation). You will probably have mental rebellions to conquer that have developed through meeting your physical wants and desires. If you have money or status, you may have a mental desire to have more money and status, or take possession of all of the material trappings that go along with having money and status. If you are in the limelight because you are a professional athlete, successful businessperson, important political figure, corporate executive, movie star, religious leader in the community, etc., then you are prone to rebellions of a mental nature. Chances are you have already grown very accustomed to all of the physical trappings that go along with your station in life.

Re-orientation towards being spiritually led is an ongoing process. With the process comes struggles, challenges, and adversities. Through these struggles, challenges, and adversities, we gain strength, wisdom, knowledge, faith, and maturity. Do you remember the first time you learned something new that was difficult? I am sure you struggled a great deal during the process of learning. When you did learn it successfully, you were able to look back and learn from the struggles, challenges, and adversities you endured along the way. In the end, you were stronger, wiser, more knowledgeable, confident, and had faith that you could do what you learned. Now you know how to successfully do what you have learned, you can also teach someone else how to do it. You are mature. Don't let the struggles, challenges, and adversities of your spiritual re-orientation discourage you. Let them serve as increased strength, wisdom, knowledge, and motivation that you are getting closer to your outcome.

31

I'll refer to Mama, my most influential spiritual mentor, by referring once again to her most memorable spiritual paraphrase that she stated to me most often, "Son, the race is not to the swift, nor the strong, but to the one who perseveres until the end." Her use of this quotation was constant reminder when I struggled to master a difficult task as a child. It sustained me, and gave me the strength, motivation, patience, and maturity to keep striving in times of my greatest struggles, challenges, and adversities. This quotation is based upon Biblical Scripture in the book of Hebrews, Chapter 12, verse 1, and actually states; "Therefore, since we are surrounded by such a great cloud of witnesses, let us throw off everything that hinders and the sin that so easily entangles and let us run with perseverance the race marked out for us." Let your struggles, challenges, and adversities also provide renewed hope as you overcome them. Your successes are a sign of progress and the future successes you will have over future struggles, challenges, and adversities as long as you persevere and remain faithful to your spiritual convictions to continue the journey.

Self-analysis, self-awareness, and self-actualization are important to understanding and growing through your struggles, challenges, and adversities in re-orienting to a spiritually dominant person. These three tools, (self-analysis, self-awareness, and self-actualization), are the key tools for looking from within-without. Until you analyze self, you can have no self-understanding. Self-understanding consists of understanding your physical, mental, and spiritual characteristics, strengths and weaknesses, and areas for development. Without self-understanding, you can have no self-awareness. Self-awareness consists of understanding and defining your life's meaning, ministry, philosophies, and purpose as you acquire self-understanding. Without self-awareness, you have no self-actualization. Self-actualization consists of knowing who you are, what you stand for, Who (God), you stand for, and how you will realize and bring to fruition your God given purpose for your life. By opening your spirit, heart, and mind to the guidance, counsel, conviction, and leading of the Holy Spirit, you enter the doorway to your sacred place. Thus, your spiritual re-orientation begins to accelerate on a more mature level with the least amount of resistance.

3rd Principle: "Thoughts, Words, And Expressions Are Things"

Have you ever thought or spoken something that came to fruition that day, week, month, or year? Here's a scripture for you to consider. The book of John, Chapter 1, verse 1 states, "In the beginning was the Word and the Word was with God and the Word was God." If that is true, then before every creation in the heavens and earth came to fruition, God spoke! If you will notice in the book of Genesis which details the creation, it is also apparent. In Genesis, Chapter 1, verse 3, God said, "Let there be light" and the light became. God's spoken commands continued until all of heaven and earth were complete. When Jesus Christ lived, He also spoke the many, many wonders and miracles into fruition that were witnessed by His disciples, the Jews, and Gentiles. As with God the Father, Christ understood this: thoughts, words, and expressions are things called from the spiritual realm into the physical realm. It is not by chance that you may have a thought of someone and in a short time, you either see them in person in your daily travels or they call you some time after you thought about them. You probably even said to them, "I was just thinking about you." It is also not by chance that you may have an idea or dream you wanted to realize, you may have even expressed your idea or dream to a close friend or loved one, and saw this idea or dream come into being at a later point in your life. Let me see if I can get you thinking a little deeper. Why is it if thoughts, words, and expressions are things that we do not have the power to make our thoughts, words, and expressions manifest instantly as God does? My theory is this: the more spiritually mature and Christ-like we become, the more instantaneous our ability becomes to manifest what we speak! Our ability to manifest that thought, word, or expression at all is only a spiritual clue for us to find as we begin to grow and mature. Another way to think of it is that as a child of your parents, you probably have certain physical characteristics that resemble your mother or father, or maybe both of them. The ideas, words, and expressions that come into fruition for us are the spiritual characteristics that show our spirit within of our resemblance to God, our Spiritual Parent.

Now that you understand that thoughts, words, and expressions are things, let's go even deeper. Thoughts, words, and expressions can be good or bad. Just as we can think good things and bring about positive blessings on our lives and manifest positive realities, we can also think bad things and bring about negative outcomes and negative realities. More importantly, we can either bless or curse others through speaking and thinking good things about them or bad things about them. I am sure if you reflect back on your past, you can think of a time when you thought something bad about a situation or had a negative expectation about something you had to do, but were afraid you could not accomplish it. I am sure you saw that bad thought come to pass or did not achieve what you had to do just as you feared you would not. The point I want to put special emphasis on is it is very important to focus your thoughts, words, and expressions towards that which is positive, good, and beneficial, for you, and especially for others. Focus is very important for your thoughts, words, and expressions because without focus, there is no structure or order. Where there is a lack of structure and order, there is chaos and confusion. Where there is chaos and confusion, there is room for others and things outside your mind to control what you think and express. Here's a quick example. When the media reports something as fact, do you just accept it as fact, or do you think and analyze to validate it as fact or not? If you accept it, chances are you will at some point repeat what the media has reported as fact to someone else. Then, you have perpetuated what has been reported as fact to someone else. Not only do you report it as a fact to others, but often, you speak it as your own and thus it becomes a reflection of your perspective or beliefs. That is okay if the fact you heard was validated and true to something you believe in or ascribe to. What if it is actually diametrically opposed to the value or belief you stand for? Don't forget, the world outside us is in rebellion to, and with us, from a spiritual standpoint. Therefore, we must be careful how we accept what we hear and what we receive from it. We must focus our thoughts through careful analysis and within-without thinking. Otherwise, we can very easily take in values and beliefs that do not agree with what we stand for or that are counter productive to our continual spiritual growth and maturation. I'll leave you with one last question on this subject to consider: do your thoughts control you or do you control your thoughts?

How does a three-dimensional nature, (body, mind, and spirit), impact what we think, express, and manifest? Until you become spiritually re-oriented, (spirit, mind and body), your thoughts, words, and expressions are physically oriented. Because you are naturally physically dominant, you are also naturally inclined to think and mentally process things that satisfy physical wants, desires, and needs. As a baby, you think of and long for food, warmth, and attention. As a child, you think about things that are fun and pleasing your parents to get their attention. As you become a teenager, you think about being liked by your peers and looking attractive. So you want to do things that are popular with your peers and also keep abreast of the fashion trends that are popular among them. You also begin to mature into a young adult and begin to get curious about your sexuality. By the time you reach adulthood, these same physical wants, desires, and needs, (eating good food, having fun, looking attractive, being popular among our peers, and having sexual appeal), are still dominant. Our minds, (the place where our thoughts, words, and expressions are formulated), grow through these stages, and are well formed by the time we become adults. Given that our nature is naturally physical it is no wonder that our thoughts, words, and expressions create dreams, hopes, ideas, and fantasies of worldly things. It is no surprise we seek career success, material possessions that indicate our success, sexually attractive mates, exotic foods that are pleasing to the eye and taste, and recreational activities that excite and stimulate us physically. While this is physically natural, it is not fulfilling to us in our entirety, because the spirit within is not fulfilled by these things. Have you ever known people who were rich, famous, and successful, but still not happy? Have you known people who were rich, famous and successful, but miserable? It is very important that you realize it is possible to exist living with a physically dominant focus that leads to a person being two-dimensional, (body and mind with mind focused on physical wants, desires, and needs). A two-dimensional life is very dangerous. It is dangerous because it is the most basic level of our being that has no other guidance beyond what the physical body craves. These physical cravings are not tempered with any spiritual rationale and thus are purely selfish. A two-dimensional, physically dominant life is also our most immature state of existence. A good analogy is our physical desires we have as babies. As babies, we crave food and sleep; however, our adult parents have to know what types of food and how to allow the proper amount of rest because they have the mental and spiritual rationale we as babies have yet to acquire. The baby merely responds to physical urges. If you seek after life for physical and mental satisfaction in the absence of your spiritual needs, you will never find true, complete happiness. You must be fully, three-dimensionally fulfilled, (spirit, mind, and body). That is why so many people who have great wealth, fame, and popularity still remain unhappy. They expend all of their energy, focus, and time towards living to satisfy their physical needs and have lived a two-dimensional lifestyle. They have never sought spiritual fulfillment and become whole. Until they understand and incline their hearts to the spirit within, which needs to be fed, they will never fill that void they feel within. Often, materially successful people conduct interviews and express that they have everything physically and economically that life can offer but just feel they are still missing something. When they seek and find spiritual nourishment and begin the process of becoming whole of spirit, mind, and body, they then profess they now have complete happiness.

When our natural physical and mental development focuses on our physical wants, desires, and needs, there are challenges and issues we must be aware of. The first challenge is we become selfish. What we want, desire, and need physically all center on us. The characteristics of the flesh come along with that selfish physical nature. The Bible calls them the "fruits of the flesh." Galatians, Chapter 5, verse 19 states, "These fruits of the flesh are sexual immorality, impurity, debauchery, idolatry, witchcraft, factions and envy, drunkenness, orgies and the like." Our selfish physical qualities are mentioned another way in Colossians, Chapter 3, verse 5, which states, "Put to death, therefore whatever belongs to your earthly nature, sexual immorality, impurity, lust, evil desires and greed, which is idolatry." Many of these selfish physical characteristics described in Galatians and Colossians can become obsessive behaviors that lead to destruction of the body, mind, and spirit. If you destroy the body, the mind and spirit are destroyed as well. If you destroy the mind, the body and spirit are useless.

I'd like to take my analysis further by analyzing one of these selfish physical desires, sexual desire. One of man's and woman's greatest downfalls and weaknesses is sexual desire. This downfall is as old as we are. There are numerous examples in the Bible of great men, (David and Solomon) and women, (Delilah and Jezebel), who succumbed to their sexual desires. One of the greatest Biblical disciples, authors, and preachers, Paul made reference to this weakness by saying, "Would that I had never known a woman," when speaking about his weakness to his sexual needs. While the world today is very much physically and mentally focused on sexuality with all of the excitement, pleasures, and passions marketed and impressed on us in television ads, magazines, books, and movies, even this is not new to man and woman. Sodom and Gomorrah, ancient Rome, and Pompeii are all places where sexual perversion existed in ancient times. Sexual perversion is nothing new. God gave man and woman the commandment to procreate and multiply. In Genesis, Chapter 1, verse 28, He states, "Be fruitful and increase in number." Sex is necessary and essential for procreation and it is natural for man and woman to crave sex. Sexual development begins at the beginning of physical life as man and woman are biologically equipped for reproduction. Most humans begin to experience some curiosity about the opposite sex as young children. Their childhood curiosity grows towards attraction as teens. By the time they are of legal age, the attraction is well known and recognized. Although physical and biological maturation is Godly, and normal, it becomes a problem when men and women take sexual desires, wants, and needs out of the original context God intended it for. When that happens, they become obsessive, over indulgent, and compulsive in their desire to satisfy themselves sexually. The actual act of sexual pleasure becomes the focus, not the act of procreation through sexual intercourse, as God intended. Since the act of sexual pleasure is one that is physical in nature, pleasing physically, and centered on physical actions in a physical world; it enables men and women to separate themselves, just as Adam and Eve did. They focus, indulge, and seek after all things that fulfill that need. I hope you are realizing how dangerous this is by now! It becomes very dangerous! The separation from the spiritual intent, and God through inaccurately choosing to seek only physical gratification through sexual acts, results in two-dimensional living. This two-dimensional focus results in the body and mind focused on the physical pleasures of sex in the absence of any spiritual and moral consciousness. It is also dangerous because the need to have more exciting sexual pleasure leads to gluttonous, compulsive, and reckless behaviors all for the sake of more and greater thrills and pleasures. Through this gluttonous, compulsive, reckless behavior comes even more perversion of thinking, so societal morals and views become more and more tolerant of sexual perversion to the point that it becomes socially acceptable. Does that sound a little familiar? Through this progressive, increasing perversion comes a variety of sexual problems, (diseases, immoral relationships, domestic disturbances, violence, and physical destruction). Also, through this progression, men and women continue to let physically stimulating sexual things of the world motivate them more than anything else. They buy homes, clothes, cars, and foods based on advertisements, commercials, and celebrities who promote sex appeal.

I chose sexuality as an example for a reason. It has become one of our biggest challenges since that original fall from grace. It is also one of the difficult inner rebellious natures to conquer. We have countless historical examples of great men and women of the Bible, and also countless examples of entire cultures, as clear examples of how difficult sexuality is to conquer. If great men and women of the past, and great thriving cultures of the past failed to overcome sexuality, we need to be consciously aware of the great threat our inner sexual natures pose, and seek to avoid past mistakes. If you are from a family of alcoholics, then the best way to avoid alcoholism is to always be conscious of the threat of alcoholism and it's impact on your family. The absolute best way to assure that you do not repeat that threat in your own life, is to avoid drinking alcohol altogether. It is probably more realistic that you will choose to drink on some level because you have grown up in an environment where drinking is encouraged and accepted. If you do choose to drink, constantly remembering your family's history of alcoholism and the risk that you are vulnerable as well should help you find ways to manage drinking without becoming an alcoholic. Let me make one thing clear at this point about sexuality. Sexual desires, wants, and needs are not wrong. In the proper context, God intended for man and woman to enjoy and utilize sexual intimacy for procreation. We just need to be continually mindful and conscious that we are sexually vulnerable to our desires. By keeping our focus and consciousness on our weaknesses, we can keep it in proper mature perspective and under control.

How does becoming spiritually re-oriented, (spirit, mind and body), change how we manifest our thoughts, words, and expressions? Spiritual re-orientation brings about a tremendous change! What is the difference between two dimensional, (body and mind) focus and three-dimensional, (spirit, mind and body) focus? The difference is the completeness of one, (three-dimensional focus is completely whole as God made you), versus the other, (two-dimensional is lacking the spiritual perspective and is centered on physically focused wants, desires, and needs). I have already talked about the dangers of two-dimensional living. So, what if a person is oriented in body, mind, and spirit? How does this orientation compare to a spiritually oriented person who is spirit, mind, and body focused? As a physically-oriented person; physical needs are first and dictate mental focus, (their minds are accustom and controlled by physical desires). Their spiritual wants and needs are last, and least. With a spiritually-oriented person, spiritual wants and needs are first and control and dictate mental thoughts with physical needs last. A good analogy of how tremendous the comparison can be derived by comparing man to Christ. Christ understood WHO He was, (first and foremost), spiritually. So while He lived as a man, His mental and physical actions were always controlled and under dominion of His Spirit. This proper spiritual-orientation, (spirit, mind, and body), is what will ultimately allow us complete access to the Sacred Temple where God resides. Because Christ understood and remained properly oriented throughout His entire life, He always had intimate interaction and communion with God. It is also through this proper orientation, that we will achieve the greater works Christ spoke of. Just as there are physical characteristics, (sexuality, greed, lust), there are also spiritual characteristics. The "fruits of the spirit" were defined in the book of Galatians, Chapter 5, verse 22. This passage states, "But the fruits of the Spirit is love, joy peace, patience, kindness, goodness, faithfulness, gentleness, and self-control." The book of Colossians also refers to these fruits in Chapter 3, verses 12 and 13 and state, "Therefore, as God's chosen people, holy and dearly loved, clothe yourselves with compassion, kindness, humility, gentleness, patience. Bear with each other and forgive whatever grievances you may have against one another. And over all of the virtues, put love, which binds them together in perfect unity."

One thing should be very apparent in comparing physical characteristics to spiritual characteristics; they are diametrically opposed. The virtues of our spiritual nature, (just like the nature of God's all-consuming love for us), are as selfless as our physical natures are selfish! Yes, it is possible to love yourself, be compassionate, and kind, but love, compassion, and kindness cannot be demonstrated without sharing and giving those virtues to someone else. These wonderful virtues focus on the positive things about us and others. Through spiritual re-orientation comes a shift in perspective and focus off satisfying physical wants, desires, and needs to focusing on spiritual wants, desires, and needs. Through spiritual re-orientation, we can satisfy that inner longing and unrest we seem to have when we have fed our bodies physically, our minds mentally, yet still yearn for something to give us inner joy and peace but are not sure what that something is. Through spiritual re-orientation, we can have peace that we just cannot find in the body and mind, or in the world around us that caters to all that is physical. As we begin the process of spiritual re-orientation, we begin to restore wholeness again and enter into that sacred place we lost through being physically oriented. We now consistently begin to listen to that quiet, still voice of the Holy Spirit and trusting the guidance, convictions, direction, and insights on how to order, control, and envision our thoughts, words, and expressions. We begin to become the Christ-like person we ultimately are destined to become. As we grow and mature, we are more empowered, (as Christ was), to manifest our thoughts, words, and expressions on a higher level. Through this progression, we are ultimately completely and fully re-oriented and whole with the proper order, (spirit, mind, and body), restored. When that occurs, we have the same intimate access to God that we originally lost.

One key benefit of being spiritually re-oriented is the fulfillment of that selfless giving nature that develops in you. Nothing brings more joy than giving. When we are young, we delight in receiving from our parents. As we grow, we desire to give back and get great joy out of giving back. Can you remember the first time you did something that really pleased your mother and how she praised you? Can you remember how good it felt receiving that praise? Can you remember how important it became for you to continue pleasing her so you could receive the joy of her continued praise? The book of Luke, Chapter 6, verses 38 and 39 state the following on giving: " Give and it will be given to you. A good measure, pressed down, shaken together and running over, will be poured into your lap. For with the measure you use, it will be measured to you." So, the old saying, "it is more blessed to give than receive" is validated in the Bible. The spiritual text speaks of pressing down, shaken together, and running over in relation to giving. These terms are related to farming. I grew up in the country as a young boy. We grew vegetables for our household. If we had a good harvest that resulted in more than we could eat, we would give (as Daddy called it) a "mess" of our vegetables to other family members and friends in need. A "mess" is a basket shaken and pressed to the point of overflow so the amount is more than enough. The point with giving until it overflows is if you give in excess, God will see that you receive in excess in your time of need. Giving is unique and specific to what talents, skills, interest, and passions we have in life. However, we all have something of value to give to others. I encourage and challenge you to seek out what your talents and skills are and give it with joy and sincerity and watch what returns to you as a result.

Being spiritually re-oriented also allows you to be different from what people expect of you and this is another important key benefit over being physically oriented. Being different from what others expect sets you apart as a unique example, positive influence, resource, mentor, and leader for others to learn from. People are used to others who are physically dominant, selfish, and after their own selfish interest, seeking to satisfy the bodily needs of food, sex, materialism, etc. Once they realize you are not seeking those things at their expense, they become drawn to why you are not. They become intrigued that you are not and curious about why you are different, especially since they are so accustomed to the world all around them being physically absorbed and focused. They want to know what makes you different. Has anyone ever made these statements about you, "There is something different about you and I can't quite figure out what it is." "What is it?" If they have, it was them seeing that you were spiritually focused in your life and governed yourself with less physically dominant wants, desires, and needs than they were used to. Being set apart in the eyes of others due to being spiritually re-oriented is a good thing. I am sure some of you may be thinking you do not want the pressures, burdens, and responsibilities of being set apart by others. My response is whether you choose to be set apart or just go with the worldly norms, you are still an example to others in your life. The question is this, are you a good example or a bad example? Will you be of positive benefit and blessing to others, or reinforce the worldly norms? Do not fear being set apart as different. By accepting the responsibility of your spiritual re-orientation, you can be used by God to help others in their growth towards spiritual re-orientation. You may be that unique example, positive influence, resource, mentor, or leader that people need to enter that sacred place within them they have been seeking. Just as you are used for that person's benefit, God will see that you also receive, "pressed down, shaken, and poured over" what you need through the unique examples, positive influence, resources, mentors, and leaders in your path to continue your progression. God will also make sure you have something of benefit and value through your talents and skills for others in their time of need for those drawn to you. You will receive the joy of giving of yourself. That spiritual joy is unparalleled to any physical and mental joys life has to offer! You are now well on your way towards spiritual re-orientation. I have one more important point. I have already talked about the mind earlier in Chapter 1 and how it develops and shapes along with our natural physical development and growth. I have also talked about our physically rebellious nature and how the mind is the battleground where that inner rebellion is fought. We process and do naturally, mentally, what we are physically or spiritually oriented to do. I want make is this important point now that you are becoming spiritually re-oriented, you can now gain spiritual focus, order, and control over your mental processes. It is critical that you continually seek to develop and understand your spiritual environment. It is also critical to listen to the Holy Spirit. As you do these things, you will continue to get more and more properly ordered of spirit, mind and body. You must seek continued understanding by reading the Bible and other spiritual works. You must also seek spiritual fellowship and interaction with others. That allows further perspective, nourishment, guidance, and sustenance. As you read and seek fellowship, think over, meditate, analyze, and reason within-without, you will continue to acquire increased knowledge, understanding, guidance, and direction. Getting the mind and body under your spiritual control will not come without rebellion and struggle. However, it will come, so do not give up the effort. Always look back and assess your successes and failures, but make sure you remember your successes and progress. By looking back, you can measure your course, see your shortcomings, and gain strength to proceed. Looking back provides maturity, strength, wisdom, and hope for the progress to come. Count and measure each growth, step, and victory as they come and realize there are more struggles to come that you will endure and overcome!

4th Principle: "The Spiritual Laws Work EVERY Time, ALL The Time"

There are societal laws created to bring order to society. There are also universal Spiritual laws. There is a difference between God's divine universal Spiritual laws and man's societal laws. Man's laws are often developed and written to benefit the men and women who write the law. I'll make a slight change to an old phrase to make my point "The man with the gold, makes the rule." I am not saying the laws of man and woman are not good laws. A society without laws and a governing body, be it local, state, or federal, is one that allows chaos to dictate. However, the man and woman with the most economic, political, and material power will always have complete freedom and liberty under the laws. They are the ones who have the status, influence, and authority to create the laws and create laws to protect their economic, political, and material power. Those with economic, political, and material power are placed above the laws because they have enough money and power to overcome the laws through exceptions they have created that poor people cannot. This does not mean poor men and women are not protected by the same laws because they are. What it does mean is this poor people are often victims if they are accused of violating the laws because they may not have the resources to hire top-dollar legal counsel who specialize in knowing the exceptions to the laws. More often than not, poor, innocent people are convicted of violations they did not commit. Also, rich, guilty people, find ways to overcome, find exceptions, or convince the judicial system of their innocence through top-notch legal counselors who specialize in creating just enough reasonable doubt to win their cases. How the judicial process is administered must be considered also. Why is it that certain crimes receive stiffer penalties? Does blue-collar crime like petty theft, robbery and burglary really warrant harsher penalties than white-collar crime like embezzlement and corporate fraud? How do racial profiles, stereotypes, and prejudices affect how people are convicted? Although I pose these questions for your consideration, you already know the answers to them. It is clear that societal laws have biases and protections toward "the man or woman with the gold," so societal laws are hypocritical.

God's divine universal spiritual laws are not hypocritical like man's laws. God's laws apply to everyone, regardless of their culture, race, economic, or political stature. God's laws work the same for everyone, whether they are the wealthiest of the wealthy, or the poorest of the poor. God's laws cannot be changed by man's laws and are above man's laws. God's laws confirm their truths in our actions and the reactions returned to us. The Holy Spirit speaks God's laws to our hearts and spirits, if we listen. God makes sure everyone knows of and has a chance to know His laws through the course of their lives. God's laws are presented to our minds through the Bible and other divinely inspired spiritual texts (the Koran, Kabala, Torah, 47 Negative Confessions to name a few, and other ancient spiritual texts all over the world). God's laws are universal. They are the same the world over and also the same in heaven and earth, (as above, so below). Since God created us, we all know His divine laws in our hearts and spirits once we open our hearts and spirits.

I have laid the ground rules above in clarifying how God's laws are different from societal laws. In societies that truly seek to benefit their people, their laws are often in agreement, reflective and supportive of God's divine universal laws. Great cultures the world over, and there have been many, were great and powerful because their leaders understood God's divine universal laws and the importance of devising rules and laws for their citizens that were consistent with God's laws. The greatness and power of these cultures lasted as long as they preserved the integrity of their societal laws consistently with God's divine laws. However, when their laws were compromised due to their physically dominant wants, desires, and needs, then their cultures began to deteriorate. Over time, the selfish "fruits of the flesh" lead to continual perversion, and in the end, laws that are hypocritical. One theme is consistent throughout this work as it relates to great civilizations and their contributions to their people and all people of the world. Those cultures and civilizations that stand out as models of success and achievement were governed by societal laws, principles, and statues that were consistent with

45

God's divine universal spiritual laws. For their leaders to govern their societies with consistent success, they had to have proper spiritual orientation, focus, and three-dimensional, (spirit, mind, and body) completeness and maturity. Conversely, civilizations that are models of failures, great tragedies, and evils, are those civilizations who established societal laws, principles and statues consistent with physically dominant wants, desires, and needs. There are seven basic divine universal laws I will discuss: love, reciprocity, faith, truth, wisdom, prayer, and grace. The principles of these laws are important keys in your continued maturation. Now that you are aware you are a spirit in a body, made three-dimensionally, (spirit, mind, and body), in God's image, and there is a sacred place where you can renew intimate communion with God, it is time to give you the basic principles you will need as you enter your sacred place!

Law 1 – "Love, The First and Greatest Of All Laws"

Of all the commandments God gave man and woman to live by, His most important was: TO LOVE! Deuteronomy, Chapter 6, verse 5 states, "Love the Lord our God with all of your heart and all of your soul and with all your strength." Christ also confirmed this commandment in Matthew, Chapter 22, verses 37 and 38 when He stated, "Love the Lord your God with all of your heart and with all of your soul and all of your mind. This is the first and greatest commandment." He also extended that commandment further to include love of fellow man and woman in verses 39 and 40 of the same spiritual text when He stated, "And the second is like it: 'Love your neighbor as yourself.' All the Law and the Prophets hang on these two commandments."

THERE IS NO FORCE OR POWER GREATER THAN LOVE! THERE IS NO FORCE OR POWER EQUAL TO LOVE! Nothing can overcome love, nothing can compare to love, and love is the only thing that is never, ever wasted. Love is also the one thing that everyone and everything craves more than anything. Yet, love is one thing there is clearly never enough of in the world today. Why is that true? While it is true for a number of reasons, I'll point out a few very basic ones. Love, in the spiritual context God and Christ spoke of, is a SELFLESS act. When love is sought from a physically dominant perspective, it becomes a selfish act, (to satisfy physical wants, desires, and needs). We are in a world that is physically dominant, born into a physical body, and naturally oriented to think and seek those physical wants, desires, and needs first. So we are selfish first, not selfless! We use the term "love" loosely to get those physical wants, desires, and needs satisfied from others. Others who seek real, selfless love from others therefore allow themselves to be taken advantage of, or hope they will in turn receive the love they so desperately desire. Our physical nature is a deceptively selfish nature. We, ourselves, are often fooled through those physically powerful cravings, (sexual pleasure for example), and use the disguise of love towards those we are attempting to satisfy those desires through to fulfill our aims. We are programmed from an infant to capitalize on our deceptive abilities. Babies quickly learn that crying will get a new parent to give them anything they cry for. The baby may cry just because it desires to be picked up every time its new parent is nearby. The baby does not know, nor care, that if the new parent picks it up every time he is nearby, he would not have time to do anything else in the household. The baby knows and realizes if they cry, their new parent picks them up, and that is all that the baby cares about. This is deceptive for the parents and the baby. The new parents' pride and joy of being new parents and their inexperience are being taken advantage of. Due to their excitement and inexperience, they are unaware that the baby is crying because of its selfish desire to be held. The parents are also not initially aware how time consuming this will become and by always picking the baby up when it cries, they are forming a habit that reinforces selfish behavior in the baby. The baby is deceived into thinking it is okay to continue to cry every time it wants to be held because the new parents will always hold it when it cries. My point in this analogy is not that babies are intentionally selfish. My point is: our physically dominant natures are self-centered on physical wants at an early age. Parents must start teaching their children, as infants, how to be less prone to selfish physical wants, desires, and needs. An experienced parent, unlike a new parent, understands that picking a baby up every time it cries will reinforce to the baby the selfish need to be held all of the time. Experienced parents teach babies not to be selfish by doing other things such as talking to them, playing with them with toys, singing to them, etc… to give them attention. In time the baby does not cry just because it wants to be picked up. If the baby does cry, the experienced parent realizes the baby must have some other need that needs to be addressed, either a wet behind, or hunger.

Babies will learn whatever behaviors their parents teach it, (either to be selfish after what it wants or to understand to trust parents for its physical needs). Giving and teaching the principle of love must start at infancy. Our first perspective about love comes from our home environment. A baby needs to know that he is loved. He also needs to know other siblings and family members are loved as well. Parents must be consistent in giving love to everyone in the family. Then, their children will realize love is for everyone. With teaching the principles of love at infancy, parents teach their children not to be selfish in their love, but selfless in sharing their love with others. In order to teach selflessness, you must be selfless in giving your love to others, not giving for the sake of your own gain, (be it physical, economic, or otherwise).

Isn't it interesting that the one thing we desire most, love, is the one thing we struggle to give in our physical aims to get it from others? It does not have to be that way. Once we stop letting our selfish physical wants, desires, and needs dictate how we give of ourselves to others, we can begin to give just for the sake of helping, benefiting, and blessing others. As we do, we begin to apply the principle of love. As we give love unselfishly, we begin to see the actions of our giving in return. It does not always return from the person we have given it to. It may return from that person; or, it will return from someone else. Love applies to every relationship we encounter in life: family, friend, child, parent, boyfriend, girlfriend, husband, wife, acquaintance, co-worker, boss, enemy, and stranger. Sexuality is one of our most dominant physical characteristics we use to express love, so we tend to think of love only in the context of boyfriend-girlfriend, husband-wife relationships. Love is not just intimate, sexual interaction in relationships. It is also acts of patience, sympathy, compassion, support, encouragement, understanding, giving, caring, and kindness to others in need in all relationship capacities. I trust that you noticed I included enemy and stranger in my list of relationships. Why are your enemies and strangers important to show love to? By showing love to your enemies you receive whatever you need to overcome them. You convict your enemies to receive the love and understand where they stand in the principle of love. Your love towards the enemy is the strongest tool you could ever use to secure your own blessings. You will often find your enemy has never had love returned from another person whom he or she considers an enemy. This enemy may have never truly experience love in a selfless way but is more used to the conditional, worldly love of "take what you need from others" for your own needs. In the end, he will learn what true, selfless, Christ-like love is.

It is also important to love strangers because at some point in the course of your life, you, or someone you love dearly, (your spouse, child, family member or friend), will be a stranger to someone else. By giving your love to strangers, you insure you and your loved ones will receive love "shaken, pressed down, and pouring over" from others in strange places. Christ emphasized loving enemies especially in Matthew, Chapter 5, verse 44. He stated, "But I tell you, love your enemies and pray for those who persecute you, that you may be sons of your Father in heaven. He causes the sun to rise on the evil and the good, and sends rain on the righteous and unrighteous." He also used a parable about a good Samaritan in the book of Luke, Chapter 10, verses 30 through 37. In this story, a passing Samaritan gave assistance to a Jewish man who was robbed and beaten on his way to Jericho. A Jewish priest and fellow Jewish countryman passed this same man. Yet, the Samaritan, who was an enemy to Jews, felt compassion and helped the injured Jew. By loving your enemy and strangers, you accomplish one of the most difficult, mature, selfless loves possible. It is of course easier to love those that love you. However, it is hard to love others who seek to do harm and damage, as enemies do, or others you do not know, strangers. If you are selfless, loving and compassionate enough to love your enemies and strangers, you will find your blessings and joys truly "shaken, pressed down, and poured over" as you enter your sacred place.

The principle of love requires hard work, discipline, and compassion. It is a process that we learn to improve along life's way. Christ put forth some very high standards in pointing out our need to love our enemies and strangers. We have enough difficulty loving those closest to us! He put the ideal before us so we can understand it is possible. More importantly, when we practice the love of our enemies and strangers, we see the benefit and blessings occur in a powerful way. When we are able to aim at the most challenging, highest ideals God has established, He gives us higher, more powerful rewards, (growth, insight, understanding and blessings) in return. I often think of my personal relationship to God as a parent-child relationship. Parent-child analogies help better relate to how God views us. For those of you, who are parents, think of the following comparison. If your child, who is an average student, gets C's on his report card, aren't you more proud when he tells you he wants to improve and make A's instead? When your child works especially hard, improves his study habits, does all of his homework, does extra special projects in his classes, and does, in fact, receive A's on his report card, wouldn't you give him extra special "shaken, pressed down, and poured over" rewards? You will also give him rewards for earning B's if he is a C student. How much greater would you now reward him, having watched him work really hard to get the results for his efforts?

Although the principle of love does require hard work, our spiritual natures are as naturally inclined towards love as our physical natures are inclined toward physical wants, desires, and needs. Love is an awesome, yet strange, thing to us until we become spiritually re-oriented. That does not mean that those who are physically oriented are not capable of giving and receiving love. It does mean that they may not understand how to define the things needed to give, receive, or practice love beyond seeking it from a physical perspective. If my last statement is confusing, let me make it clear. If you are physically dominant and oriented, chances are, you are confining love to what you desire and need physically. Therefore you are only pursuing this satisfaction of your physical wants, desires and needs through others to seek love. You also think giving your love means giving physical things, i.e. sexual interaction or material things. Your focus is self-centered towards receiving from others what you want to please your physical needs; consequently, you are missing the wholeness of the principle of love from a spiritual perspective, (selfless giving, caring, compassion, etc...) as it relates to every relationship you encounter on life's journey. You are also missing the fulfillment of the love your spirit craves to be fed through giving love in the form of your time, knowledge, resources, talents and insights to others. Whatever physically oriented love you have experienced is not wasted. It is very important because we are still physical. We can build on love from any capacity, and physically oriented love is a starting point. Even with physical love, there are strong emotions, feelings, and motivations. Once we start understanding the fullness of the principle of love, we can apply a lot of the same emotions, feelings, and motivations toward acting on our new spiritually focused love. We can also re-organize and remove any physical wants, desires, and needs that are not true to our spiritual principles. My final commentary on love is this: applying the principles of love from a mature, Christ-like standpoint is a progression that is ongoing. It takes continual, consistent time, energy, effort, work, and patience. Don't be hard on yourself if you find you still have physical wants, desires and needs that are not true to your spiritually re-oriented principles. Keep trying knowing that you will overcome your challenges, or learn from them for continued growth and maturity. In time, you will put those physical wants, desires, and needs in their proper perspective.

I know I have spent a lot of time and attention on love. However, I feel as if I could spend even more time on this principle because it is so important, yet so misunderstood in the world we live in today. However, we should not feel bad. It has been misunderstood throughout our entire history of existence as it was during the days of Christ some 2000 years ago.

Law 2 – Reciprocity, "As One Soweth, So Shall They Reapeth"

Reciprocity is very specific. Galatians, Chapter 6, verses 7 to 9 state, "Do not be deceived: God cannot be mocked. A man reaps what he sows. The one who sows to please his sinful nature, from that nature will reap destruction; the one who sows to please the Spirit, from the Spirit will reap eternal life. Let us not become weary in doing good. For at the proper time, we will reap a harvest if we do not give up." This passage is concise and to the point. What we do in life, good or bad, comes back in like measure. While it is concise, there is more to think about. In order to be true to reaping that which is blessed and good in life, we must stand on the principle to do and be good to others. Sure that sounds simple enough, but actually doing it is another thing. Allow me to relate an example of how it may be more difficult than you think. Someone can mistreat, betray, and hurt you. That someone may even be someone you are very close to and cherish dearly. The pain he causes can be deep, severe, and lasting. The damage can be so significant that it damages you in your home, at work, and in your other environments, such as in the church and other social environments. The damage is also so severe that it has a lasting impact on your self-esteem and emotional state of mind that leads to depression. Through all of this pain, suffering, and damage, you survive. In time, maybe even much, much time, you begin to recover and heal and go on with your life. Your total recovery and healing may take several years if not more than several years. Most of us have gone through an experience like the one I just described at some point in our lives. Your first, natural, physical instinct is to get revenge, to get him back! If he has done all of this to you, shouldn't you do the same thing back to him? If you are applying the principle of reciprocity, wouldn't you reciprocate towards him the same way he has treated you? The answer is a resounding NO! Unfortunately, many of us do in fact reciprocate based on our natural, physical nature and attempt to get back at them and mistreat, betray, and hurt them even more, or at the very least, as much as they have hurt us. Or, even worse, we hurt someone else who is totally innocent of the original violation to us to make us feel better because we have at least gotten revenge on someone.

I challenge you to think about what your natural, physical inclinations are. I also want you to know this; reaping what you sow is not sowing back what you have reaped from someone else. With this realization in mind, I will add some key perspectives for your consideration. One key perspective is: you are not responsible for the seeds someone else sows. You are only accountable for the seeds you sow unto others. So, even though you have been mistreated, betrayed, and hurt by a person whom you love dearly, that person is responsible for sowing those seeds of hurt and pain unto you. His bad harvest will return badly unto him. Another key perspective is: while your natural, physical inclination is to do harm in return to the person that has hurt you, you are only perpetuating and increasing the harm which will return a harmful outcome to you as well. It is a very subtle deception you need to be aware of. It seems logical and correct at the time to react by doing harm to that person or someone else because the pain you are suffering creates strong, painful emotions, (anger, frustration, and depression). Out of these strong, painful emotions, you are susceptible to react quickly and impulsively. When you react quickly and impulsively with strong, painful emotions boiling within, you fail to reason with the spiritually-oriented focus tempering your actions. Can you see how these powerful physical emotions, acted on impulsively, can snowball quickly to wrong actions?

A third key perspective is: the right action to apply the principle of reciprocity properly is to do the opposite of what has been done to you when you are mistreated. Do what is right and good to the person who mistreated you, or do what is right and good to someone else. Doing what is right and good requires you to get past all of the negative emotions and pain. It also requires you to endure that emotion and pain and resist the obvious temptation to inflict that same amount of hurt and pain onto others. Doing what is right and good forces you to control your physical inclinations by being spiritually-focused enough to listen to your heart, spirit, and the counsel, guidance, and direction of the Holy Spirit on what is truly the right action to take. When you do what is right, the outcome for you is always blessed. You may still have to endure the pain, but God will give you comfort, strength, and also use you as an example for others on how to respond in the same proper way when they are challenged.

The fourth and final key perspective is: always do good and you will always reap exponential good returns. That is far more difficult to do than say because we all have human weaknesses and flaws that we must struggle to overcome. Through your weaknesses and flaws, you can very easily become self-absorbed, self-centered, and seek self-gratification of physical wants, desires and needs. Once in a self-absorbed, self-centered mindset, it is really easy to get so caught up in satisfying your wants, desires, and needs instead of thinking about how others are affected and what will return, good or bad, to you in the end. It is equally easy to rationalize that it is okay to get revenge and hurt someone else because your revenge is worth their pain to help you get past your own. We have all, and will all sow some bad seeds during the course of our lives. When you do sow bad seeds it will come back to you exponentially bad as well. Be mature, strong, and humble enough to suffer your consequences without sowing more bad seeds to others. If you can endure without sowing more bad seeds, you will not continue to reap bad outcomes after you endure the consequences. Learn from that bad outcome. Sow good seeds next time. It is important to think and reason within-without about what you do in your life when it comes to your own wants, desires, and needs, and to consider the source, spiritual or physically motivated, for those wants, desires, and needs. This is especially important if others are affected. If you are thinking from within-without, about how your actions will affect others, you are more likely to be spiritually oriented, more selfless, and inclined to do what is good towards others. If you are mature and humble enough to allow the Holy Spirit to convict you of your wrong actions, you can also avoid taking that wrong action again. You will find ways to cope with your pain until there are positive ways to release it without causing harm to others. In time, you will perfect the proper way to reciprocate so your outcomes are always spiritually proper and blessed "shaken, pressed down and pouring over!"

Law 3 – "Faith: Spiritual Emotion In Action"

How important is the principle of faith in our journey to the sacred place? Hebrews, Chapter 11, verse 1, state, "Faith is the substance of things hoped for and the evidence of things yet seen." Faith is one of God's most essential characteristics because it is through our faith, or lack of faith, that God develops the experiences that shape our lives as we seek Him. Someone once asked me, "How do you know there is a God?" "Have you ever seen Him?" I used the principle of faith in responding. I told him I have faith that God exists based on my life's experiences. I then asked him this question to make an analogy for him to relate to. Have you ever been to New York? Since he was from New York, he responded, "Yes." At the time of our discussion, we were in North Carolina. I then asked him, "Can you see New York now?" He replied, "No." So then I asked him, "Since you cannot see it, how do you know it is still there?" I realize my example is a overly simplified one for relating a very complicated concept, but it makes a very critical point about faith. Physical, visible, tangible things in this physically dominant world we exist in do not always reflect faith. Yet, faith is still a very real part of our existence.

As physical beings, we have a very diverse range of emotions. These emotions are not visible at all times. In fact, they are not visible most of the time. Although these emotions are not always visible, they usually result from physical, tangible things in our experiences. Love, fear, anger, and passion are four very strong emotions everyone experiences at some point during the course of their lives. These very strong emotions are within and not visible except through physical behaviors. We do have facial gestures and other bodily gestures, physiological traits, (increased heartbeat, nervousness, upset stomachs, and increased blood pressure), that are physical signs of these strong emotions. We even have chemical indicators such as increased adrenaline, increased endorphins, increased perspiration, and other chemicals released in our body's response to these strong emotions. However, it is also easy to suppress outward signs of these emotions. A gifted criminal can suppress his physiological traits when taking a lie detector test and pass the test because it measures physiological traits to determine whether that person is lying or telling the truth. My point is: love, fear, anger, and passion are four very strong emotions, which we cannot see on the inside. They are only visible through physical behaviors. They are even invisible when suppressed. Yet, they are a very, very real part of our life experiences. We cannot always count on the physical gestures of others to show their emotional state. Someone may be approaching you with a gun in his pocket to rob you as you walk past him. Yet, he may be smiling as you approach him and looking at you like you're someone he knows. You could be deceived and approach him trusting that he is friendly and safe to approach, when, in reality, he is not.

Faith is the emotion of the spirit. Let me tell you why. In the biblical passage I referenced earlier, there is a subtle, yet important clue. That clue is the two simple words that conclude the phrase, "yet seen." Physical emotions result from actual physical, tangible experiences and occur naturally as we live in this physical world. We all become accustomed to acting and reacting to life's experiences through our physical emotional state based on whether those experiences are positive or negative. However, those natural emotional responses, from a physical standpoint, are still generally based on the tangible things we experience and see. Faith requires trust, belief, and confidence in God, Christ, and the Holy Spirit, (the unseen Spiritual Trinity). Through this trust, belief, and confidence in the unseen, the substance for all we desire, hope, and dream are possible. So our faith can manifest from nothing, (our substance of what is hoped for), or a physical outcome or action in our lives, (that evidence we are hoping for through belief in God, Christ, and the Holy Spirit). Our physical emotions are reactions to life. Faith brings to life our hopes and dreams. So, physical emotions are "reactionary" while the spiritual emotion of faith is an "ACTIVATING" power that is evoking the unseen powers of God to bring into fruition our spiritual desires, wants, and needs. The power of belief is a tremendous force. Through this power, all things are possible. As my Daddy says, "The possible things we do, the unpossible things, we let God do." For that faith to work to the fullest, we must have confidence beyond our physical capabilities in the all-powerful, unseen force of God. That faith, combined with the proper words and expressions, (through prayer, meditation, and focus on within, without reasoning), produces positive outcomes and actions for others, and us. It is possible through either physical emotions or faith to generate the internal motivation to act and react in life. Our physical emotions generate actions and reactions to physical wants, desires, and needs that are centered on the physical. They generally serve our own selfish physical wants and desires. Because these physical emotions are more specific to our internal physical wants and needs, others are not always positively affected. In fact, if we are not careful, others may be taken advantage of due to these selfish wants and desires.

There are similarities between faith and physical emotions. Just as your body reacts to physically emotional experiences, faith can also affect your physical and physiological state. When you are trusting God will answer a prayer for something you are seeking, you have peace of mind that it will occur. You are emotionally calm and at rest. Christ provided a good example in the Bible in the book of Mark, Chapter 4, verses 35 through 41. During a violent sea storm, the disciples were getting increasingly fearful and worried as Christ rested peacefully below the deck. Finally, they awakened Christ and He chastised them for their lack of faith. He then calmly went onto the deck of the boat and commanded the sea to become calm. The sea became calm. Christ conveyed several lessons to the disciples through that experience. Christ knew it was not His appointed time to die because He still had works to fulfill in His life; therefore, He had the faith of knowing that storm on the sea was not going to end His life. Through this faith, He could rest calmly. Through this same faith, He commanded the sea to become calm and it did. He called that which was not, (a storm, choppy, hostile sea), into being, (a calm, peaceful sea). Christ's faiths provided a peace of mind and spirit that the disciples witnessed, being with Christ firsthand, and applied to their own storms. The disciples could also go forward with peace of mind through their own faith that they would endure storms as well. The disciples also learned they could, through the proper prayers, meditations, and with-in, without reasoning, have the power to conquer and subdue their challenges, just as Christ conquered the raging sea.

On the other hand, your physiological state of mind may be one of excitement and high emotion. When God performs a miracle in your life, your adrenaline is very high, your heart is racing, and your state of mind is one of extreme joy. Your state of mind is also very quietly confident and stable when you endure storms and overcome them when God answers long awaited prayers for things you have been seeking. As you grow and mature, your faith grows stronger through the many experiences where you receive the outcome of God's blessings through the storms, trials, and challenges in your life. It is that increased level of faith that will give you even greater strength and peace of mind for future storms to follow because you know the past storms you have survived. A good example to consider that is physically emotional to compare to my above examples of the extreme responses we experience to our faith is successfully working in a job environment that is highly stressful, like performing surgery. A surgeon's very first surgery is one of high stress level because it is his first opportunity to actually practically perform what he has learned to that point through textbooks. I am sure he experiences a high level of adrenaline, racing heart, sweaty palms, mental, and physical anxiety as he anticipates and performs the procedure from start to finish. At the conclusion of a successful procedure, I am sure there is tremendous joy, relief, and happiness. In addition, I am sure he now has a certain level of quiet confidence that he can in fact practically apply all that he has studied and learned in his textbooks and classes. A surgeon gains continued peace of mind, confidence, and trust in his ability to successfully perform that surgery with each surgical procedure he or she does. The surgeon also gains the same level of peace, confidence, and trust in his medical team because they work together on each procedure and thus mature together. Your faith and trust in God, (founded and based upon each subsequent occasion God has blessed, guided, and answered your needs), should be your vision of God's promises that will manifest in your life. That vision will begin to form and take shape as you seek to understand, through becoming spiritually reoriented, what your spiritual ministry, gifts, and purpose in life are. God's promises for our lives are not only related to spiritual wants, desires, and needs but also abundant life in every aspect, physically and mentally as well, as we grow into wholeness of spirit, mind, and body. Consequently, He also desires we have the tangible, physical, material, and mental desires of our hearts when we are mature enough to manage them. Seek out what promises God has in store for you and hold fast to them. The way you hold fast to promises that have yet to be realized, (yet seen), is to recall all of the blessings, guidance, and answered prayers God has already given you, (those that are seen and already realized).

Through the course of experiencing the excitement, anticipation, or quiet confidence of waiting for God's promises to manifest, we go through the very same inner emotions we go through with life's physical emotional experiences. As I described in my comparisons earlier, our bodies create the same various chemical and physiological reactions to our faith as it manifest through fruition just as our bodies do in response to life's physical emotional experiences. Take time to reflect on, introspect on, and consider your emotional response to your faith as it relates to life's experiences and get in tune with all of the emotions you have just as you do with your physical life experiences. This additional perspective will give you the maturity and patience to wait for the fulfillment of God's promises in your life. You will truly have the patience to wait for "that which is hoped for but yet unseen" to manifest from the unseen to the seen.

Faith only requires a small measure for results. Christ stated in Matthews, Chapter 17, verses 20, 21, "Because you have so little faith, I will tell you, if you have the faith as small as a mustard seed, you can say to this mountain, 'move from here to there' and it will move. Nothing will be impossible for you." Why does faith require such a small measure when we seem to exhaust such a large amount of physical emotions in our day-to-day lives? It is really very simple.

Faith is the formula, through our confidence, trust, words and prayers, that activates the power of God to bring into fruition what we seek. Our physical emotions activate the physical and mental capacities we have within our physical being. When we act and react purely to physical emotions with purely physical and mental capacities, we are far more limited because we act without God's promises and power to change the issues we are facing. Therefore, we expend far greater energy with far less benefit to affect those day-to-day issues. As we become whole of spirit, mind, and body, (spiritually reoriented), we begin to combine that spiritual faith to our mental and physical capacities. That spiritual faith, even in a very, very small measure as Christ said, restores the wholeness needed for results with more balance, power, and maturity and less physical and mental energy expended. Let me pose a question for your consideration that relates to this topic. Which emotion is more damaging and stressful, love or hate? The answer should be obvious but I'll provide my view. Love is far more positive, uplifting and beneficial than hate. Yes, loving others can be stressful at times because when you love others, sometimes you have to sacrifice your needs and feelings for them. You may also worry out of your love as a mother does for her child or a man and woman does during times of crisis in their relationship. It is still very much clear that the few stresses are minimal to the tremendous positive benefits you get from love. Love heals, nurtures, uplifts, supports, and develops us spiritually, mentally, and physically in ways no other force in life can. The healing, nurturing, uplift, and support you receive from love are both mentally and physically therapeutic. Studies show that people who are married live longer than people who are single. The common theme for these studies is the consistent nurturing and support that exists in a marriage. Hate, on the other hand, eats away at us internally. As it eats away, it causes health issues through the emotional stress and energy needed to sustain that hate. Yes, hate can be a strong motivator for change. You can hate something so much, like a job, that you finally take action by leaving it. Unfortunately, often by the time you seek that change, you have already undergone tremendous stresses and anxieties mentally and physically. You may have ulcers, high blood pressure, depression or other physical ailments as a result. When your hate is channeled at another person, that desire for revenge can be equally damaging due to the negative emotional energy you exert in exacting that revenge. Along with that anger and revenge comes your need to be on the defense for their retaliations to your attacks upon them, which also brings added mental stress. Faith is strengthened through our trials and challenges. As the old saying goes, "There is no testimonial without a test." There will be trials and challenges along the course of life's journey that shake your faith. However, do not give up. When these trials and challenges come, reflect back on previous ones you have come through and realize this one is no different in the end. Even if you do not overcome the trial or challenge immediately, you gain some insight and perspective as you introspect, analyze, and reason "within-without," what you need for your continued growth. In the proper time, you will overcome it. As you continue to grow and mature in your faith, let it be a marker and example for others. As you do, you will also uplift them in their daily walk towards wholeness and completeness. Faith is one of your most essential keys. Grow it and use it wisely as you grow. If you do, you will find that you will always have God's ear as you enter His Sacred Temple.

Law 4: Truth – "The Highest Standard"

When I was a young boy, Mama was extremely strict on me about being truthful. I grew up with an old-fashioned mother who did not believe in "sparing the rod." My brothers and sisters and I had more than our fair share of good old-fashioned switch whippings for our childhood transgressions. However, Mama was not a cruel disciplinarian. She normally gave us at least two, even three times to make a mistake that was a violation of her rules that led to punishment by her dreaded switch. Even with all of those chances, we normally ended up getting whipped. I now realize, growing up in a rural area with very little to do, some of our misdeeds resulted from sheer boredom. There was one rule she never, ever gave us leniency on and that was lying. Mama always believed in being truthful. If she caught us lying, there was no second chance. I remember getting some of my most painful whippings due to lying. Although I did not understand, as a little boy, why lying was so much more important the other offenses, I now understand. Mama was trying to teach us to embrace truth at all times. She always lectured us before punishing us and I recall her often emphasizing the importance of truth in our daily lives. Her goal was to help us understand that no matter what, it is always best to be truthful. There were even times when I did something wrong and when I confessed truthfully to Mama, she praised me for being honest and did not punish me. There were also times when I did something wrong and lied about it and was severely punished. Mama was more upset and disappointed in me lying than she was with my misdeed. So Mama was teaching me a very important spiritual concept; that I must always stand behind the principle of truth. Even if it meant I had done something wrong to accept it. Without realizing, or having the consciousness to seek truth, we cannot incline our hearts, minds, and spirit to God's will to seek repentance or change from our misdeeds in life.

Truth has and always will exist in the midst of our existence as a barometer and measure of God's highest standard for us to compare our actions to. Looking back on Adam and Eve's original fall from grace, Adam knew he was wrong for eating the fruit from the Tree of Knowledge of Good and Evil. That is one of the reasons he and Eve were hiding from God when God came to commune with them in the coolness of the evening, (see Genesis, Chapter 3, verses 8 through 10). That same voice of reason for truth for us, the Holy Spirit, was that little voice of conviction that Adam was reasoning with to arrive at his awareness of his failure and transgression. Christ confirmed the Holy Spirit is our counselor and companion for truth in the book of John, Chapter 14, verses 16 and 17. In these scriptures, Christ stated, "And I will ask the Father, and He will give you another Counselor to be with you forever, the Spirit of Truth. The world can not accept Him, for he lives with you and will be in you."

If truth has been always present with us through the Holy Spirit, as a voice of conviction, counsel, and reason, and in us, in our spirits, the dimension of our image that most closely relates to

God; then why has it been so difficult for us to grasp, aspire towards, and incline ourselves to it? The answer to this question is the same answer that has been consistent throughout this text; our physical orientation is inclined towards that which is not true in spirit until we begin to re-orient ourselves back towards spiritual maturity. Christ also spoke of truth as the Jews were persecuting him in the book of John, Chapter 8, verses 32 to 34. He stated, "Then you will know the truth and the truth will set you free. But I will tell you the truth, everyone that sins is a slave to sin." Given that our natural physical orientation is programmed towards physical wants, desires, and needs, we are susceptible to sin and that which is not true in spirit. As we begin spiritual re-orientation, we open "the book of truth within" that we each know through accepting the voice, counsel, and conviction to the principles of truth through the Holy Spirit. I hope you are curious about "the book of truth within." If you are, I will tell you what I have been led to share about it.

In our spirits, we all understand, know, and recognize truth when we hear it. However, since we begin to grow, mature, and develop physically dominant over our inner spirits as we are born and grow in a physical world, that innate, inner knowledge is buried and hidden. As young children, we are more prone to hearing and accepting the inner spiritual truth because we have not yet grown enough physically for our physically dominant wants, desires, and needs to suppress that inner spiritual intuitiveness of our youth. It may seem strange, but young children are far more open to their inner intuitions because at their young ages, they are closer to having been spiritual before being born physically. Young children often know truth when they hear it. As we grow older, and more physically dominant in a world that is physically focused, we become tainted towards the world and away from inner truths. In spite of being in a world that wants to influence us away from truth and towards sin, most of us are fortunate to still receive some portions of truth through our spiritual environment. What becomes a challenge is inclining our self to hear those truths against our physically rebellious natures to pursue physical wants desires, and needs. Unfortunately, the more inclined and physically dominant we become, the harder it becomes to seek after truth from a spiritual perspective, and the easier it becomes to rationalize worldly views, that conform to physical wants, desires, and needs, as the truth we now accept. These physical wants, desires, and needs are inclined toward sin and thus we become, as Christ said, enslaved to that sin. Since we are a spirit in a body, that inner, innate spiritual truth may be buried, but it is still present. How and when do we uncover it? The process of uncovering the truth begins in our childhood as our spiritual environment is molded and shaped around us. At some point, as we grow towards adolescence, we begin to hear that inner voice of reason of the Holy Spirit as He speaks to our conscience to confirm and reinforce the truths we are learning in our spiritual environment. Since we are all uniquely specific and specifically unique, the age that we begin to uncover and accept truth is specific to everyone. It is more likely, however, that it begins in childhood since we are more open to accepting our spiritual intuitions as children. It is never too early for parents to shape and inspire their children towards truth. In fact, children desire that direction from their parents and mentors. The earlier we are taught to seek uncovering that inner, innate truth, the easier it becomes for us to properly re-orient ourselves to wholeness of spirit, mind, and body. By learning to seek after inner, innate truth at an early age, we become less tainted towards worldly perspectives and also become less susceptible towards being mentally influenced by our physical dominance as we grow. So, we begin the uncovering process through our spiritual environment. Through that environment, we are led to seek, analyze, introspect within-without, to relate the truths from our spiritual environment to day-to-day life and the world around us. Next comes the ongoing development physically that is selfish towards physical wants, desires and needs. Unfortunately this natural, ongoing physical development is often diametrically opposed to inner spiritual truths. Can you see why it is important to begin to seek that inner, innate spiritual intuitiveness as early as possible?

One major key for accepting the truths we seek is the Holy Spirit. As you accept your true, three-dimensional character, (you are a spirit, mind, and body), at that point spiritual re-orientation starts. As re-orientation starts, you have now aligned your spirit to the guidance, conviction, and counsel of the Holy Spirit, which is the voice of truth for God. Prior to reaching that point in your maturity of spiritual awareness of your wholeness, the Holy Spirit is still present to speak to, guide, counsel, and convict you. A good way to think about it is to think of the voice, guidance, counsel, and conviction of your parents. As you venture into the world as a young adult, your parents have already spent the years as you grew under their roof to shape and mold you to make choices that are right and good so you will have success and happiness in life. Any time during the course of your life that you stray off the path they have worked hard to guide you towards, they are present to speak with you and remind you that you are going astray. They are there as the voice of guidance, counsel, and conviction based on what the circumstance or life issue you are dealing with calls for. They have warned you many times of wrong choices, actions, and directions to avoid. However, you may still choose, as an adult, to make those choices. If you do, you review over and over in your mind their guidance, counsel, and conviction but still choose to ignore it and go forward. Your decision to go forward may be due to physical wants, desires, needs, curiosity, or just because you can. You may ultimately endure suffering and hardships from your choice and learn to accept that what you were taught by your parents was in fact correct. It is also likely that you will tell them of your experience and acknowledge their wise direction, counsel, and conviction. As you do, they are there to support and nurture you and encourage you to get back on the path they have directed you towards. The parent, child comparison is an important one in understanding our relationship to God. The Holy Spirit, as the parent of Spiritual Truth, is ever present. It is not Him that changes in the course of our lives as we develop. It is our understanding and relationship to Him. Prior to reaching our spiritual re-orientation, we are much like a rebellious child. We hear His quiet, inner voice of reason, guidance, counsel, and conviction as we pursue physically selfish wants, desires, and needs that are true to worldly needs but counter to spiritual truths. But, we still choose to ignore His voice and pursue our own physically dominant selfish wants, desires, and needs. At the point we begin spiritual re-orientation, we change from a rebellious child to an obedient child. We begin to seek, analyze, introspect – reason within -without, and incline our hearts and spirits to the parenting of the Holy Spirit. As we begin to uncover, unravel, and reveal spiritual truths, we ultimately begin to understand that we are kindred with the Holy Spirit and the truth we are uncovering and discovering is within us. The Holy Spirit, much like the parent who has taught his or her child the proper direction to take, only reminds us of what we already know. Sometimes in the midst of life's day-to-day struggles, we forget to focus on basic spiritual values and truths that provide the foundation, strength, and reason to make good choices and actions. These choices and actions keep us at peace and blessed. As we continue to get caught up in additional day to day struggles, we get further and further out of focus with our core spiritual values and beliefs. Parents and close friends often remind us of these values and beliefs and get us back into focus. They are not telling us anything we do not already know, just reminding us of what we already know. Just through that reminder, we get back on track with renewed focus and strength to choose and act what we already know. Through this renewed focus and strength, we regain the proper choices and actions to renew peace and blessings from those choices and actions. As we grow, we no longer need that reminder from our parent or friend as it relates to those issues but remember through having endured and made proper choices and actions. In time, as we grow towards full, Christ-like maturity, we will have more knowledge of the truth within and need less guidance, counsel, and conviction from the Holy Spirit.

Seeking, acquiring, understanding and applying truth in your life requires self-analysis, reasoning, reflecting, and introspection within-without thinking. You must look within and looking within means analyzing things about your character, physically, mentally, and spiritually. You must be mature enough to understand things about your character that you do not like and be willing to seek changes to those things. You must also appreciate the good things about your character that you can build on. As you do self-analysis, reasoning, reflecting, and introspecting, compare your good and bad characteristics to your spiritual environment and the world around you. You will also have the voice of reason, counsel, guidance, and conviction of the Holy Spirit to confirm and guide you in your self-analysis, reasoning, reflecting, and introspecting. You must be patient, strong, persevering, and mature because what you find on your own, and with the counsel, guidance, and conviction of the Holy Spirit is often hard to accept. However, as you do accept the things you find, you will continue to grow and re-orient into a more complete person, spiritually, mentally, and physically. In time, you will have mastery of "the book of truth within" again, and applying its principles will be natural and second nature, just as it was for Christ. Then, as Christ stated, "You are truly free" and well on your way to arriving at that sacred place you seek.

Law 5: Wisdom – "The Eternal Well of Knowledge and Understanding"

There is a saying, "Knowledge is power." I am not certain where it originated or if it is modern or ancient. I do know this, it is true; knowledge is, in fact, power. When you think of knowledge from any perspective, spiritually, mentally, physically, economically, socially, politically, academically, or personally, it is still true. If you have it, you have power. Yet, while knowledge is power, it is of no use without "Wisdom." Seeking, acquiring, and having wisdom will produce knowledge, and more importantly, UNDERSTANDING of that knowledge. Having knowledge does not produce wisdom. Today's world of information and technology is a perfect case in point. Our world today is full of technological, economic, academic, and scientific knowledge. Not only are we full to an overabundance, but also, the majority of the world has access to our excessive knowledge. Yet, in all of this expansive knowledge, we still do not know how to restore ecological and natural balance to the animals, plants, and environment that has been grossly damaged and destroyed through our technology. With all of our scientific knowledge, we still cannot explain the meaning of life, and how life is created and defined. With all of our economic strength and prosperity we still have millions upon millions of poor, impoverished, and starving nations. Yes, the world today has abundant, even an overabundance of knowledge. But, does it have wisdom and understanding with which to perfect its knowledge! How long can we survive without tempering our knowledge with the proper wisdom and understanding to resolve the challenges that have resulted from excessive knowledge applied in the absence of wisdom and understanding? If history is an example and lesson for the present, we should have the intelligence and insight to gleam that other great cultures, (the Romans and Kemetians), had a wealth of knowledge that ultimately did not prevent their demise and destruction. Was it due to their lack of wisdom and understanding on how to balance their knowledge to maintain a balance of spirit, mind, and body? That's a question for you to consider. King Solomon, noted for his tremendous wisdom, stated, "Give me wisdom and knowledge, that I may lead this people, for who is able to govern this great people of yours?" in 2nd Chronicles, Chapter 1, verse 10. The wisest man in the Bible asked God for both "wisdom" and "knowledge," not just knowledge alone. He understood that knowledge, in the absence of wisdom, would not give him the ability to govern his mighty kingdom successfully.

Why is knowledge in the absence of wisdom so dangerous to us? For a good analogy, think of today's teenagers. Today's teenagers, compared to teenagers just fifty years ago, have access to far more information and knowledge at a much earlier age than teenagers of the fifties ever dreamed possible. One area of major concern today is how quickly young teens mature into puberty and are knowledgeable about sex. Young people of the fifties also matured into puberty and were curious about sex. However, our culture today is far, far more promiscuous, visually open, and susceptible than ever to exposing, (over exposing), our young teens to sex. In the more innocent times like the fifties, parents were much more influential in controlling the knowledge their children had about sex. That parental insight provided wisdom and understanding of how sex and their development into puberty prepared their children for adulthood. Today's parents make the same effort to prepare their children for adulthood. It is just far,

far more difficult for today's parents to control the information and knowledge about sex their children are exposed to. Teenagers today are more strongly influenced by their peers and also the excessive amount of information overload available in the world around them. Knowing about sex does not equate to wisdom and understanding on how sex fits into life from a mature, adult perspective. I did not provide the comparison of teens today to teens of the fifties to pick on our youth. Knowledge in the hands of adults, cultures, and nations of power, in the absence of wisdom and understanding, is far more dangerous. Knowing how to make an atomic bomb or other deadly technological weapons without the wisdom and understanding of being responsible to preserve human life is a far more dangerous threat than childhood ignorance on sex as it relates to adulthood.

What differentiates man's and woman's knowledge from God's knowledge? The difference is so vast it cannot be defined or adequately explained. Let me see if I can attempt to provide a few insights for your consideration. God's knowledge is perfectly complete because it is all knowing and consists of all wisdom and understanding. God's knowledge consists of ALL existence. It is defined by ALL there is; spiritually, mentally, and physically, (past, present, and future). Can you visualize how exponentially large that difference is from the knowledge of man and woman? At our best, we can have knowledge tempered with, wisdom and understanding, of spirit, mind, and body. That, again, is at our absolute best. Even still, at our absolute best, we can only relate to our knowledge and understanding based on our past and present, absent of the future. As spirits in a physical body, the confines of our physical existence and laws limit us. Christ is a good comparison to us because He lived as a man. Yet, He was God-realized in man. Christ developed complete wisdom, knowledge, and understanding with full insight to His past, present, and future. He understood, in perfect union with God and the Holy Spirit, the completeness of all there is, was, and ever will be. It took Christ all of His years to attain and demonstrate His realized, (which He realized as a child), maturity and completeness, and fulfill His destiny. Great men and women of history have achieved many great scientific, technological, spiritual, intellectual, and philosophical accomplishments without ever reaching Christ's level of maturity. Yet Christ said in John, Chapter 14, verse 12, "I tell you the truth, anyone who has faith in me will do what I have been doing. He will do even greater things than these, because I am going to the Father." Christ realized that we have the capacity for complete wisdom, knowledge, and understanding of spirit, mind, and body, (past, present, and future), through properly re-orienting ourselves spiritually in perfect union with God, Christ, and the Holy Spirit. By re-orienting ourselves spiritually, we tap into all of God's, (God, Christ, and the Holy Spirit), perfect wisdom, knowledge, and understanding. When that occurs, all things are possible to us.

I realize I have provided an ideal comparison in choosing Christ as an example. I also realize that with my explanation of aspiring towards the ultimate, infinite, wisdom, knowledge, and understanding of God, I am providing an ultimate level to aspire towards. I hope you realize that through awareness ultimately comes attainment. You must first have awareness of what is ultimately attainable in order to strive to attain that which you are aware of. Attaining that ultimate spiritual re-orientation will not come overnight. It took Christ all of His 39 years of life to attain the maturity to fulfill all He was predicted to achieve in His life. It stands to reason our attainment is also a lifelong process. Attainment will also come through progressive growth, development, and maturation just as Christ endured. Progressive growth, development, and maturation will require struggles and triumphs along the way. It is important to learn as much as possible through each. Along the way, you will experience glimpses of perfect God-wisdom, knowledge, and understanding as you progress. These glimpses are signs and messages that you are progressing in the right direction. They are also to provide hope, strength, insight, and introspection for you to continue your journey. Through seeking after God's perfect wisdom, you will gain knowledge, combined with wisdom and understanding, for your continual total life development and re-orientation, (spirit, mind, and body).

Law 6: "Prayer – The Perfect Medium Between Us and God"

Let's go back to the Garden of Eden. Do you realize that prior to Adam and Eve's fall from grace, they had perfect communion with God? Think about it. Adam, Eve, and God, (in all of God's awesome presence), could converse as easily and openly as we do with our close family and friends any time they felt the need. It is clear, from biblical scriptures, that Adam and Eve could call upon God and get an immediate response and reaction. God Himself also sought them out, "And the Lord God called unto Adam and said unto him, where art thou?" in Genesis, Chapter 3, verse 10. God delighted in conversing and interacting with them! With God so readily at their disposal, I am sure there was no need unfulfilled for them. By having such perfect communion, there was no want or need Adam and Eve had, that God was not aware of. Why would Adam and Eve need prayer when they could call upon and have God's immediate presence at all times? Would we need prayer if we had that same unique communion that Adam and Eve had?

That is the relationship I visualize for Adam and Eve before they fell from grace. However, once they chose to separate themselves from God, the beginning of the need to call upon the Lord in prayer and supplication started. One Adam and Eve chose physical dominance they lost that spiritual frequency and interaction with God. A good analogy is AM radio frequency verses FM radio frequency. Before their original sin, Adam, Eve, and God were on the AM, (I AM God's) frequency. After their fall, Adam and Eve automatically switched to physical dominance and FM, (fallen man's and woman's) frequency. Adam and Eve lost far more than their banishment from the Garden of Eden. When their fall from grace first happened, I am sure they were still dialoguing, conversing, and calling unto God, much like we do when talking on a cell phone whose service has been interrupted without our knowledge. At some point, they thought God was not hearing them, which we eventually realize when we discover our cell phone connection has been lost. It wasn't God failing to hear them at all. He was hearing them as clearly and distinctly as before. God knew Adam and Eve's frequency had changed through their new physically dominant orientation; so they could not hear Him. God also knew, in His omniscient capacity, that they would not realize their transition from His AM frequency to their FM frequency. I am sure Adam and Eve thought God had forsaken them because they could not hear Him. Yet, God was ever-present as He was in the beginning, and always will be. As Adam and Eve began their journey back towards their spiritual natures, I am sure they caught snatches of God responding much like we do when we hear broken dialogue on our cell phones when we are in an area with poor service. At that point, they realized God had not forsaken them and was still responding. Hearing God's broken response was, I am sure, encouraging to Adam and Eve that they were not forsaken. Thus, they continued to communicate with the hope that they would fully hear Him again as they grew and matured spiritually.

Prayer was created out of this initial fall. Not because God ever left man and woman's side, but prayer was created because man and woman changed frequencies through their new physical dominance and orientation, and they needed prayer to re-discover their connection to God's frequency as they begin to become spiritually re-oriented. Along the way towards maturity and wholeness, God continues to respond and even answers our cries knowing that only some of His responses will get through to us. He also knows that more and more responses will get through as we continue to re-orient from physical dominance to three-dimensional wholeness of spirit, mind, and body.

I hope that my perspective on how, why, and when the need for prayer began has impressed upon you how vitally important it is. If there is one ingredient that is essential for our sustained spiritual development, it is PRAYER! Of all principles, prayer is the one we learn at an early age. Most parents teach their children simple childhood prayers, "Now I lay me down to sleep…" These early prayers form the beginnings of teaching us to utter important wants and needs to God for our life's existence.

Prayer is a universal custom and has been throughout history. While I don't want to provide a history lesson, I would like to spend a brief moment discussing prayer from an Afro-centric perspective.

The ancient Africans have always had an oral tradition at the core of all other traditions they developed. They understood the power of the spoken word. Moreover, they recognized that only through uttering their wants and needs to a "Higher Source" could they bring to fruition and physical reality these wants and needs. They also realized the "I AMNESS" principle of God in relation to all life. They understood, as they pondered and became self realized spiritually, mentally, and physically, that this Spirit of "I AMNESS" was, is, and always will be. Consequently, utterances, supplications, libations, and prayers have always been very significant principles in their practices and traditions. One conclusion I have drawn from studying great African cultures that made significant philosophical, spiritual, scientific, technological, and cultural contributions to the world is they all had one key common denominator; as a whole they were self realized, spiritually re-oriented and whole spiritually, mentally, and physically. These cultures had leaders who led their collective people through their spiritual wholeness and maturity. These leaders understood how to tap into the AM, (I AM God), frequency and hear and receive all that God had to offer. Thus, they became empowered to view life fully spirit, mind, and body and live life fully and also teach their collective people to do the same thing. When this occurs on a collective basis, men and women achieve great things in the world.

Although I have chosen to highlight African cultures, this simple truism applies to all cultures, Eastern, European, Western, Asian, Indian, etc… Yet, I felt compelled to make a point about the African cultures because it is now common knowledge that Africa is where life as we know it as humans originated. Africa is where the original fall from grace occurred. Being the oldest, it is where men and women have had the longest to mature towards many of the spiritual principles essential to gaining wisdom, knowledge, and understanding of how to get back to spiritual re-orientation and wholeness.

Does prayer have a definition? If it does, what is that definition? In asking the Father that question one day, He responded to me, as He often does through input from the Holy Spirit on my meditations and introspections, by first saying, "Son, I'm glad you asked." He went on to define prayer as follows.

"Prayer is Divine Utterances, the Anointed-Sacred Expression, the manifestation of My Perfect Will, the Substance of My Grace unto thee, The Power behind the Word of 'My' chosen, a seed of Grace, a small token of My Perfect Love for thee, a direct reflection of thy inner Spirit and Person, a pathway to My Throne of Mercy, an immovable force, an un-shakeable foundation, an intercessory bridge from Me to thee, the Beginning of all communication to Me, the End of all communication to Me, a channel of Divine Love, a measuring stick which shows thy faith, an Intimate dialogue tempered by the Holy Spirit and Christ, a Sacred-Hallowed spot between Me and thee, conviction of thy walk through the Holy Spirit, a Covenant, Promise, Miracle and Blessing between Me and thee, a higher calling, a discipline for my disciples, instruction and guidance through and by the Holy Spirit, life for the spirit, essential for the spirit, a living and breathing servant of Me, a cry from My distressed, downtrodden and burdened, a call for My Power, Works, and Action, a means of worship, reverence, humility, and praise unto Me, pleasing to your spirit, and My Spirit, the highest expression of self, one of the Sacred Keys to life, My Perfect Response to your every need, a small sample of My Power, a healing force, Unconditional Love from Me to thee. You see my son, Prayer is infinite in its scope, definition, capacity and purpose. Continue to grow and seek the fullness of self and you will continue to grow in the fullness of your prayers. The Holy Spirit and Christ shall continue to intercede on your behalf and make your prayers perfect to meet your needs."

Introspection, (within-without thinking), reflection, analysis, and meditation are essential to understand the substance of God's profound revelations in our lives. It is important as you begin to mature and re-orient into fullness of spirit, mind, and body, to introspect, reflect, meditate, and analyze what God lays on your spirit, heart, and mind. As you do, you will continue to increase your wisdom, knowledge, and understanding. Here's an analogy to make my point. At the age of 5, most children go to kindergarten. In kindergarten, they are introduced to many of the elementary concepts for their future educational development. In the beginning, they learn many new, wondrous concepts. Many of these concepts may not make sense and seem foreign initially. In time, these new, wondrous concepts begin to make sense because during the teaching process, children are taught to think, reason, and understand. In time, they are taught more advanced concepts to add to their initial elementary concepts. They begin to see how their initial new, wondrous concepts fit and make sense as they progress to higher grades through thinking, reasoning, and understanding. In time, they put all the pieces together and begin to know, understand, and learn. They are acquiring wisdom, knowledge, and understanding through the process of learning. The process of learning requires thought, introspection, reflection, and meditation in order to acquire wisdom, knowledge, understanding, insight, and clarity. This is a truism whether that learning is spiritual, mental, or physical.

A lot of perspective and insight lies within the definition of prayer God revealed to me. One of my purposes in writing this humble work is to share what I have been blessed to receive and understand for your benefit. By sharing my perspective, I can also show you how I have applied my own personal introspection, reflection, analysis, and meditation to seek wisdom, knowledge, and understanding. While many, many phrases within the definition stand out, I am only going to highlight the ones I have been led to. I encourage you to do your own introspection, reflection, analysis, and meditation on any others that stand out to you.

The first phrase that stood out to me is Divine Utterances. It is not by chance that God began His explanation with Divine Utterances. All that is, was, and ever will be, would not exist in this wondrous existence we call life without God having uttered three critical words: "LET THERE BE!" The majority of chapters one and two of the book of Genesis is filled with those three critical words. Let me take you a little deeper. It is clear that utterances, words, ideas, and thoughts are things. If this is true, what differentiates Divine Utterances from our utterances? One very clear and simple difference is man and woman are not all knowing, so our utterances are limited to our perspective of past and present without any insight to the future. God is omniscient and knows all past, present, and future. So, our utterances are never fully and completely divine in nature until we re-orient ourselves spiritually. Until that occurs, we tend to utter and seek things from God without the benefit of His omniscient counsel. Our focus for what is uttered and asked for is designed to satisfy our physical wants, desires, and needs, and based on our present and past wants, desires, and needs. As we transition towards fuller spiritual maturity, we learn to think, reason, and utter tempered with the Holy Spirit's input. In aligning our thoughts, reasoning, and utterances with the Holy Spirit's, we also align our utterances to God. This process is one that improves and is mastered through time and experience.

Let me explain. Often, we think about a situation or issue we need to pray about. In our physical and mental nature, we also think about what we think we need in response to that situation. In meditating and pondering over what we think we need to utter in prayer, the Holy

Spirit chimes in with His small, quiet voice and convicts us with what God wants us to utter in prayer. However, what God wants for us and expresses through the Holy Spirit's small, quiet whisper is not what we wanted physically or mentally with the situation or issue. So, we ignore or rationalize away that small, quiet, inner Holy Spirit voice and pray for what we want based on physical and mental insights and impulses. You see, God gives us the free will, just as he did Adam, (see Genesis, Chapter 2, verse 17), to choose what we seek from Him in prayers and utterances. So we pray what we want based on our physical and mental insights and impulses and eventually get what we prayed for. However, in time, we realize we got what we thought we needed physically and mentally only to realize it is not what we needed entirely. In many such cases, we get what we uttered, and realize it is not at all what we need. Or, we do not get our prayer answered and wonder why God has chosen not to answer it. The point is: when we seek to pray for a want, desire, or need without the benefit of spiritual insight, maturity, and orientation unto God, it is seldom, (in fact, almost never in total), what we need for that want, desire, or need.

76

Let's look at the same scenario from another perspective. We are once again at that point where that small, quiet, inner voice of the Holy Spirit is telling us something different from what we physically or mentally thought we wanted to utter in prayer. This time, although we disagree or are begrudgingly listening, we do. We pray for what we are led to by the Holy Spirit. In time, our prayer is answered and we realize what we prayed for was entirely what we needed. In most cases, we realize immediately what we have gotten is what we needed. In other cases, we have to look back after further growth, or after more experiences, to realize what we received was what we needed.

Growing from our human tempered, (physical and mental impulses), to Divine Utterances, (hearing and trusting the Holy Spirits voice of reason and tempering), is a process that takes time. It is also a process that is continual through life as you evolve into the fullness of your spiritual re-orientation into a spirit, mind, and body centered adult. Interestingly, as you grow, you will get it right sometimes and fail at other times. Failures can result for a number of reasons. Sometimes failures are due to a physical weakness or selfish want. In other cases, it is a mental weakness or selfish perspective and we think we know better than the God who made us what is best. We can also succeed at one level with an issue or challenge and fail with that same issue or challenge at a higher level. For example, a person may be very prayerful and seek God's guidance when it comes to matters of his career as he begins to work for a living. Over the years, he prospers and enjoys the enormous success that results. In time, he reachs the top of his careers and is now very wealthy. If God tries to steer him towards a more benevolent career that does not have the wealth and success attached to it, that same person now struggles with making that career move. Yet, he has listened and followed God's guidance every step of the way with his career to this point. He may even, at this point, begin to reason more based on physical and mental impulses and attach more of his career success to his own knowledge and hard work as the reason for his success, instead of God's guidance. He now begins to block the Holy Spirit's voice of reason that is telling him to trust God and also go where He is leading, as he has in the past with his career decisions. Several outcomes are possible. However, remember that our own prayers and utterances, without spiritual tempering and guidance, are seldom, (to never), what we need entirely. Let's say in this instance, he has chosen to ignore the Holy Spirit and chooses not to change careers. The success and prosperity he has enjoyed in the past is no longer grounded in the spiritual tempering and guidance that got him there. Since he has chosen to follow after physical and mental impulses, his focus for guidance is susceptible to physical and mental wants, desires, and needs. The spiritual guidance behind making career choices he once trusted is no longer a part of his decision making. Eventually, he will make unwise career moves that could result in him losing all of the success and prosperity he has gained. Or, he could continue to grow more materially successful but gain that success through having to make unscrupulous choices that are against his spiritual principles. Or, he is now are so self-absorbed through his physical and mental impulses, wants, desires, and needs that he makes career choices that help his continued material gain at the expense of all others in his work environment. At the end of this vicious cycle, he remain wealthy but unfulfilled because he now has material and physical wealth without wholeness of spirit, mind, and body. Or, just as he has made unscrupulous choices or gained by hurting others, someone else will come along and do the same thing to him to get ahead. His suffering will be far greater because the law of reciprocity always assures far more exponential returns, good or bad, than we send out. I realize I have painted a pretty drastic picture here but the purpose of painting such a drastic picture is to make a point.

Let's pick up this same analogy at the point where the Holy Spirit is now seeking to provide guidance and explore another outcome. Under the same situation, he again still chooses to ignore God's leading to pursue a more benevolent career that has less success and wealth. However, he now begins to struggle greatly because he is not choosing the path he is being led to. Through his struggles, he realizes how he arrived at past successes and accepts the Holy Spirit's leading, and ventures into the new career. Now, he has restored the spiritual orientation and his prosperity and success can continue. God may choose to increase his wealth outside of his job, but to a point that his job is just a career that allows him to be used to help others who need to know how to seek God's guidance to have model careers. Or, in time, he may find that while the job did not initially offer the success and wealth his old job did, in the long run, he grows to be far more prosperous. Or, he may find that the job is not as lucrative as his old job, but it offers far more satisfaction and enjoyment, and he now loves his work and looks forward to going to work. Again, the possible outcomes are infinite.

Revisiting our analogy at the point where the Holy Spirit is seeking to steer him to a new job again, let's say he choose not to change and follow their spiritual leading. As a result, he continues to have the economic success in their present job, but starts to have major changes and problems in the work environment. At this point, he reflects back and realizes he never had major changes and problems before of such drastic measures. In thinking back, he also realizes he has never chosen to make a career move against the reasoning and tempering of the Holy Spirit. He also thinks about any problems and challenges in the course of his career in the past, and realizes how smoothly and efficiently he was able to address them compared to his present chaotic mess. He now realizes the difference is he made a career move of his own free will and ignored God's guidance through remaining in his present job. He also realized he has failed in applying one very key thing that has enabled his successes, following God's guidance in his career decisions. At this point, he decides to get back to what has worked and chooses to enter the career he had chosen not to pursue. Failure is not always bad. In fact, it is sometimes very essential to our growth and development. Through our failures, we are convicted to seek after changes in our approach, our perspective, our orientation, and our understanding. Also, we realize our need to seek spiritual guidance, growth, development, and communion. We most definitely do not forget failures and gain great maturity from them. A failure is only a failure when we fail to seek conviction, improvement, growth, and proper perspective from God on why we failed. If we seek sincerely, He will help us learn and continue in our growth and progression towards spiritual maturity.

Why is God's guidance, tempering, and conviction through the Holy Spirit such an essential ingredient for making our prayers complete? The whole point of providing you drastic outcomes from my previous analogies should make it clear. ONLY GOD HAS OMNISCIENCE! So when we temper, incline, and modify our prayers to our inner leadings, we take advantage of God's omniscient wisdom to assure we are completely seeking what is best for our needs. That omniscient wisdom enables us to know that God already knows when He gives us guidance through the Holy Spirit, what we need completely, and thus what we are lacking in our prayers and utterances to make our prayers complete. Let me pose a question to make the point. If you could have complete insight, understanding, and knowledge about each choice that you face in life before you make it, would you be able to make the decisions that give you the perfect outcome to each choice? Through allowing the quiet, inner voice of the Holy Spirit to temper your utterances and prayers, you have just that. The toughest aspect to spiritual guidance, conviction, and tempering is accepting that some of our own physical and mental impulses and wants are not what we need. That is especially tough because we still have veto power in the form of free will to choose those impulses and wants even when given wise counsel and direction.

It takes practice, patience, discipline, and maturity. Through practice, we become naturally better. Through patience, we remain steadfast and stick to it through the end. Through discipline and maturity, we remind ourselves to stay focused and also recall past successes, or failures, when we have applied the proper process or failed to apply the proper process.

I must make one last point on Divine Utterances. As you grow into a mature spiritual adult, you have a responsibility on what and how you speak, utter, and pray. That's why Christ gave us the model prayer, (see the Lord's Prayer in Matthew, Chapter 6, verses 9-13). It is true that you must be careful what you ask for and how you ask for it! Moreover, it is important that you be thoughtful, meditative, introspective, and inclined towards the Holy Spirit before asking.

What you ask and pray for, as a mature spiritual adult, can great impact your life and others. What you ask and pray for can greatly hinder or greatly accelerate your growth. What you ask and pray for can bring great joys or great pains. Hopefully you will seek good things for you and others in your prayers and utterances. I often think of God in a parental capacity because He is the most gracious, patient, and loving parent that ever existed. He is tolerant and forgiving of our errors. Yet, as we mature, He expects us to know how to ask and utter in a more mature way. If we fail to ask in a mature way, He allows us to bear the consequences of our lack of insight and maturity for that which we utter and ask, much like our parents let us make mistakes as children as long as they are not dangerous to us so we can learn from that mistake for growth and development. The lack of thought, introspection, and an inclining nature towards the Holy Spirit often brings strife, pain, and challenges we must bear and get through.

The next key thought that needs further emphasis is pathway. A pathway is a course that leads to and from a destination. Going back to my original premise that man and woman have been trying to get back the keys to that sacred and anointed place where God resides, we must realize that finding, traveling, and following the proper path that God created is essential. It is also a process that is ongoing and challenging, but well worth it! The path, as it relates to prayer, also has to be discovered and followed as we grow and mature. If we get off the path, we lose time and struggle for growth that is far easier to reach when we are on the path. However, it is sometimes necessary to lose the path for the sake of understanding the difference to being on the proper path and not being on the proper path. Sometimes you do not know which path is right until you have definitively experienced the wrong path. You do not know your prayers are Divinely complete until you have reaped the results, or failed to reap the results of one that is not. A pathway is also a two-way route. People can either go to or from on this pathway. God did not choose to separate Himself from man and woman. Man and woman chose to separate themselves from God. Yet, God loves man and woman so much; He still left a pathway back to His most intimate and cherished children. God welcomes the chance to travel back to us as well! Often, we feel as if we are the only ones traveling when actually, God is the only one traveling towards us as He waits patiently for our further growth and development. A good comparison to clarify my point is many adults are much like infants who need physical nourishment to grow strong and healthy mentally and physically when it comes to spiritual nourishment. They only call to God in times of major, earth-shattering crises and turmoil, just like a baby cries when it is hungry. Babies rely on the parent to provide the proper nutrients when they are hungry. We must also rely on God for spiritual nutrients as we grow and develop spiritually. A path has a definite beginning, course, and length and is traveled by you and others. You will find others that will provide guidance and direction along the way. You will also provide guidance and direction for others on the same path, but at different stages as you progress.

Intimate dialogue is critical in prayer and essential to discuss further. A good way to think about intimate dialogue is to compare and differentiate it from other types of normal daily discussions we have in different settings in our day-to-day lives. We talk with co-workers, strangers, friends, and family. Not all of those discussions are intimate. Many are very necessary and essential, but few are intimate. A new mother and father cooing, singing, and complimenting the beauty of their newborn baby is an intimate dialogue. A newlywed couple discussing their hopes and dreams for many years of happiness together is an intimate dialogue. A newfound lover expressing his love to a soul mate in as many ways and words as possible is an intimate dialogue. A cherished friend comforting his best friend during a time of crisis and need is an intimate dialogue. When one has intimate dialogue, he has the attention, compassion, love, nurturing, support, and guidance of the person with whom he is talking to. Yet, with God, there is even more involved in our intimate utterances. Man and woman, in their infinite smallness, could never fully measure the Grace, Compassion, Love, Joy, Anointing, and Power God makes available when our intimate prayers are sincere and Divinely uttered. We can combine the attention, compassion, love, nurturing, support, and guidance we offer with unlimited, unconditional love, grace, and power. That is as close as we can get to understand how powerful an intimate dialogue with God is for us. One thing intimacy requires is private attention and space. It is very difficult to have an intimate interaction with a child, friend, or soul mate in a public environment. Most intimate discussions are held in a very quiet, peaceful, serene setting. The people involved in the intimate discussions also set aside all other concerns and issues and focus on the topic at hand. That intimate issue is priority. It is treated with urgency over all else. We need to be just as mindful and respectful of our prayers. We should give the same special space, focus, urgency, and attentiveness to our prayers. That is why great prophets, religious teachers, leaders, and figures of the Bible, (including our model example-Christ), often went into seclusion to a private place to speak with God. They understood the special power of intimate dialogue with God. They also knew that giving homage and reverence to God through giving special space, focus, priority, and urgency to those intimate dialogues enabled them to get the same in return from Him and enabled tremendous growth, expediency, and power to their prayers. Try making your prayers private and intimate with God. As you do, you will find fuller understanding, growth, power, blessings and results. God will smile upon you and your prayers as you make them special, intimate, and sincere. The more mature and divinely insightful your prayers, the more potent and blessed the outcomes become. As that occurs, you are growing more spiritually mature and oriented.

Prayer is necessary and "life for the spirit." Let's probe deeper with this important perspective. Food and water are necessary for the physical body. Prayer is the food and water for the spirit because it provides the sustenance for the spirit. Our spirits grow, flourish, and are nourished through communion with the Holy Spirit, Christ, and God. The spoken utterance creates interaction between our spirit and the Holy Spirit, Christ, and God. Once the AM, (I AMNESS), frequency is re-established, our spirits can mature. Through prayer, we mature into all of the fullness and spiritual oneness that we have to re-discover in our journey to become a fully mature three-dimensional, (spirit, mind, and body) adult. Consider the food and water analogy from another perspective. Proper food and water foster a healthy physical body. Proper focus and discipline, through prayer, foster a healthy spirit. If we do not have the proper focus and discipline through prayer, our spirit is not conscious of the convictions, counsel, and guidance of the Holy Spirit, Christ, and God. Without this focus and discipline, we are not open to the spiritual truisms in our environment that form from spiritual fellowships, worshipping customs, spiritual texts, mentors, and guides who come our way to help us seek awareness, introspection, insight, and growth. We are not conscious of, nor do we appreciate, the examples of others who have come before to show us how to become fully three dimensional and thus live as completely as God made us. Prayer is also necessary and life for the spirit because since the spirit is not physically visible and tangible, Divine Utterances are the ONLY source through which to AWAKEN, SPARK, TOUCH, and REACH our inner spirits and the spiritual essence of the Holy Spirit, Christ, and God. Remember: thoughts, words, and expressions, though not physical and tangible, are things that in time manifest physical things. We call those thoughts, which are not, into a physical realm, which is, just as God did in creating all with speaking all that is through His spoken word. The spirit of man and woman becomes visible in our tangible, physical realm through the thoughts, words, expressions, and ultimately the good works we perform for others and ourselves; just as the spirit of Christ was visible through the signs, wonders, and miracles He performed among the masses. A good concept to make my point is love. Love is not a physical, tangible thing. Yet the evidence of love is clearly visible through the acts and actions one performs in the interests of those he or she loves.

Prayer as a call for God's works and action is a vital point, especially as we grow into fully mature spirit, mind and body adults. When people call, they are seeking to be heard. They are also seeking to fill a need or express a need or want. I am sure most people know the fairy tale about the boy shepherd who cried wolf to his village. The young boy had no discretion about crying wolf to alarm the village to respond, even when there were no wolves present to threaten the sheep he was guarding. When the wolves finally came, the boy cried wolf, as he had countless times before, the village did not respond. This fairy tale makes an important point about our calls to God or His work and action. Our cries and utterances seeking God's works and actions should be important. We should not call out for help for things we can do for ourselves. Daddy's favorite saying is; "The possible things we do, the unpossible things, we let God do." If we are diligent in seeking spiritual nourishment, growth and development, we will find that God has already made accessible many of the things we need for development without even having to call unto Him for work or action. If there is a life issue or challenge that is blocking your progression and you have exhausted all resources and ideas within your grasp of spiritual morals, knowledge, and principles, then it is time to call upon God to provide help, guidance, clarity and deliverance. Often, God answers your prayers by pointing you towards solutions through others in your life: family, friends, co-workers, the Holy texts, or even total strangers.

How does one know when to call on God and when not to? That is a very important question because our normal nature is to think from a physical and mental perspective that we can solve most of life's issues on our own. Yet, in order to be spirit-led, spirit-convicted, and spiritually re-oriented, we have to shift our natures away from physical and mental alone when dealing with life's issues. It is a fine line to tread. The best answer I can offer is to try calling on God and see how He responds. Call Him for all things and analyze what the outcome is. Keep in mind the parent-child analogy. A young child realizes at some point when he cries the parent will pick him up or give him food. Yet, there are many times when the parent does not pick him up or give him food. As the child grows, he has to reason to understand that at times when he cries, the parents do not pick him up or feed him. The child has to understand why. Thus, as with a baby, you must seek to understand how, why, and when God responds to your calls. As you begin to understand how, why, and when God responds, you must also begin to understand when He wants you to act on your own with your present resources and maturity to get what you are seeking. Or realize you do not, at that point, need what you are seeking. Babies eventually reason they do not need to be picked up or fed when the parents do not respond because they remember that their parents respond when they need attention and nourishment. Eventually, the child stops crying just to get picked up or fed. Maybe the child cries because it is sleepy. The parents know the child does not need to be picked up to go to sleep and does not pick him up. In time, the child will stop crying and go to sleep on its own. As the child grows older and begins to talk, crying does not get the same response from the parents because the parents can now ask the child what it is crying for. As you mature spiritually, you will be able to communicate with God through your prayers and utterances and also understand His response through your practice, analysis, and meditations. Although calling for God's works and actions is a fine line, it is better to start out calling on Him too much and see the outcome than not calling on Him at all. The baby cries initially for a variety of things and as it grows, the baby learns what the parents will respond to as the parents also learn which needs the baby is crying for that need to be filled. While God already knows our needs, He is waiting for us to understand our needs and call out accordingly as we grow. If you do not call Him at all, then chances are you are not becoming spiritually re-oriented but remaining physically and mentally focused. Learning the proper measure of when to call comes as you grow.

Prayer is the perfect medium, and understanding why is one of the key perspectives for spiritual re-orientation. Think about the different aspects of what, how, and why it is essential for your growth into fullness of spirit, mind, and body. Continuing the comparison of the development of a baby earlier, an infant cries to let its parents know there is some need. Our prayers let God know of our needs. As the infant begins to talk, it can tell parents what it wants and needs instead of crying to express these needs. As the child becomes a teenager, it asks for more complicated things and often does not understand if the parents do not provide them. When the child becomes an adult, and a parent themselves, it better understands that many things, infants, children, and teens want are not best for their growth and development. In fact, many things they want are actually detrimental and potentially damaging to their healthy growth and development. This can be true for our prayers as well. Often what we want is not what we need at the time for further spiritual growth and development. In fact, what we want can be detrimental and damaging to our continued healthy growth and development. If you have ever wondered why a prayer that you thought was critically important was not answered, it is because God knows far better, as the consummate parent, than you that you do not need it at that point. Further, as the consummate parent, He knows the proper time and season for responding to your prayers. It most definitely is not a failure on your part; nor God's, if a prayer goes unanswered. It is, instead, God responding as a loving Guardian should by not fulfilling your want because it is not best for you. As you progress into maturity, you will better understand why some of your past prayers were not answered. More importantly, you will better understand what to pray for tempered with the proper spiritual guidance from the Holy Spirit. Until that occurs, Christ intercedes on your behalf to make sure your prayers are acceptable to God and also good for your continued development and growth.

Prayer is a multi-faceted resource. We can pray for our needs, pray on behalf of others, (intercession), pray through intimate dialogue just to have a private conversation with God, pray to offer thanks and praises for His infinite Blessings, pray to call God's promises to us into action, pray to remind God of His commitments, covenants, and promises to us, pray to claim those commitments, covenants, and promises to us, pray for anointing and power in times of battles, crisis, and challenges, pray for strength, wisdom, power, and understanding to do works for us, others, and Him, pray a testament of our victories in times of battle to give us strength for the present battles, pray a prayer of healing for ourselves and others, pray a prayer of encouragement and support, pray for confirmations, wisdom, knowledge, understanding, clarity of thought, focus, and reason, pray for guidance and development, pray for repentance and change in our lives. There are few, few resources at our disposal more powerful than prayer. As we mature into the fullness of spirit, mind, and body, our prayers increase in the full benefit, power, attention, and anointing God has available. It is no mystery when we examine the example set by Christ that He prayed consistently and continually to deal with every aspect of His life. Although Christ had all power and authority of God the Father, He still acknowledged, as a physical man, the need to Divinely Utter unto God for all challenges, issues, works, and deeds He performed to confirm the prophecies of His life. In order for us to realize fully all the growth, blessings, victories, joys, promises, and greater works we long to achieve, we must follow Christ's example and be diligent in prayer. Use this invaluable medium because it is one of the most important keys to unlock the path to that sacred, hallowed place to God. I'll conclude by asking you to ask yourself this question. What frequency are you trying to reach God on? AM or FM?

Law 7 – Grace, "God's Unconditional, Total Provision"

How much does God love us? How forgiving, compassionate, caring, empathetic, patient, understanding, and supportive is He of us? The answers to these two important questions is so simple, it is almost unbelievable! He LOVES us so infinitely much that He holds Himself to an unconditional provision that offers us His Heritage, Protection, Guidance, Blessings, Anointing, and Power even if we fail in every chance to follow His Laws, Voice, Teachings, Statues, Principles, Precepts, and Commandments. That unconditional provision is GRACE! How awesome is that? I'll answer my own question but ask you to answer it for yourself as well. It is so much more awesome and an ultimate expression of God's intimate, special, unique love of us that only God, in all of His magnificence, is capable of. Grace is one of many other laws and provisions that testify to us how special God sees us in all of this existence we call life.

I would like to attempt to show you a small perspective into the mind of God. I am sure I cannot do it adequate justice but hope my attempt does provide a perspective to further your understanding and growth. Here is the glimpse I see. At the dawn of creation of all that God thought first, then spoke, then became, God was so awesomely omniscient that He knew, before His creations began to manifest, the beginning, middle, and end of all that is, was, and is ever to be at that instant. I know it is very difficult to grasp the mind of God. In fact, it is impossible to grasp, in its entirety, the mind of God when we are but a very, very small spec in comparison to the whole of all that God is. I am but a lowly man who, like many others throughout the histories of our existence, has been blessed to seek after God's infinite wisdom and understanding. So any small perspective I can share is still infinitely beneath the reality of just how great, wondrous, all encompassing, and infinite – and any number of other adjectives I could use to give an accurate picture. However, I am humbly thankful for any portion of His Omniscient Mind He reveals to me, and through me, to share for your understanding. Stick with me here. I promise there is a point for clarity and I hope He has already allowed me to give you some points of clarity for your uniquely specific and specifically unique needs thus far in this work. I also trust that His promise to me to: "Bring clarity through the word for my people and His people" is being fulfilled. I further trust that they have because God knows my intent is to be of use for Him.

Continuing with my theme of providing a glimpse of the mind of God, only He knows the beginning, middle, and end. Man and woman, to compare, never, ever from a mental and physical perspective – know the beginning, middle, and end of any sequence of our life events and experiences. We only have the present and past to draw from in understanding life. We can take a calculated, educated guess about our future life experiences based on our past experiences. We can even take calculated, educated guesses about future life events and experiences based on intellectual, factual knowledge we have from our past experiences or read of from others who have had similar experiences. We can also take calculated, educated guesses about future life events and experiences based on the vicarious experiences of our closest friends, family members, and loved ones. However, while we do gain wisdom, understanding, and insight, we still do not know the outcome of that event until it has passed. We can reflect back on that experience and fine-tune our perspective so we can learn how to better deal with that event if we experience it again in the future. We can duplicate the experience or event if it was pleasant, positive, or favorable. Or, if it is challenging, negative, painful, or unpleasant, we consider what we could have done to bring about a more positive outcome or avoid that experience altogether. In some cases, our changes and adjustments work; in some cases, they do not. So, we, as humans, are limited to the now and past, to experience life's events and adjust, grow, and change as life goes forward. We cannot go back and retrieve an experience after it has occurred because it is not physically possible to go back in time. We can recall past experiences and use that knowledge, insight, wisdom, and understanding to plan and anticipate how to deal with similar future events to come. Here is the point of my glimpse into God's mind that I want you to consider and reflect on. Who is in a better position of knowing how, why, where, and what we need to become fully spirit, mind, and body adults? God – who knows all there was, is, and ever will be – or us who only knows past and present? I am sure the answer is clear, God!

What does glimpsing into the mind of God and the comparison of our differences have to do with grace? It has a very significant impact on our need for grace. You see, God knew instantly all past, present, and future as it pertains to our entire existence when He thought the first thought of conceiving all of this existence of the lives of all men and women throughout our entire history. In His awesome, all-knowing capacity, He realized all the Laws, Teachings, Statutes, Principles, Precepts, and Commandments He would create were not sufficient without His unconditional provision of Grace. He loved us so very much from the very dawn of creation that He provided His grace as a fail safe provision to assure that if all else failed, we would still have His Grace to find that sacred place between Him and us.

Wouldn't you think all the many laws, teachings, statutes, principles, precepts, and commandments God made should be sufficient for man and woman to live fully realized, three-dimensional – spirit, mind, and body – lives He intended them to live? The answer should be clearly a resounding yes! Yet, Adam and Eve proved early on that the answer was no. I'll use an analogy to bring it to the natural. A teacher who is passionate, loving, and caring about his students makes certain that every possible resource available is used to insure his students have the chance to learn everything he teaches. In addition, the teacher sacrifices his time, energy, and experiences and is ready at all times to make sure all students have the best possible opportunity to learn, under the best possible conditions in which to learn. However, the difference between the teacher, as a human, and God is clear and simple. If the student fails unequivocally after the teacher applies all teaching resources, time, energy, and experiences, the teacher cannot wipe the grade slate clean through unconditional love and give the student an A. God has always known that man and woman were not capable in their physically dominant natures to live life in accordance with His laws and statutes, which were rooted in their spiritually dominant natures. Thus, through His unconditional provision of GRACE, He allowed room for physical and mental errors as man and woman became fully, maturely "Spirit-Realized." Even in man and woman becoming "Spirit-Realized" and growing towards three-dimensional – spirit, mind, and body – adults, He also realized they would still need His powerful GRACE along the way. Grace is still very essential because man and woman will continue to make many mistakes along their journey towards complete maturity.

One of the best ways to remember how God's grace applies is to remember how parents and families allow room for errors in their relationships. Parents must give their children the spiritual, moral, cultural, social, legal, and personal principles and rules to live by. Equally, a large family of people consisting of parents, siblings, uncles, aunts, and cousins must also have a common base of spiritual, moral, cultural, social, legal, and personal principles to live by successfully in their community. Parents must give their children room to make mistakes in properly learning to adhere to the spiritual, moral, cultural, social, legal, and personal principles and rules they were taught. By the same token, parents – just as God does us – monitor, evaluate, and provide guidance and correction in a loving, nurturing, and caring manner to their children when mistakes are made. They also provide leeway by not always punishing, chastising, or disciplining their children every time the child makes a mistake. Given that the parents have had to learn through making some mistakes themselves, they should use their own experiences to reflect upon their own errors and empathize with how the error their child made could have happened. If after proper guidance and correction, the child continues to make the same errors, then discipline may be required. In all of this process, the parent is applying parental grace to his child. That parental grace is giving the child the proper measure of guidance, correction, support, leeway, and patience to see that the child is growing as it tries and fails to apply life's principles properly. On a larger scale, the same grace must be given with the community of parents, siblings, uncles and aunts, cousins and friends. While it becomes far more complex in that each individual family in a community is unique, grace becomes the bridge that allows peace, communication, tolerance, reconciliation, support, and trust to see that ultimately everyone grows towards the same spiritual, moral, social, legal, and personal principles to function as a whole.

I realize that I have thrown a lot of information, knowledge, and insight at you. Since this chapter has far more information because each chapter continues to build on the previous one, I am providing the chapter Spiritual Truisims from this chapter segmented by their appropriate subject for simplicity and clarity.

Chapter 2 Foundation and Fundamental Spiritual Truisms
- How God Defines You -

- From a spiritual perspective, God sees you as a "chosen people" a royal priesthood. Once you accept and realize you are a spirit in a body and begin the process of spiritual awareness and re-orientation, you are accepted into God's priesthood. If you are a priest, or priestess, how should that role affect and effect your purpose and direction in life?

- Our Lives Are A Ministry -

- Our lives are a ministry. Everyone's life serves to minister to others they encounter along life's wondrous journey. That is ESPECIALLY TRUE for those who seek to walk a spiritual path in life. Your actions, reactions, expressions, behaviors, and spiritual platform – what you say and how you define your spiritual principles and beliefs – are all under observation by everyone you meet in day-to-day life. It is essential that what you say and how you define yourself is clearly reflective in your acts and actions to and for others.

- Once you accept your spiritual platform and life as a ministry, you become set apart from viewing life as a purely physical existence. You are therefore set apart from a world that is physically focused and oriented. If you are no longer dominated by your physical urges and desires, but are in a world that is dominated by physical urges and desires, then it is no wonder that you are PECULIAR to the world.

- How will you change your life's choices and the acts and actions you take in dealing with others in the context of your own personal ministry? You must realize how critically important it is to espouse, stand firm, and act on and react to others in a manner that reflects who you are in the truest aspect of what you stand for spiritually.

- You DO NOT have to be perfect to be of ministerial benefit to others. You just have to be open to be of benefit and have faith that you can give perfectly that which you are purposed to as you seek to be of use – just as great men and women throughout the history of the Bible did.

  - You MUST Re-orient From Physical to Spiritual -

- In the process of re-orienting ourselves from physical consciousness and dominance to spiritual consciousness and dominance comes physical rebellion.

- The first battle of rebellion starts within you. You must concentrate on your own personal, inner rebellion. The world around you is the battleground that contains all of the worldly weaponry that makes your inner struggle more challenging and difficult. By concentrating your thoughts, energies, and efforts within – being introspective and reflective of you you can fight a focused, strategic battle that will overcome your rebellions. Don't let the outside world distract you from working on your inner self.

- Re-orientation towards being spiritually lead is an ongoing process. Struggles, challenges, and adversities come with any process. Through the struggles, challenges, and adversities, come strength, wisdom, knowledge, understanding, experience, faith, maturity, and growth.

- Don't let the struggles, challenges, and adversities of your re-orientation discourage you. Each and everyone that has or will ever live – even Christ Himself went through them. Let them serve as a motivation that you are getting closer to your outcome because you are. Let your successful triumphs over past struggles, challenges, and adversities give you FAITH and STRENGTH to face your future struggles, challenges, and adversities.

- Self-analysis – introspection – and actualization are VITALLY IMPORTANT to understanding and growing through and past your challenges to re-orient yourself into a Spiritually dominant person. It is through being dedicated and strong enough to look at YOU from "within-without" that you gain insight, understanding, wisdom, and guidance to allow continued development. Don't get down on yourself for finding flaws. Until you find your flaws, you cannot rid yourself of them.

- Listening to that soft, quiet, inner voice of the HOLY SPIRIT is the path to overcoming physical rebellion. You will find that simple task far more difficult for some rebellious challenges than others. However, that soft, quiet, inner voice will patiently speak TRUTH consistently until you are mature enough to hear it, receive it, and grow from it.

- Thoughts, Words, and Expressions Are Things -

- Thoughts, words, and expressions ARE THINGS. Before everything in the heavens and earth were created, God SPOKE. Thoughts, words, and expressions begin in the mind and spirit, and ultimately materialize in the physical world. God first thought in His infinite mind and visualized all that is, was, and ever will be.

- The more spiritually mature – Christ-like – we become, the more powerful our abilities to manifest that which we speak! Our ability to manifest our thoughts, words, and expressions at all before we are fully mature, is a sign of our full potential yet realized.

- It is very important to focus your thoughts, words, and expressions towards that which is positive, good, and beneficial for you and others. This is vitally important whether you are immature or mature. In fact, it is probably more important when you are immature because you can do great harm to yourself and others because you do not have the wisdom, awareness, and understanding of how your thoughts, words, and expressions shape your own outcomes and the outcomes of others. A mature spiritual person knows the awesome power behind using his thoughts, words, and expressions and also the responsibility to use them for the good of him and others.

- If we are physically oriented, our thoughts, words, and expressions are focused on and controlled by our physical desires. Most physical desires are selfish in nature and geared towards physical, worldly wants and needs – sexual pleasure, material possessions, wealth, and popularity. Our physical needs are natural and important to sustaining physical life, but must be put in the proper context for which God intended them – sex is for procreation in a marriage and not selfish, wild pleasure at the expense of others – for example.

- Physical wants and desires CANNOT satisfy the spirit. If you put all of your energies on pleasing your physical needs, you will still find something lacking and missing in your life. Only by seeking that in you that is spiritual, can you become completely whole as God intended.

- As you acquire increased spiritual knowledge, you must ponder, meditate, and incline your heart and mind to the Holy Spirit for continued growth, insight, and understanding. This enables continued growth and maturation.

- Think about WHAT you allow to enter your mind and GUARD your words, thoughts, and expressions. After all, the more Christ-like you become in your walk, the MORE POWERFUL is your ability to make REAL –good or bad that which you think, say, express, and envision for you and others.

- God's Spiritual Laws Work Every Time -

- God's Spiritual Laws work EVERY TIME. In math, 2 + 2 will always = 4. It is the same with God's Laws. It is NOT God's Laws that change, but our CONSISTENT APPLICATION of His Laws that cause us to fail in using them. God's Laws are universal the world over, in heaven and earth, and consistent in all spiritual texts and Holy writings and scriptures.

- The Holy Spirit SPEAKS God's laws to our hearts, minds, and spirits, if we listen. God makes sure EVERYONE knows of and has the chance to know His Laws through the course of their lives.

- Love -

- Of all the commandments God gave man and woman to live by, His MOST IMPORTANT one was TO LOVE.

- There is no force or power like LOVE. Nothing can overcome love, nothing can compare to love, and love is the only thing that is never, ever wasted. Love is also the one thing that everyone and everything craves more than anything else.

- Love is the spiritual context that God and Christ spoke of as a selfless act. When we seek love from a physical perspective, it becomes selfish. Since we are in a world that is physical, born into a physical body, and oriented to think and seek that which is physical first, we are selfish in our love initially and seeking what we need rather than loving others selflessly as God intended.

- Once we stop letting our selfish physical needs and desires dictate how we give of ourselves to others, we begin to give just for the sake of helping, benefiting, and blessing others. As we do, we start to apply the principle of love in its truest sense. As we apply and give love unselfishly, we begin to see the actions of our giving in return.

- Love is not just a physical, intimate, sexual interaction in relationships. It is also acts of patience, sympathy, empathy, compassion, guidance, understanding, support, caring, giving, sacrifice, charity, and kindness to those in need in all relationships.

- Spiritual attributes – love, compassion, patience…are as SELFLESS as physical attributes are selfish. Spiritual attributes also require us to give of ourselves to others. This giving gives us inner, spiritual joy like no other joy and also allows us to open up and listen to the Holy Spirit. The Holy Spirit can then provide guidance, wisdom, conviction, insight, and understanding as we continue to seek to become spiritually re-oriented and complete –spirit, mind, and body.

- Our spiritual natures are naturally inclined towards love.

- Reciprocity -

- What we do in life, GOOD or BAD, comes back in like measure. We REAP what we SOW.

- You are not responsible for the seeds someone else sows. You are only accountable for the seeds you sow unto others.

- When harmed or hurt by someone, do not follow your physical nature and inclination to harm that person in return, or harm an innocent person. You perpetuate the harm if you do and it will return more harm to you later.

- Do what is right and good to the person who mistreated you or the other person, "turn the other cheek." To do what is right and good requires you to get past the emotion and pain. It also requires you to endure the emotion and pain and resist the temptation to inflict that same emotion and pain upon others. To do what is right and good forces you to control your physical inclinations by being spiritually-oriented enough to listen to your heart, spirit, mind, and the Holy Spirit on what is truly the right action to take.

- When you do what is right and good, the outcome for you will ALWAYS be blessed. You may still have to go through the pain, but God will give you the strength and comfort to get through it. Your example will also teach others how to respond in the same way when they are in that situation.

- Faith -

- Faith is one of God's MOST IMPORTANT tools because it is through our faith, or lack of faith, that He manifests situations that shape our lives as we seek Him.

- Unlike physical emotions, faith requires trust, belief, and confidence in God, Christ, and the Holy Spirit, and that requires confidence in that which is UNSEEN. Just as thoughts, words, and expressions are things, our faith for that which is to be, becomes a physical thing, act, or action that affects our lives in a powerful and wondrous way. So unlike physical emotions, faith can emanate from the unseen nothing to a physical thing in our life. We think and trust that it will become, and it DOES IN FACT BECOME.

- Your faith and trust should be your vision of God's promises to emanate in your life. Seek out what promises God has for you and hold on to them until they are realized. Faith serves and feeds the inner spirit, which helps nourish us to become more mature, wise, and complete.

- Faith only requires a very SMALL measure to have a very POWERFUL outcome.

- Truth -

- In our spirits, we ALL understand, know, and recognize TRUTH when we hear it.

- Our awareness is innately a part of our being through our spirit. Our spirits relate to the Holy Spirit, who provides counsel, guidance, and conviction and Christ, who provides a perfect role model or pattern for us to follow when we attempt to analyze our thoughts, actions, and deeds that are contrary to that which is truthful and right spiritually.

- Since this awareness is innate, it is there at the very beginning when we are born. It is never too early to shape and teach our children to inspire towards truth. In fact, children desire that direction from their parents and mentors.

- The more we allow ourselves to be physically lead, the harder it becomes to seek after truth from a spiritual perspective. It is also harder for us to receive and hear truth from the Holy Spirit or Christ's example, because our physical desires, wants, and needs become what we accept as right. These desires, wants, and needs are inclined toward sin. We become, as Christ said, "enslaved to those sins."

- Seeking the truth of the Holy Spirit through the counsel, guidance, and convictions of the Holy Spirit, leads to the re-orientation from physical to spiritual and sets you free, as Christ said.

- God's Spiritual Truth, written on our spirits and spoken to us through the Holy Spirit, is the HIGHEST TRUTH there is. It is the ABSOLUTE measure to which we should continually aspire with the understanding that it is a progression.

- Our spirits and the Holy Spirit are KINDRED, and the truth in us resides in our spirit. The Holy Spirit only REMINDS us of the truth we already know within and provides mentoring, counsel, guidance, conviction, and direction to that inner knowledge until we are mature enough to realize what we know. Sometimes in the midst of life's daily struggles, we forget to focus on basic spiritual principles and beliefs that provide the foundation and strength that keeps us blessed, at peace, and secure. As we continue to get caught up in those daily life struggles, we can very easily get further and further out of focus with our core spiritual principles and beliefs. Close friends and loved ones remind us of these spiritual principles and beliefs as we share those daily struggles by jogging our consciousness with a word, phrase, or belief that reminds us of those principles. Through that reminder, we get refocused and use those spiritual principles and beliefs to overcome life's issues. Through that renewed focus, we gain strength and maturity for the next challenge. As we continue to grow towards full Christ-like maturity, we will have more inner knowledge, wisdom and experience and need less guidance from others around us.

• Seeking truth requires self-analysis and introspection. This means looking at things about yourself that you may not be happy with. It means knowing your greatest flaws, physically, mentally, and spiritually. It also means knowing your greatest assets and strengths physically, mentally, and spiritually. Do not be so critical of yourself that you only look at your weaknesses and flaws. Let your assets and strengths motivate you to continue overcoming your weaknesses and flaws.

• Seeking truth requires a lot of patience, strength, perseverance, and maturity. It is often very hard to accept when we are wrong and convicted by the Holy Spirit. As we persist to aspire toward better results, we continue to grow stronger and better. We will eventually succeed through our sincere persistence.

- Wisdom -

• While knowledge is power, knowledge is of no use without WISDOM. In fact, knowledge can be dangerous in the absence of wisdom. Seeking, acquiring, and having wisdom will produce knowledge and more importantly; UNDERSTANDING of that knowledge.

- We can have COMPLETE wisdom, knowledge, and understanding of spirit, mind, and body only through properly re-orienting ourselves spiritually in perfect union with the Holy Spirit, Christ, and God. By re-orienting ourselves, we tap into God's PERFECT Wisdom, Knowledge, and Understanding.

- In the absence of God's perfect wisdom, knowledge, and understanding; which is past, present, and future, man and woman can only have knowledge of their past and present. God's wisdom, knowledge and understanding are all encompassing.

- Prayer -

- If there is ONE ESSENTIAL INGREDIENT in our sustained spiritual development, it is PRAYER!

- As we grow into fuller spiritual maturity, we learn to think and reason through listening to the Holy Spirit and aligning our utterances more closely to His voice. In aligning our utterances to His voice, we begin speaking after God's own Divine Utterances.

- When we seek and utter for a want, desire, or need without the benefit of spiritual insight, maturity, and orientation unto God, it is seldom – in total – what we need.

- What you ask and pray for can greatly impact your life and the lives of others. What you ask and pray for can hinder or greatly accelerate your growth. What you ask and pray for can bring great joys or great pains.

- If we fail to ask in a mature way, God allows us to bear the consequences for our lack of insight and maturity for that which we ask. That lack of thought, introspection, and inclination towards the Holy Spirit often brings strife, pain, and challenges we must bear and get through.

- Prayer is food and water for the spirit because it provides sustenance for the spirit. Our spirits grow, flourish, and are nourished through the communion with the Holy Spirit, Christ, and God. The spoken utterance creates interaction between our spirit and the Holy Spirit, Christ, and God. Once the AM – I AMNESS – frequency is re-established, our spirits can mature into wholeness.

- Prayer is also necessary and life for the spirit because since the spirit is not physically tangible and visible, DIVINE UTTERANCES are the only source through which to awaken, spark, touch, and reach our inner spirits and the spiritual essence of God, Christ, and the Holy Spirit.

- The good works of man and woman become visible through the good works we perform for ourselves and others, just as the spirit of Christ was visible through the signs, wonders, and miracles He performed amongst the masses.

- Our cries and utterances seeking God's works and actions should be important. We should not call out for help for things we can do ourselves.

- Although calling for God's works and actions is a fine line, it is better to call Him too much and see the outcome, than not to call Him at all. If you do not call Him at all, then chances are you are not becoming spiritually oriented but remaining physically oriented or physically and mentally focused in life.

- If you have ever wondered why a prayer that you thought was so very important was not answered, it is because God knows far better than YOU, what you need. Further, He knows the proper time and season for responding to your prayers. It is not a failure on your part, nor God's part, if a prayer is not answered. It is instead God responding, as a loving guardian should, not to fulfill your want because it is not best for your development and growth.

- Grace -

- God LOVES man and woman so INFINITELY much that He holds Himself to an unconditional provision that offers us His Heritage, Protection, Guidance, Inheritance, Blessings, Anointing, and Power even when we fail to consistently and continually follow his Laws, Voice, Teachings, Statutes, Principles, and Commandments. That unconditional provision is GRACE!

- God allows room for physical and mental error as man and woman become spirit-realized. Even in man and woman becoming spirit-realized and growing towards three-dimensional – spirit, mind, and body – adults, He also realizes they would still need His Grace along the way. Grace is still VERY ESSENTIAL because man and woman will continue to make mistakes along their journey towards wholeness.

- Just as God give us Grace, we must extend grace to each other as we seek to provide guidance, mentoring, and direction to others in our life's ministry. Just as God's Grace provides just what we need to overcome, our grace unto others is often just what they need to overcome their challenges and issues to continue to grow. If we fail to provide grace, we hinder others' growth. We also fail to secure God's continued Grace unto us since we are not mature enough to teach others what God's Grace stands for through our example.

Chapter 2 "Foundations and Fundamentals" Workbook

I realize this chapter is much longer and more detailed. It is not by chance, but by divine intentions, that this chapter is so lengthy. In order to grow and shape you from being physically-oriented into a fully realized and whole spiritually-oriented person, you must have a solid, strong, stable foundation. Therefore, as with a perfectly constructed house that requires a solid, strong, stable foundation, you must also take as much insight, knowledge, perspective, wisdom, and understanding as you need from this chapter to insure your foundation is secure and complete! The following questions should provide your continued introspection.

Question 1:

If God sees you as "a chosen people," "a royal priesthood," then how should you see and define yourself in relation to your life's goals, works and purpose?

Thoughts, Insights, and Reflections

Question 1-Thoughts, Insights, and Reflections

Question(s) 2:

How does the four basic spiritual principles: 1. "Our lives are a Ministry," 2. "We must reorient from physical consciousness to spiritual consciousness," 3. "Thoughts, words, and expressions are things, and 4. "The Spiritual Laws work every time, All the Time," change your approach to daily living? How do these principles change your approach to spiritual worship, fellowship, and development?

Thoughts, Insights, and Reflections

Question(s) 2- Thoughts, Insights, and Reflections

Question(s) 3:

How do the seven basic divine universal laws of love, reciprocity, faith, truth, wisdom, prayer, and grace apply to decisions in your own personal life experiences? Which of these principles come naturally to you and why? Which of these principles are most difficult for you to apply and why?

Insights, Thoughts, and Reflections

Question(s) 3 Insights, Thoughts, and Reflections

Question(s) 4:

What other personal perspectives and understandings have you gained from this chapter that will help you better understand yourself or further understand your spiritual development and growth? What topics do you need to seek further knowledge and understanding of from additional spiritual texts and sources?

Thoughts, Insights, and Reflections

Question(s) 4 Thoughts, Insights, and Reflections

Give Us This Day, Our Daily Bread

Chapter **3**

Each stage of life serves as a building block and progression to the next level. The building of this life is much like constructing a home from all the pieces and materials scattered and strewn in a huge pile at the beginning of a construction project. Yet, constructing our lives from the beginning back to that "Sacred Place" from whence we came is far more complicated than simply constructing an animate, physical object from its many pieces. Although constructing our lives is far more complex, the construction of a home is a good analogy. One key benefit of good analogies is they convey, through physical and mental images, spiritual principles and concepts. They bring a physical or mental perspective that we can relate to, that enables us to understand spiritual perspectives which we may not otherwise grasp. Since we are naturally physical, and in a physical world, it is easier to understand spiritual principles and concepts through physical and mental images tied to things we relate to every day. There are several significant reasons this analogy is an ideal comparison. Just as we were originally a thought and desire of our parents to conceive children before we were born, the thought of building a home has to occur before the physical materials are compiled to construct one. That initial thought eventually brings into fruition the components to build a home just as God thought FIRST before creating all that He made. The next phase of eventually building a home is the assembly of the materials. Assembling the materials requires wisdom, understanding, knowledge, (a blueprint – or plan), the skill to ensure the materials are properly assembled, and of the quality necessary to last permanently. Once the home is skillfully constructed with the proper building materials combined with the necessary wisdom, understanding, knowledge, and plan, it will last for generations and generations. By comparison, for us to become completely three-dimensional as God originally made us, and properly oriented of spirit, mind, and body, we must acquire the wisdom, understanding, knowledge, and plan for our completion to wholeness. Now that you have been provided a beginning in the first chapter, and foundation to build upon in the second chapter, it is time to provide further wisdom, understanding, knowledge, and planning by providing day to day sustenance. Through this daily sustenance, you can construct and assemble the materials to make yourself who God intended you to be in all of your fullness of spirit, mind, and body.

What was Christ speaking of in His model prayer when He asked God to "Give us this day our daily bread?" Do you think He was literally speaking of bread for physical nourishment? Or, could He have also been thinking of bread for the mind and spirit as well? One of my aims is to get you to probe deeper in seeking your understandings and leadings in the Holy Bible and other spiritual texts. One way to probe deeper is to consider things from a broader perspective. When spiritual knowledge, insight, and teaching are presented to you, try to reflect on it from as many different perspectives as you can. As you do, you will acquire a broader perspective, insight, and revelation. You begin to acquire wisdom combined with understanding. Think of it this way. God knows ALL about of everything; therefore, the more broadly you seek to view spiritual knowledge, insights, and teachings, the more clearly you understand a more complete measure of God's viewpoint. However, realize this: God reveals the level and measure of wisdom, knowledge, and understanding to you based on your unique and specific need.

Using the parent-child relationship once again for comparison, God – the parent – provides the response to us – the child – when we seek to understand. God's response is based on the level of maturity and need, (notice carefully that I did not say want), as any good, loving, responsible parent would. In other words, God will not reveal adult-level knowledge and perspective to a baby because He, being the caring, gracious, loving parent that He is, realizes the baby needs baby knowledge. When a four-year-old asks a question, the parent does not prepare a response for a full grown adult. The parent has to consider how to relate the response to the four-year olds' scope of understanding. As we continue to seek after and grow from infancy to adolescence to adulthood, God, as any proud parent would, rewards us with a higher level of wisdom, knowledge, and understanding. We earn the right to more and more through our continued efforts to grow and develop. I need to make another very important point regarding spiritual texts, teachings, and leadings. If you only seek to understand it from a literal perspective, you could miss the spiritual meaning. The Holy Bible is a great example to draw from. Reading the Bible and understanding it literally limits your perspective to a physical and mental interpretation absent of the spiritual meaning. In many cases, reading it literally reduces the perspective to a purely physical perspective. Whether the perspective is just physical, or physical and mental, which work together naturally, they fall short absent of the spiritual essence behind them. By viewing the scriptures this way, you fail to seek God's mind through the Holy Spirit, Christ, and God to understand the "Spirit" behind the literal word. Physical and mental combined is so far beneath understanding the Bible through God who inspired – through His Spirit, Christ, and the Holy Spirit – the authors to write it in the first place! How can something written and inspired through God's Spirit be understood absent of our spirit seeking Him for insight? If you really want to understand how something works, go to the person who made it. He will always intimately know best how his creation works and how it was intended to work. This point is extremely critical because man and woman have been deceived since their original fall from grace because they failed to understand the need to seek spiritual teachings, texts, and leadings from all perspectives – spirit, mind, and body. When man and woman are separated from seeking the spirit behind their spiritual teachings, texts, and leadings, they never understand or realize the true power, essence, and perspective needed to become whole of spirit, mind, and body. That is what Christ meant when He challenged the Pharisees about the laws in the book of Matthew, Chapter 23, verses 2 – 5. He was making the point that the "Spirit" behind the laws was important, not their literal interpretation of the laws, which the Pharisees used to condemn and judge the people of their times. Christ was the model reflection of the spirit behind the laws because He put into action the compassion, love, patience, respect, and humility to show others in a positive way how to apply the spiritual principles instead of judging them for their shortcomings and failures against the laws. He provided a high moral standard in living the principles of love for all consistent to His acts, and actions which taught His followers how to use those same principles actively in their dealings with others. When God first revealed to me I would write this book, He stated: "The same way man and woman have been deceived with the Word, you Shall bring clarity with your words." I understood then just how lost man and woman have been in spite of all of the spiritual teachings, texts, and leadings God has provided because they did not understand how to seek complete analysis –spirit, mind, and body in synergy – of their teachings.

Now, I'll answer the questions I posed earlier about daily bread. I am sure you have already reached a conclusion of your own as well. Since man and woman are three-dimensional, (spirit, mind, and body), and Christ was mature and knew He was complete and fully conscious of His spirit, mind, and body as God made Him, He would have known that daily bread was needed in equal measure for His spirit, mind, and body. I want to make a suggestion. As you read the Holy Bible and other spiritual texts, try thinking how it applies to you in spirit, mind and body. Try to understand which aspect of you the text relates to. As you begin to reason in this manner, you will find fuller, deeper, richer perspectives in your development.

The concept of viewing daily bread as a spiritual, mental, and physical process should provide a new, fresh perspective of how you look at each day. In the world today, most people confine spiritual sustenance to their weekend ritual of Sunday worship, or to other rituals like Bible study and church programs only. Daily bread means just that, BREAD EVERY DAY! We should receive, or give, spiritual nourishment every day. That is the ideal we should strive for. Consider physical and mental nourishment in comparison. We eat daily several times a day for good nutrition and we exercise our minds in our work and play and keep a sharp, healthy mind. Why do we, then, restrict seeking spiritual nourishment to weekend and other limited church rituals? Does not the spirit deserve, in equal portions, the same nourishment as the body and mind? That's a question for you to consider. I am sure you are thinking of spiritual nourishment based on the traditions and rituals related to your spiritual worship and church environment. It is easy to think of spiritual nourishment as a sermon, Bible class, or church office, such as ushering, singing in the choir, or visiting the sick. I am not saying these rituals are not necessary and important because they are. Any deeds and works giving of one's self in love and compassion, and to edify God and others in need, are extremely important. Day-to-day spiritual nourishment, like physical and mental nourishment, is more individual, simple, and specific. Using the traditions and rituals mentioned above as a comparison, when you focus on eating and exercising the mind, you eat as an individual in individual portions, or work and play in individual portions. Your physical and mental nourishment is individualized and specific to your needs. When you seek daily spiritual nourishment, it should be specific to you and your relationship with God. A daily dose of spiritual nourishment may be a very, very small thing, like providing an uplifting word or encouragement to someone in need. Or you may also receive an uplifting word from someone in your time of need. It may be something as small as being friendly, humble, and polite to the people you work with; even if they are not friendly, humble, and polite to you. It may be lending your spiritual insights and perspectives to someone in need. It is possible it could be something larger also. You just may provide much needed assistance to someone experiencing a major crisis. Just as physical and mental nourishment requires focus and intent, spiritual nourishment also requires focus and intent. You must be open to the possibilities that you will have the opportunity to give or receive it daily. If your focus is open to that possibility, you will be focused and intent when the opportunity arises. You do not need to focus on the size or scope of the act or actions, but just be open to seeking that daily nourishment. In order to be open to seeking spiritual sustenance, you must first be aware of the need to be open to that need. Once you are aware, you will look for opportunities to give and receive something of yourself spiritually. The beauty of spiritual nourishment is it can be given or received, and either way you become nourished and fulfilled.

Another wonderfully awesome thing about spiritual nourishment is God knows uniquely, specifically, and intimately what each of us needs for proper growth and development. It is uniquely different for everyone. One person seeks nourishment through prayer, another may seek it through music, another may seek it through kind acts towards others, another may seek it through reading and studying spiritual texts, another may seek it by leading others by example, and so on... While spiritual nourishment is unique, and intimately specific, there are some basic universal ways to seek daily nourishment.

Prayer, (especially prayers seeking guidance, praise, and intercession on behalf of others), kind acts, giving love, having compassion and caring, seeking to understand from within-without, having spiritual interactions and dialogue with others, reading spiritual texts and works, and helping others in need are all basic universal ways to receive nourishment. One essential ingredient needed for spiritual nourishment is a sincere desire and an inquisitive will to acquire nourishment. Unlike physical nourishment, which you become obviously aware of through hunger pains, a growling stomach, or headache, there are no physical or mental urges that motive us to seek spiritual nourishment. The Bible emphasizes the fruits of the spirit in Galatians, Chapter 5, verses 22 and 23: "But the fruits of the spirit is love, joy, peace, patience, kindness, goodness, faithfulness, gentleness, and self control." It is not a coincidence that these character traits produce the acts, actions, and behaviors that allow us to give and receive spiritual nourishment. These good fruits bear good nourishment and benefits for us.

By seeking daily spiritual nourishment, we also activate and bring to life the spiritual teachings, texts, and leanings we receive in our spiritual environment. When we receive spiritual guidance and knowledge in our home environments, worship environments, and life experiences, we can use each day as a forum to apply the principles, laws, and precepts that we hold sacred. This enables an active daily spiritual walk instead of confining spiritual development and nourishment to the occasional weekend church services or occasional church programs. Just as food provides physical energy that allows us to be physically active in our physical capacities to work and live healthy physical lives; spiritual nourishment provides spiritual energy that allows us to be spiritually active in our daily life experiences. Through this energy, we produce the good works and fruits which reflect the energy of our spiritual natures. In actively applying this energy and producing the good fruits and works, we develop and grow healthy spiritually. Mama was a living example of daily activating her spiritual walk in her life. She was always helping any and all in our community in need. She also gave love and compassion to everyone. She fed her children and every hungry child in the neighborhood in need providing spiritual, mental, and physical nourishment. She also set a positive example of how to give unconditional love and compassion to others even when they gave her pain and scorn in return. I feel fortunate that I learned of the fruits of the spirit in my spiritual environment and actually witnessed her apply them every day. Can you imagine going all week long without eating and just eating on Sunday? How healthy and strong would you be physically? If that is what you do spiritually, how strong are you spiritually?

Daily bread can also be defined as bread every day. What am I saying? One of the many important keys to a "Sacred Place" is a daily walk. There is an ancient proverb that many attribute to the Chinese culture that states, "A journey of a thousand miles begins with the first step." Just as we need spiritual sustenance every day as a part of our daily focus and intent, we must also take it a day at a time. We do not eat seven days worth of food on Monday. We eat one meal at a time, a day at a time. The best way to progress is at the proper increment, at the proper speed. Most complicated tasks are more easily achieved through breaking them down into simpler, easier segments.

Another good outcome of taking things in the proper increment, at the proper speed is it allows you to stay focused. When things get too complicated and overwhelming, we tend to lose focus, direction, perspective, and understanding. We also become stressed and worn by seeing the complexity and overwhelming nature of the situation in its entirety. Have you ever been given a new assignment on your job, or taken a subject in school that you really dreaded taking? If you have, I am sure the dread, coupled with the fear of failure, anticipated difficulty, and complexity made the task seem even more impossible. Yet as you began the task, or class, it became less and less dreaded, feared, and complicated as time passed. After a year of performing the task, or after completing the class, you reflected back and realized it was not as difficult or impossible as it initially appeared. That's because through time and experience, you learned to master comfortably the task or class. You also learned how to manage in the proper doses and increments the task or class in a way that allowed you to deal successfully with it. Through this experience, you matured to have less fear of similar tasks and classes in the future. Our spiritual walk is sometimes shrouded in confusion and mystery because we overwhelm ourselves with looking at too many challenges. Or, we get confused with a situation, experience, or information, and dwell on the complexity or confusion. When we are confronted with a lot of challenges, it is important to take them in the proper increments, at the proper speed. It is also important to take them a step at a time, and a day at a time. Once one challenge or several are resolved, move to the next one and the next until they are all resolved. If a challenge remains unresolved, realize that it may not be the time for resolution and trust that God knows the proper time and season for it to be resolved. Continue to try to understand what you are doing to impact the situation to make sure you are not doing something that is preventing resolution. When confused, do not linger in that state of confusion. Instead, go back to a common point of understanding and re-establish your confidence and trust in what you know. It is okay to be confused. It is okay not to know. In many cases, we do not know because God, in His All Know, loving parenting, realizes we do not need to know at this point. Have patience and faith to progress without knowing and also the maturity to understand if you are meant to know, you will know in the proper time and season.

What should daily bread consist of? The answer to this question is as uniquely specific and individualized as we are. Everyone is unique and special in his or her own way. Just as there are different basic ingredients in the makeup of different breads, wheat, rye, pumpernickel, flour, etc… there are some basic ingredients to our spiritual daily bread common to all, such as oil, yeast, baking powder, and salt are common to all breads. The first and foremost is application. It is important to actively use, in acts and actions, the spiritual teachings, laws, precepts, and principles in dealing with life's daily issues, experiences, and challenges. Think of the application process as the yeast or baking powder in your bread. It gives you the rise, growth, development, anointing, and blessings to your own life. How can you know and understand the "spirit" behind your spiritual teachings, laws, precepts, and principles without applying through your acts and actions, them to life's daily issues, experiences, and challenges?

The "spirit" behind our teachings needs further discussion. In an absolute sense, God is "The Spirit" of all there is. His all-knowing, all-encompassing, all-inclusive Spirit is the very "Essence" and "Spark" that provides the energy to ALL that is, (spirit, mental, and physical). God's Spirit is the life force, energy, and infinite will behind all that was, is, and ever will be. Infinite will and energy combined are two key components of the spirit. Man and woman have a finite will and energy in comparison to God's Infinite Will and Energy, yet we are a very, very, very minute, small fraction of the greater Whole, (God). The reason man and woman have a finite spirit is because we have a finite physical and mental body that houses our spirit. In essence, the spirit component of man and woman, (being a smaller part of God's), is infinite but bound to a finite existence within the body and mind. If your spirit is infinite, how do the acts, actions, and experiences of your finite existence during your brief life here shape your spirit's life? Is this finite existence we know of as "life" really a fundamental training ground for further spiritual growth during and after this life begins? My last two questions for your consideration are the most profound. Do you have to leave this existence to have that perfect relation and communion with God? Or can you arrive at that point while living here? Since God's Infinite Spirit is the "Absolute Spirit" behind our spiritual laws, teachings, precepts, and principles, the will and energy we put behind our actions in life's daily experiences reflect the spirit behind our beliefs. How strong are your actions and how strongly do you act on your spiritual convictions? Are they reflecting your true spiritual beliefs?

Another aspect to the spirit behind our teachings is the absolute authority God has over our acts and actions. A good comparison is the civil laws we use to govern criminal behavior in our culture. The laws are defined and explained in detail along with the acts and actions that violate these laws. Adherences to these laws have benefits and privileges while violations of them have defined punishments. Similarly adherences to our spiritual teachings have benefits and privileges as well while violations of our spiritual teachings that we know to apply, yet fail to, reap punishments according to the degree of our violations. How does God exercise His absolute authority? God gives blessings, enlightenment, wisdom, knowledge, understanding, joy, peace, love, prosperity, etc… when we honor His spiritual teachings. He also punishes us when we fail to adhere to His spiritual teachings. The parent-child analogy is again a good example. When parents teach their children the principles of discipline, hard work, dedication, and reasoning, they hope their children will apply them to excel in school. When their children do apply them and excel as expected, parents reward and reinforce the application of these principles by doting on and giving their children special gifts, privileges, clothing, toys, etc…they desire. God often allows our own failures to exact the punishment upon us when we fail to adhere to His spiritual teachings. Often our action, or inaction, results in a reciprocal act or inaction. Using the parent child analogy again, if a parent teaches a child it is wrong to fight, yet the child fights anyway, eventually the child will attempt to fight an opponent that will beat him. The parent may initially tell the child it is wrong to fight again to reinforce what he was taught.

Instead of punishing him, the parent may just let the child continue to fight, knowing full well sooner or later that child will meet an opponent that will beat him far worse than anyone he has beaten and the child will finally realize it is wrong to fight others.

God can also remove the opportunities to realize His blessings, enlightenment, wisdom, knowledge, understanding, joy, peace, love, etc… That, in and of itself, is a tremendous punishment. I am sure that Adam's and Eve's choice to separate themselves from the intimate contact they had with God before their disobedience was far more punishing than any other punishments God gave them. Adam and Eve caused the separation, not God. If God had given them the choice, they would have chosen any other punishment over being separated from God. Yet, they chose, through sinning, to separate themselves and they would have never been separated from God had they not chosen to sin. I see God as the consummate Parent in disciplining us, not the fire and brimstone God He was interpreted as by earlier traditional religious leaders. I remember Mama, (just as I envision God does), whipped me on occasion after I repeatedly violated one of her rules, or violated a rule she clearly told me would lead to immediate punishment if I broke it. Yet, often I could see her suffering and hurting far more for having to punish me. She preferred to let my wrong actions or inactions result in troubles, struggles, and strife I eventually suffered serve as my whipping instead of having to whip me herself. Then, she would remind me of her teachings and help me through providing guidance on the proper way to deal with my troubles. She also preferred denying me certain things I enjoyed instead of whipping me when I failed to follow her rules. One common thread in all instances is that Mama had to punish me, or see me suffer for my mistakes because of her tremendous, unconditional love for me. She suffered with and endured with me through my troubles. Yet, she suffered much, much, more for having to punish me directly by whipping me herself when she had no choice but to exact pain on her child whom she loved so dearly. God suffers and grieves when He punishes us as well. He often allows our wrong actions or inactions to bring the pain, troubles, struggles, and strife that become our resulting punishment. However, He also waits for us to seek His guidance to readily provide that direction we need, just as Mama did to resolve our problems. He does love us enough to punish us directly if necessary, just as Mama did. So God's absolute authority goes both ways, in a good way when we apply our spiritual teachings or a not-so-good way by exacting the proper punishment if we fail to apply our spiritual teachings. Ultimately we determine whether we are blessed or punished by our actions and inactions just as Adam and Eve did.

Giving and receiving love is the next important ingredient for our daily spiritual bread. If application is the yeast or baking powder, love is the flour for our daily spiritual bread. Flour is the chief ingredient and makes up the majority of the substance of the bread. In the seven key laws outlined in Chapter two, love was the first and most important. It is not by chance that love is the substance of our daily bread because love is the one thing that no other power or force known to man and woman can overcome. Love is the strongest, deepest, most powerful part of our being. Analyzing the dimensions of humans as God made them three-dimensionally, (spirit, mind, and body), it is clear to me that love is not of the body or mind. It is of the spirit. This is true because love from the physical sense is limited to that which gratifies one's physical needs; food, shelter, sex, recreation, material things, etc… Love from the mental sense is limited to what one has learned mentally to desire, which is also dictated by the physical needs. Love from within one's spirit is the only love that has the same character as God's love. It is selfless and compassionate for and on behalf of others. Possessing true spiritual love draws others like a magnet in the world today. People have become accustomed to living to satisfy life from a one-dimensional, (physical), or two-dimensional, (physical and mental), perspective in the absence of the spiritual dimension which offers the inner, selfless, compassionate love not capable of the body and mind alone. You will find as you seek to have selfless, compassionate love for others, they will be drawn to you and often they will not even know why. They may even ask you in the course of a discussion what it is about you that makes you different. Or, they may say something like; "There's something different about you but I can't quite put my finger on it." When we offer that inner love of our spirits, we have an aura or glow that others are drawn to. That's because it speaks to their latent, buried spirit within them beneath their mental and physical natures and is screaming to be activated, awakened, and applied. Love is of the spirit also because in order for it to pass the test of selflessness and compassion, it has to be unconditional. When people try to mask selfish love as real, unconditional, selfless love, the true natures of their intentions eventually come to light. Since the physical mind and body are finite, love has to come from the spirit because it is infinite. Here is an analogy to prove my point. A man can love his brother, sister, pet, best friend, girlfriend or wife, mother, father, sports, music, art, hobbies, and work. Yet each is uniquely specific, different, and special to him. Each is also equally meaningful and important to him. While each is independent of the other, none of them take away any measure of the love he has for the other. He can give the fullness of himself to each love and still have the fullness of himself for each subsequent love without diminishing or depleting his love. Each has the capacity to last the duration of his life. Thus, all of his various loves will never end until his life ends. Even after he has succumbed and no longer lives, the memory of his love lives with each brother, sister, pet, best friend, girlfriend or wife, mother father etc… through them. So although he is gone, the essence of his love lives on through the memories and positive experiences they recall to keep his love perpetually present in their lives. Furthermore, they can also duplicate the principles of his love through loving others the way he taught them to love perpetuating his love throughout their lives and so on, and so on. The mind and body, on the other hand, progresses through the normal stages of life on a time continuum that goes from infancy to childhood, adolescent, adult, elderly, and ultimately expiration. When the physical body expires, the mind also expires and is gone.

Giving and receiving love on a daily basis comes with challenges because you must first continue to mature into the proper fullness and re-orientation of spirit, mind, and body and also seek to give and receive in a world that is largely giving and seeking physical and mental substance. Many you meet on a daily basis are foreign to understanding love in its pure form. There is also an internal struggle of self going on, (physical verses spiritual, or physical and mental verses spiritual). At the same time, there is an external struggle waging, (giving love to a world that is seeking only physical and mental gratification). In your internal battle with physical and mental self, you still have to sustain your physical and mental needs because God made us with a body and mind as well. What you must do is analyze your physical and mental wants and needs compared to your spiritual environment to find proper balance. You should analyze your physical wants and needs in comparison to your spiritual laws, principles, and precepts to make sure you are not violating them in meeting your needs. It is very important that as you assess how what you desire physically and mentally impacts others. Are you taking advantage of or using someone else for your own selfish and mental desires?

As you practice giving of yourself selflessly, you set an example to others that may not fully understand you. Some of them will be drawn to you for it and seek to better understand you and thus awaken and open themselves to seeking more than just physical and mental needs and wants because they have experienced a more complete love, (spiritual love), through you. Some you meet will be seeking to find them-selves spiritually and grow from what you give them through your example. Others will be convicted from within to better understand what they are missing when receiving selfless, compassionate love from you. Their inner spirits will cry out to seek more than they have gotten through physical and mental gratification. Have you ever met people who were materially wealthy but just did not seem happy? If so, chances are they may have put all of their energies into seeking physical, material gains but never sought to understand the wealth within their spirits. They may have never realized the wealth of love they could give and receive to and from others. There will be others who seek to take advantage of you for giving of yourself because they are physically oriented, or physically and mentally oriented, and see your giving as an opportunity to further their selfish needs. If that happens, do no worry. God knows the intent of your heart and will bless you accordingly for giving of yourself out of love and compassion for others. What they get, or take, will be replenished EXPONENTIALLY! If it is not, you do not need it or God has something far better for you. In time, these people will suffer from the laws of reciprocity and reap exponentially what they have sown unto you. They may gain momentarily but in the long run, they will lose far more. Continue to strive to give love and receive love as you focus on your self-analysis and you will continue to acquire the keys you need to enter that sacred place you seek.

Along with our daily bread ingredients of application, which is the yeast, and love, which is the flower, there are several other very essential ingredients for completion of life's daily bread. The next two key ingredients are introspection and reflection. Think of them as the liquid and oil in our daily bread. I remember seeing Mama make buttermilk biscuits from scratch during most of my childhood. She made fresh biscuits twice a day; in the morning for breakfast and in the evening for dinner just before she went to work. Her milk of choice was buttermilk and her oil of choice was lard. Whether you use water, sweet milk, condensed milk, or some other liquid, you must have liquid in your bread. Whether you use lard, olive oil, corn oil, canola oil, or butter, you must have oil in your daily bread as well. Why is introspection essential in your spiritual daily bread? Here is one of my old sayings surfacing again. Through introspection, we begin to think "within-without" not "without-within." Introspection is the liquid of our spiritual daily bread because like the buttermilk in Mama's bread, it is the ingredient that holds and binds everything else together. It is the glue of the mixture that allows the flour, yeast, oil, and other spices to be formed and molded into the biscuit or loaf.

I hope the phrase, "within-without" not "without-within" has forced you to pause and think to understanding its meaning. I realize when the Holy Spirit placed it on my conscience during the course of this work in progress; I had a clear understanding of what it means. Let me offer more clarity since the intent of my writings is just that to bring clarity, perspective, and understanding.

"Without thinking" is thinking controlled by the physical senses alone. Going back to my earlier reflections on physical orientation, it is normal and natural for us to begin the process of thinking through physical senses alone because we are initially physically oriented. "Without-within" thinking is physical and mental combined and results from our natural progression as we grow and mature in the absence of spiritual awareness, consciousness, and maturity. "Within-without" thinking reverses the order to allow the spirit to govern the mind and body. It results as we become spiritually conscious, awakened, and begin to become spiritually orientated. The subtle deception of life in this world is we naturally progress towards physicality of body and mind without an urgent need to become whole of spirit, mind, and body. Yet, as we are exposed to our spiritual environment, we begin to form a consciousness and awareness of the spirit and begin the process of spiritual orientation and becoming whole of spirit, mind, and body. Because of the subtlety of physical dominance, the struggle of spirit verses physical begins the battle of whether we will think "within-without" (spiritually led), or "without-within" (physically led). This occurs even as we become aware and conscious of our spiritual self and the need to become whole. I am sure Adam and Eve had no clue how much they were giving up in choosing to be physically led over being whole of spirit, mind and body. There is no appropriate analogy that comes fractionally close to explaining how much less they settled for in making their choice.

The process of introspection, then, is one of looking within. That sounds fairly simple I know. Yet it is probably one of our most challenging tasks! It is far, far easier to look at others and criticize, analyze, and assess their weaknesses, shortcomings, and faults than look at your own. Looking within can be painful because it often forces us to be convicted to hear the voice of the Holy Spirit and seek change, (repentance) for our wrongs, shortcomings, and failures. While it can be painful, it is vital and essential for us to grow stronger and more mature. Adam and Eve's story provides a good perspective for understanding. I am sure once they realized their new state of physical dominance was far less than their original three dimensional, (spirit, mind, body) one that it was a very painful reality for them to understand just how much they had lost. As the old saying goes, "You don't miss the water till the well runs dry." Their pain was far greater than we could ever comprehend because they had experienced the fullness of being whole of spirit, mind, and body and having an intimate relationship with God first before choosing to be far less. We have not had the choice they did. Introspection from a scriptural reference point is the two edged sword the Holy Bible speaks of in the book of Hebrews, Chapter 4, verse 12, "For the word of God is quick and powerful, sharper than any two edged sword, piercing even to the dividing asunder of soul and spirit, and the joints and marrow, and is a discerner of the thoughts and intents of the heart." When the inner voice of the Holy Spirit tells us we are wrong, it is sometimes painful to accept that we are wrong. Since some of our wrong ways are developed through selfish physical wants, desires, and needs, it is truly painful and difficult to change our ways. This becomes increasingly challenging because we struggle to balance what is physically essential from what is physically desired. Much of what we learn to desire is not essential, but it is very much wanted. It becomes very much wanted through our habit of allowing our physical urges and needs to be our sole focus. Over time, these habits become very challenging to change once we begin the process of re-orienting ourselves from physical to spiritual. Just as the liquid holds the ingredients together and allows the baker to mold and shape the ingredients into a roll or loaf, our introspection allows us to mold and shape our flaws, challenges, and shortcomings as we mature towards wholeness. Introspection is not all pain. Just as the Holy Spirit convicts our wrongs, He also uplifts and praises our successes. We receive positive encouragement and support as we do the right things as we grow. We also have positive experiences and successes to draw from when facing new challenges. Remembering positive experiences and successes provides a good frame of mind and motivation to seek more successes and also strength to draw from to endure more struggles and failures.

Reflection is very closely kindred to introspection. The oil used in making bread serves a very similar function to the liquid. It helps to bind and mold the ingredients into the biscuit or loaf. The oil also lets the bread separate smoothly from the pan it is baked in. Reflection assures a measure of smoothness to our daily bread as well. It is very important as we introspect, (look inside and listen to the Holy Spirit), that we also reflect, (look back over our own experiences and evaluate them and the outcome of our acts and actions based on those experiences). This wondrous and mystical journey we call "life" is a progression of steps and stages. How can we progress without looking back? Is it possible? Let me ask the question another way. Can one know where he is going, or progressing towards, without knowing where he has come from? How do you know how far you are going unless you measure how far you have already traveled? Reflection provides the mature perspective to our introspection and progression. A child grows from childhood to adulthood. The child's parent, as the mature perspective, reflects on the child's development to make sure he is properly and completely developing into a well-rounded adult. The child is wrapped up in the process of growing and could care less about reflecting on its development. As children become young adults, they then begin to look at the process of growing into adulthood. The benefit of reflection is it enables us to adjust, amend, change, and try new things to continue our development and progression. It also provides the actual hind sight for us to assess how well, or poorly, we grow through our experiences. Reflection allows us to compare past to present and understand what has changed to determine if we are moving forward, going backwards, or are exactly at the same point in our efforts to grow.

Introspection, combined with reflection, provides wisdom and understanding. Through introspecting and reflecting, we analyze thoroughly. Through thorough analysis, we force ourselves to do more than just go with our natural physical inclinations. Through analysis we also question. As we analyze and question, we seek to understand. As we seek to understand, we incline our hearts, minds, and spirits to the voice of the Holy Spirit. As we seek, we also explore our spiritual environment, resources, and knowledge to further our understanding and growth. Thus we learn and grow through our efforts. All of this combined brings wisdom, understanding, and maturity.

Our spiritual daily bread is nearly complete. There are still a few remaining essential ingredients. Prayers and utterances must also be added in ample measures. Prayers and utterances provide the heat that cooks the bread. I know I have already spoken a great deal on prayer and utterances but as I stated earlier, prayer is the medium that ties all else together in our spiritual walk. My specific intent in talking about prayer earlier was to provide a broader view of it because prayer is much, much, more than just a plea during times of crisis. Prayer and utterances in the context of our daily bread is even more specific.

From a day-to-day perspective, it is important to listen to the Holy Spirit. It is also important to pray and utter, (have dialogue with God the Father, Christ the Son as needed). Keep in mind the parent-child analogy. God is the ultimate and consummate parent because He is both Mother and Father. If you seek to talk to Him as the ultimate parent, you then lend yourself to the guidance you need for continued development. A child looks to his parents for direction, food, shelter, knowledge, and understanding about life. The child also interacts with his parents. He asks questions, makes requests, pleads to them in times of crisis, reflects, and introspects on their corrective discipline, asks for his wants, expects his needs to be fulfilled, and models himself after his parents. As a result, the child grows healthy, full and complete. Active, continual dialogue and interaction is the essential medium for the child to receive all the guidance, nourishment, and development from his parents he needs. With God the Father, Christ the Son, and the Holy Spirit as the parent, we, their children, must actively, continually engage ourselves in prayer and utterances just as children do with their natural, physical parents.

How does God provide guidance for our continued growth and development? My oldest brother always told me: "God never does in the supernatural what He can achieve in the natural." Most often, God uses everyday life experiences, resources from our spiritual environment and upbringing, family, friends, and acquaintances to provide the guidance we need to develop and grow. One problem we often have is we are looking for the awesome, dynamic miracles of old, the "burning bush" or "pillar of fire" to identify that God is providing the very guidance we have asked Him for. Since we are so intently looking for the awesome, dynamic miracle, we look right past or overlook the obvious guidance God brings to us through the natural course of daily events. I am not saying God does not bring awesome, dynamic miracles into our lives because He does and can if they are needed. He is more than capable to do so. What I am saying is we often receive what we are seeking in a normal, natural way in day-to-day life without all of the pomp and circumstance we expect. The real challenge for us is to realize that we have received the guidance we seek and not get wrapped up in how that guidance was delivered. Reflection and introspection are valuable to us here because we must analyze from "within-without" all things great and small to see God's hand in the smallest of things, as well as the greatest of things in our lives. I encourage you to look for Him in the smallest of things in your life. Trust me, if you see Him there, you will definitely see Him in the magnificent things He does. Do not be afraid to relate to, dialogue with and pray to God as your ultimate, consummate parent. As you seek to relate to Him in this way, you will enhance your continued spiritual reorientation. Your daily bread will have the spiritual heat it needs to bake to perfection!

Now that most of the basic ingredients have been added to our daily bread, I would like to talk about some other ingredients that add some spices to enhance the flavor. There are all kinds of spices one can add to bread to make it more tasteful. These ingredients vary from fruits to nuts, to cheeses of various types, to hot seasonings-like cayenne pepper, or other spices like ginger and nutmeg. The spices, in the context of our spiritual daily bread, result largely from problems and challenges in dealing with others and weaknesses we discover through our introspections and reflections.

Just as there are many different spices, there are many different types of problems in life. There are different types of problems because problems can result from many different perspectives, (personal, internal, external, physical, mental, cultural, societal, etc…). All problems fall into two simple categories: good problems and bad problems. Be that as it may, my oldest brother and mentor taught me another excellent saying regarding problems, "Problems are opportunities to grow." Whether you are confronted with a good, or a bad problem, each offers an opportunity to grow. Are you asking how can a problem be good? A problem can be good because it offers you the chance to apply the ingredients of your daily bread, (application, giving and receiving love, introspection, reflection, prayers and utterances), to gain positively and to positively affect your life or the lives of others in times of need. A good problem allows for growth, development, and maturity without any pain or suffering on your behalf. In fact, a good problem allows you to give of yourself to benefit others in need and giving to others in need is one of life's greatest pleasures, joys, and blessings. A good problem also allows for continued understanding, wisdom, and evolvement from one point in your development to another point. Just as a child grows in his knowledge from first grade to second, and so on, a good problem enables progressive development for us as well. A good problem will also provide a chance or test for you to apply action to your spiritual laws, precepts, and principles to help others and/or increase your spiritual knowledge, understanding and growth on that issue. A bad problem is one that requires pain and suffering to overcome. I have found in life's journey, the bad problems are the ones that have yielded the strongest and most lasting maturity and development. When we encounter bad problems, we suffer and often feel as if we will not survive, only to get through it and realize we are far stronger from having gone through it. Mama always said, "Anything that does not kill you will make you stronger." In my own personal observation of problems, bad problems tend to result from more internal issues where as good problems are more external. Remember, our physical natures are selfish and rebellious towards our spiritual natures. Often, we act on our selfish physical wants and desires and create bad problems that we must resolve at some later point in our lives. Good problems are more external because they are often encountered through others we meet that have needs, or from other things in our environment that force us to think and reason from "within-without" to reach a solution. Bad problems have one very significant thing in common with good problems. They also provide good opportunities and outcomes for us and for others. However, bad problems are more difficult to solve and may require many years to resolve. Selfish physical habits that lead to bad problems will also continue to grow bigger and bigger and at some point pose a bigger problem to solve. If you develop a habit of drinking, it is easy for that habit to become much bigger over time. At some point, you could even develop a habit of drinking too much and become an alcoholic. Solving the problem of alcoholism is far more difficult than solving a problem of drinking before it becomes a major problem. Alcoholism is far more pervasive because it is a physically, mentally, and spiritually damaging problem. In making your daily bread, introspection and reflection becomes very important because it is through daily introspection and reflection, we stop physically selfish habits that will progress into bigger problems later by changing our physically selfish habits early on in our awareness of them.

Both good and bad problems are essential to our evolution towards that "sacred place" we so desperately desire. Otherwise, how can we truly act on that which we learn and believe? Furthermore, how can we know with certainty the proper spiritual orientation and balance of spirit, mind, and body without the forum in our lives to prove it through? Let me ask the question this way. How do we know God's laws, precepts, and principles are true and real unless we apply them to our own life's issues, opportunities, and challenges? Is there a testimonial in the absence of a test? Or is the testimonial just an idea or words that are empty without the proof of the test? If you are willing to approach life's problems with this understanding, you will find your tolerance and focus to be more mature. Put into this perspective, you should have the patience, poise, persistence, assurance, wisdom, and fortitude to see any and all problems through fruition. You will also have the same BLESSED assurance Christ had in knowing all problems, good and bad, end in a far greater good for you and others. In time, you will also acquire the wisdom, maturity, and understanding to endure bad problems that take far longer to conquer through the recognition that when solved, they result in far more significant gains for you and others. Bad problems are often the major crossroads that become major turning points in our eventual proper spiritual reorientation. Stay positive and focused through good and bad problems and seek to be introspective in knowing the lessons they are teaching you through them.

Challenges you face with others often point back to you. This is true because often that which we find fault with in others, is also our own fault within. When we are young and immature in our spiritual orientation, it is very easy to spend our time and energy judging, criticizing, and finding fault in others. As we begin to grow into spiritual awareness and towards our spiritual reorientation, that little, quiet Holy Spirit voice within begins to let us know that the judgements, criticisms, and faults we see in others are our own internal reflection. We are also convicted to spend our time looking at, (introspecting), our own faults and shortcomings instead of looking at others' faults and shortcomings. It is far more difficult initially for us to accept our own faults. Using basketball as an example, it is always easier to criticize the basketball players on the court and provide excellent critiquing on just what they are doing wrong from the stands. It is far more difficult to go onto the court and execute the same techniques to perfection we see while critiquing other players. Only those who have actually played at a highly competitive level and won championships will have complete insight on just how challenging it is to perform at that level. Yet, all of us, champions or not, seem to be experts at criticizing our respective teams if we watch the sport. Once you are aware that the challenges you face with others may be an indication of some challenge within you, you can then seek to understand, through introspection and reflection, what the challenge is. You must first have awareness before the process of seeking change, (repentance), can occur. Be patient with yourself, because, as with solving bad problems, internal challenges can take time.

Challenges with others can also result because of differences you have with others. As the old saying goes, "Oppo sites attract." Sometimes our completely different viewpoints, perspectives, and approaches in life draw others who are totally opposite to us. A good comparison here is the spirit to the physical. Many physical laws are opposite to spiritual laws. For example, in physical law, no two things can occupy the same space at the same time. Yet, in spiritual law, we possess both good and bad within the same body; the spirit occupies the physical body so two things can occupy the same space. Likewise, in my earlier analogy of man and woman being made in God's image, (with God representing the mind, Christ representing the body, and the Holy Spirit representing the spirit), God, Christ, and the Holy Spirit are separate, but one. The physical body, mind, and spirit of man and woman are not one, but separate, three-dimensional parts of one whole just as the fingers are five separate parts of one whole hand. Attracting those who are opposite from you is again good for you. It is an opportunity for growth for each person. After all, if I am a spiritually mature and enlightened person, should I not be an excellent example for someone who is physically oriented and yet to have spiritual awareness? There is an opportunity for growth for both. For me, I can grow to understand my physical capacity and limitations better. For the person who is unaware of his spiritual orientation, I can provide that spark that ignites his inner spirit. In time, I can continue to provide mentoring towards his continued development. Each of us also has the opportunity for vicarious learning through the other's experience. Vicarious learning is very important because we can learn through hearing about what others experience and acquire that wisdom, knowledge, and understanding without having to go through that experience ourselves. If I am a mentor and role model to someone who is just beginning to seek spiritual orientation, I can tell him some of the challenges and mistakes I made in my development so he can avoid making some of those same mistakes in his development. I can also show him sympathy with some of his challenges and mistakes to give him strength, support, and encouragement through them. That's not to say he will not choose to experience some of the same challenges and mistakes I made. Even if he does choose to, he will at least be wiser having had the benefit of my experience to deal with his own challenges. He could also choose to avoid some of the mistakes I made and progress faster than I did as a result. Challenges that mirror you through others and challenges that result from opposites attracting provide the opportunity to apply your daily bread ingredients, (application, giving and receiving love, introspection, reflection, prayers, and utterances), to further your progress towards spiritual reorientation.

By now, I hope I have impressed upon you that self-analysis is one of the master keys to the "Sacred Place" you are seeking. Self-analysis leads to a self-realized, three-dimensional individual. In the course of becoming fully self-realized and spiritually reoriented, we become aware, through self-analysis, of our weaknesses. As I reflected on the term self analysis, the Holy Spirit told me this: "The outer portion is just the package that hold the gift and greater portion within." It stands to reason if the greatest portion, (the spirit and mind), is within, that the outer body is the weakest portion of you. We are therefore faced with a deceptive challenge in dealing with our physical existence. That challenge is to realize that as we grow through life, we must seek full, three-dimensional balance of spirit, mind, and body without continuing to strive for what we naturally desire and want for our weakest portion, the physical body. It is the greatest deception in that we are so much more naturally inclined towards physical wants and desires and relate to and understand what these desires and wants "feel" like when met. I have already discussed physical rebellion in Chapter one. I only want to remind you without repeating myself that most of our struggles begin and end here. How does our weaknesses relate to our bread making analogy? Think of our weakness, in this respect, as the trial and error stage. If a chef conceives a new bread recipe, he may only have a general idea of the ingredients he wants to include in it. He may actually make the bread with his initial original ingredients only to find it does not have the flavor and quality he is looking for. At this point, the chef would analyze what ingredients went into his original ingredients and weed out any ingredients that would lessen the flavor and quality. He would also add other ingredients that would enhance the flavor. This weeding out and adding to process will ultimately result in the perfect tasting, quality bread he initially envisioned. In understanding our weaknesses, we also seek to weed out any behaviors, characteristics, and qualities that stop us from becoming fully balanced and oriented, (spirit, mind, and body) and whole. We also need to add more good behaviors, characteristics, and qualities that improve our growth and development. Our ultimate aim, through weeding out and adding to, is the same objective as the chef's. We are seeking to perfect our wholeness of spirit, mind, and body.

Effectively identifying weaknesses is another important key to the "Sacred Place" we are seeking. Awareness that you are a spirit in a body with a mind, analyzing your spiritual environment, thinking "within-without," self analysis, introspection, and reflection are all essential tools you must use to identify weaknesses. Each and everyone that is blessed to experience the gift of life have uniquely specific and specifically unique mixtures of qualities. So everyone has his or her own weaknesses and strengths. While this is true, it is clear from most spiritual texts and sources the world over that there are some basic common weaknesses that all men and women are susceptible to. In the Bible in the book of Matthew, Chapter 7, verses 21-23, Christ states: "For from within, out of the heart of men, proceed evil thoughts, adulteries, fornication's, murders, thefts, covetousness, wickedness, deceit, lasciviousness, an evil eye, blasphemy, pride, foolishness: All of these evil things come from within and defile the man." The seven deadly sins, (pride, envy, gluttony, slothfulness, greed, anger, and lust) are the central weaknesses throughout the Old and New Testament of the Holy Bible. Let's re-visit one of my initial analogies by going back to the Garden of Eden during Adam and Eve's fall from grace. Their choice to separate themselves from God's spirit created their own individual physical and mental self-awareness apart from God. It is significant to emphasize this point because it was at this point that any weaknesses became apparent. If you will recall, Adam responded to God in Genesis, Chapter 1, verse 10, "I heard thy voice in the garden, and I was afraid, because I was naked; and hid myself." Adam and Eve had been physically naked all along prior to their separation from God. Yet, they were not physically focused before the separation, because they were spiritually focused. So, their physical appearance was of no importance to them until they separated themselves spiritually from God. This perspective is critical because there is one common theme to all weaknesses men and women are susceptible to. They are physically and mentally oriented, just as Adam and Eve became after their separation from God. This was true from the very beginning when Adam and Eve fell from grace and it is still true today. Just like Adam and Eve, we are vulnerable because we are physically oriented, or physically and mentally oriented, without the proper spiritual awareness and maturity. Consequently, just as Adam and Eve did after their fall from grace, we get caught up in things that are centered towards our physical and mental wants, desires, and needs until we begin the process of spiritual reorientation towards wholeness of spirit, mind, and body.

Let me prove my point about our weaknesses this way. Men are generally very visually focused. Men lust after women for their physical and sexual beauty. Can you think of any product in our world today that is marketed to men that does not appeal to them through the TV and print media that does not show beautiful, sexy women? There are very, very few exceptions that come to mind. This is not a new issue. Wars throughout the annals of time have been fought over beautiful women. One of the Holy Bible's greatest heroes, King David, sent his head general off to war knowing he would be killed just to covet his wife. Women are generally more emotional. Using the same theme of lust, they are appealed to from a more romantic standpoint. A woman may fantasize about passionate romance at the office with a new, handsome stranger who is paying her the undivided attention she is lacking at home with her husband or boyfriend.

Let's analyze these scenarios a little closer. Yes, men are generally drawn to physically attractive, sexy women, and women are generally drawn to men who meet their romantic, emotional needs, regardless of how physically attractive they may be. However, the issue at hand is not that men are generally visual and women are generally emotional. The true issue at hand is both men and women are susceptible to their lustful natures and how they allow their weaknesses to affect their choices in daily life. A man who is seeking balance of spirit, mind, and body is mature and is aware that he is generally more visually focused. He is also mature enough to put into perspective that just because he is attracted to a woman because she is physically and sexually attractive does not mean he should act on his attraction. He has to assess the whole situation and listen to that little, quiet, inner Holy Spirit voice as to what is morally and spiritually proper in how he relates to this woman. Is it right morally and spiritually to act on his pure, physical attraction without considering any other moral and spiritual principles, precepts, and perspectives? It is clearly not right to act purely on physical impulses. Ultimately, any acts or actions should be based on what is morally and spiritually proper and in agreement with spiritual principles, laws, precepts, and perspectives. Just by taking the proper time to put into perspective the initial physical and sexual attraction tempered with what is morally and spiritually right will assure he makes a balanced, whole, (spirit, mind, and body) decision in relating to this woman.

A woman who is seeking a balance of spirit, mind, and body should also be mature enough to realize she is generally more emotionally focused. In the scenario explained earlier, the woman may be emotionally drawn to the new stranger in the office that is giving her the undivided attention she is missing at home from her husband or boyfriend. However, she must be mature enough to also introspect, reason, and listen to that little, quiet, Holy Spirit voice and put her emotional attraction into perspective without just acting on her emotional fantasies. Our physical and mental weaknesses are a part of who we are. The problem is not the weaknesses, but how we act and react if we fail to find spiritual insight and perspective in dealing with life's issues and challenges surrounding our weaknesses. It is okay, in fact, it is wise, prudent, and mature to know your weaknesses. It is not okay for us to NOT seek understanding on how to spiritually adapt to life's issues that cause us to selfishly act or react just because of our physical and mental wants, desires, and needs.

There is a very, very subtle deception at work in properly applying our daily bread principles. Remember, our natural inclinations are to act and react to physical and mental stimulus; therefore, it is very easy to act, then, think about the consequences later. Or, it is just as easy to hear that little, quiet, inner Holy Spirit voice and reason and rationalize that because we have the physical urge at that moment it is okay to ignore that little voice and let the body and mind act on its own natural inclinations. Can you see the deception at work? Subtle deceptions are the most dangerous because they are hidden and unconscious. The deception is to get you to act and react purely based on physical, or physical and mental reasoning and desire, without seeking spiritual reasoning. Another deception is to get you caught up in the circumstances and situations and physically acting and reacting without thinking at all. Another related deception is to get you to put yourself in a vulnerable position that you realize you cannot overcome and therefore you succumb and act or react accordingly. For example, if you have been addicted to alcohol or drugs, it is not wise to go places with friends who drink and do drugs constantly because you are not strong enough to overcome succumbing to your addiction. These deceptions are largely an inner struggle as we physically rebel against restoring ourselves to wholeness of spirit, mind, and body. But, also remember, since we are in a physical world, chances are much more favorable that the world will continue to provide support towards our physical and mental rebellion against our spiritual reorientation. Your daily bread ingredients, (application, giving and receiving love, introspection, reflection, prayer and utterances), will provide the tools and resources you need to overcome any weaknesses you encounter as you continue to perfect your daily walk. Just remember, dealing with your weaknesses is a weeding out process. It takes time, patience, and persistence. Don't forget to savor the changes and improvements in your walk along the way.

It is my desire, in concluding this chapter that you never fail to realize the importance of your day-to-day existence. It is also my hope that I have provided much needed perspective, guidance, and sustenance to help you become more whole and complete of spirit, mind, and body. This chapter has a large amount of information so it is a good time to list the Spiritual Truisms. I have segmented them in this chapter also by subject for clarity and ease of understanding.

Chapter 3 Daily Bread Spiritual Truisms:

- We must seek daily sustenance in all ways to achieve wholeness. It is especially important to seek spiritual sustenance daily because we naturally take care of getting physical and mental sustenance but think of spiritual sustenance as a more occasional need.

- Analyzing and evaluating spiritual texts, and teachings in a literal way, restricts your understanding to physical, or physically dominated, mental insights and brings literal knowledge without full spiritual understanding.

- Complete understanding of that which is spiritual is not possible without seeking to understand God's "Spirit" behind spiritual texts, teachings, and leanings.

- Though our efforts, God provides the proper measure of wisdom and understanding as we seek to understand spiritual texts, teachings, and leanings in a more complete manner.

- Do not be deceived into trying to understand God's inspired texts, teachings, and leanings from a purely literal, physical perspective. Seek through your spirit, the Holy Spirit, Christ, and God to get the full measure of wisdom and understanding God has for you. Realize full understanding also comes with time as you progress and grow each day, week, month, and year.

- In seeking to grow into the fully realized, (spirit, mind, and body) person God intended you to be, you must seek daily bread and nourishment of the spirit as well. That requires daily emphasis and attention just as we do physically and mentally.

- The main ingredients for your spiritual daily bread are: application, giving and receiving love, prayer and utterances, introspection, and reflection. These powerful ingredients will provide the nutrition for your daily spiritual needs.

- Good and bad problems, as well as dealing with challenges and weaknesses are also very important spices that supplement your spiritual nutrition, growth, and development.

-Application-

- Application, (practicing your spiritual laws, teachings, precepts, and principles) allows you to understand "the Spirit" behind your spiritual laws, teachings, precepts, and principles. How can you know that your laws, teachings, precepts, and principles are true unless you try them through applying them in your day to-day life experiences?

- The spirit behind our spiritual laws, teachings, precepts, and principles is God's Infinite Will and Life Force. As it applies to us, the will and energy we put behind the acts and actions we take daily to life's issues and challenges reflect the spirit behind how we exercise our beliefs. How strong are your actions and how strongly do you act on your spiritual convictions? How are your actions reflecting God through you? Are your actions reflecting God through you?

-Love-

- Giving and receiving love is of the spirit, not the body and mind because it is an act of selflessness and is unconditional. Physical and mental wants are selfish towards sustaining the body and mind and are opposite to unconditional giving of one's self to others as love requires. Through spiritual reorientation, we transform the selfishness of the physical and mental body to the same selfless love and compassion God has for all.

- As we practice the principle of giving and receiving love, we attract others in the world that are seeking love in a world that is physically and mentally oriented towards only fulfilling physical and mental desires dominated by the physical. This allows the opportunity to awaken the spirit of love in others advancing them towards continued growth and development.

- Don't worry about those who seek to take advantage of your giving love for their own physical and mental selfish aims. God knows the intent of your heart and spirit and will see you are rewarded EXPONENTIALLY for giving selflessly of your love to others. You will also be a shining example to those around you of God's all consuming love. They will learn from your example when they are open to learn.

-Prayers and Utterances-

- Prayers and utterances are a powerful, valuable means of communicating daily experiences, issues, and challenges in order to get specific guidance and nourishment. As children of God, He responds to our needs when we communicate them, just as we as parents respond to our children's needs. God tempers the response to our needs so we receive what we need based on where we are in our growth and development, just as parents temper with their wisdom, their response to their children's needs. Parents know which needs are important and which are detrimental based on how their child is developing. So does God with us!

-Introspection and Reflection-

- Introspection is the process of beginning to think "within-without." Seeking your spiritual perspective and hearing the quiet, inner voice of the Holy Spirit in analyzing your flaws and weaknesses and how these flaws and weaknesses affect your daily application to life's experiences.

- Introspection requires looking inside. Not focusing on the flaws and weaknesses of others. It can also be a painful process to look inside because you must commit yourself to seek change and also accept conviction for your flaws.

- Introspection rewards us with tremendous growth, development, and maturity when we are committed to seriously work at changing our flaws.

- Reflection is kindred to introspection. Through reflection, we look back to make adjustments, amendments, and changes to try improving our progression and development. It is important as we introspect to also reflect at the same time.

- Reflection also provides strength and the faith for each new challenge because we can reflect back on the challenges we have already overcome before the next one arrives.

- Introspection combined with reflection brings wisdom and understanding.

  -Problems, Challenges and Weaknesses: Daily Spice-

- Much of our spice in our day-to-day lives results from problems and challenges in dealing with others and weaknesses we discover through introspection and reflection.

- Problems may be good, (usually external and brought through others), or bad, (a result of inner challenges we are seeking to overcome). Both good and bad problems are opportunities to grow and allow us to help others learn through how we handle them. Both good and bad problems result in our growth for our continued progression. Introspection and reflection are essential in overcoming all problems.

- The challenges we face with others are often a mirror reflection of flaws and weaknesses we share in common. It is important to look inside when faced with challenges with others.

- Challenges with others may also exist because they are diametrically opposite to you. If that is the case, it is your responsibility to help them grow while also growing your perspective in how they are different.

- The weaknesses of men and women have a central theme. They are physically and mentally oriented. It is not the weakness that is significant, but how we act and react to the weakness. Being spiritually mature and balanced requires aligning life's day-to-day challenges with spiritual laws, teachings, precepts, and principles and also seeking counsel, guidance,e and conviction from that small, quiet voice of the Holy Spirit to make certain acts and actions are properly tempered.

- As we mature into the proper spiritual reorientation and balance of spirit, mind, and body, we are mature enough to act and react properly to manage our weaknesses in a spiritually ethical manner. Thus we act and react within the spirit of our laws, teachings, precepts, and principles.

The "Daily Bread" of the spirit is the most neglected nutritional need of our daily lives. It is my hope that I have given you some very simple, clear, yet essential, ingredients of your "spiritual" daily bread that will provide you FULL and COMPLETE sustenance in your life's journey to wholeness of spirit, mind, and body. **Introspect, reflect, and respond to the questions related to Chapter 3 as you seek to digest the ingredients from this chapter.**

Question(s) 1:

What spiritual ingredients do you possess in the recipe of your spiritual daily bread? What spiritual ingredients do you lack and need to add to make your daily nutrition complete?

Thoughts, Insights, and Reflections

Question(s) 1-Thoughts, Insights, and Reflections

Question(s) 2:
How will you change your approach to nourishing your physical and mental needs to assure proper alignment of those needs with daily spiritual nourishment and sustenance?

Thoughts, Insights, and Reflections

Question(s) 2-Thoughts, Insights, and Reflections

Question(s) 3:

How will you utilize the Chapter 3 "Daily Bread" ingredients of application, love, prayers and utterances, introspection, and reflection to shape and enhance your daily life experiences, actions, and reactions? How will you utilize these ingredients to understand and relate vicariously to others you meet in your life?

Thoughts, Insights, and Reflections

Question(s) 3-Thoughts, Insights, and Reflections

Question(s) 4:

How will you process, analyze, and solve the good and bad problems in your day to day life with your spiritual daily bread ingredients to ensure your continued growth, maturation, and development of spirit, mind, and body? Which particular spiritual daily bread ingredients, (application, love, prayers and utterances, introspection, and reflection), are most critical to solving good and bad problems? When do you apply them and at what stages during the process are those you apply important?

Thoughts, Insights, and Reflections

Question(s) 4-Thoughts, Insights, and Reflections

Questions(s) 5:
What other personal perspectives and understandings have you gained from this chapter? What other spiritual texts and resources can you use to further enhance your wisdom, knowledge and understanding?
Thoughts, Insights, and Reflections

Question(s) 5-Thoughts, Insights, and Reflections

New Perspectives

Chapter **4**

The Apostle Paul stated in 1st Corinthians, Chapter 13 verse 11; "When I was a child, I spake as a child, I understood as a child, I thought as a child; but when I became a man, I put away childish things." He was referring to his progression from a boy to a man. It is my sincere and earnest hope and prayer that what God has enabled me to express thus far has assisted in your transition from spiritual infancy towards adulthood. If so, it is time for new perspectives! Now that the basics have been provided, it is my hope to challenge you to "put away childish things" in your approach to thinking, analyzing, acting, and reacting to life. One good thing about Divine Understandings and Revelations is once you receive them, your perspective, thoughts, actions, and reactions are changed from your old physically dominant way of functioning. Have you ever watched a baby learn something new? Have you ever watched a young child fully understand something for the first time? If you have, you could probably see in his eyes and facial expressions the excitement, joy, and happiness in having arrived at a new perspective. My hope and prayer is that you have gained something in this humble work thus far to bring about the same childlike wonderment as it pertains to realizing how awesome you are in your full, (spirit, mind, and body) creation and capacity.

I fully believe the physical self is the baby of your total being. If you have chosen to view life purely from a physical viewpoint, you choose to be an infant in this wondrous experience we call life. Amazingly, you can live your entire life in a physical state of focus and grow to become a ripe, old age and die. I realize I have already discussed this in Chapter 2, (Principle 2), but it is important to mention again. It is my hope, by now, when I make bold statements that you are doing your own introspections, analysis, reflections, and seeking counsel to understand why I would make such a statement. However, you know if God has led me to espouse something, He has led me towards a perspective to share as well.

Let me expound on my initial analogy regarding babies as they relate to physical life from Chapter 2. Babies of all species of life, human or animals are precious. It is not by chance that babies are small, cuddly, adorable, irresistible, vulnerable, and precious. Without these endearing qualities, they could not receive the support, care, and nurturing from their parents to grow into adults. Yet, make no mistake about it, babies are selfish to their own wants, needs, and desires. Their very survival from infant to adolescent to adult requires selfishness. Like the baby, the physical self is the most endearing, tangible, visible part of our being. We cannot see our mind or spirit. We can only see, touch, and feel our bodies in a physical world that has physical things we can also see, touch, and feel. Like the baby, our physical self also demands what it desires, wants, and needs over all else for it's survival. I want to challenge you to think from a new perspective at this point. While one can live with a physically dominant focus, one cannot really exist on a purely physical level alone. Since the physical focus is so dominant, it dictates and governs one's mind, and a physically dominant focus is actually two-dimensional with the physical body also dictating and controlling the mind. In this case, the spirit is suppressed and buried beneath the body and mind.

In my personal analysis of the histories of man and woman, it is clear that two-dimensional, (physically dominant body and mind), existence is the norm. When humans have achieved their greatest achievements culturally, socially, scientifically, spiritually, technologically, philosophically, etc… they have done so when they were fully realized and three dimensional, (spirit, mind, and body). I feel very comfortable making this statement with respect to any culture and society in any part of the world. That doesn't mean men and women have lived in the absence of being fully realized. It does mean that humans, as a rule, have not used the fullness of their capacity through which to live life to the maximum potential as God intended us. Adam and Eve are one of the best examples. In their choosing a physically-dominant focus in their original fall from grace, they then realized just how much less they were than when they were fully spirit, mind, and body before their fateful choice. Let me pose an important question for you to consider. Will you choose to seek the fullness of your being – spirit, mind, and body? If so, what greater works for your life, (for the world), will you leave as your legacy if you do?

There really are a number of great cultures and individual examples where there was a cohesiveness of spiritual focus and balance of spirit, mind, and body. These cultures and individuals achieved some of the worlds' greatest accomplishments. My intent of this work is not to get caught up in the politics of world history views. I encourage you to think on it and draw from your own individual cultural point of reference. There is one universal individual that is safe to point to: Christ. The figure and person of Christ is the most dominant example in many historical and spiritual texts throughout the world. Christ is mentioned in the three most dominant world religions: Islam, Christianity, and Judaism. I feel very comfortable lifting Him up as an ideal of living a fully realized, (spirit, mind, and body), life. Now is not the appropriate place to deal with Christ, unless I get ahead of myself and the flow of the Spirit. But I want to make two key points about Christ at this point and leave it for now. He is the MODEL EXAMPLE of three-dimensional living. He also spoke of our capacity to do "Greater Works" than He Did!

In the newness of your thoughts and perspectives, (as I am challenging you to seek and realize), I want to pose more food for thought. How do you understand and grow your infant, physically dominant self into maturity? I trust that you will apply any guidance and foundation you have gained thus far to seek wisdom and understanding. I also trust that you will retrospect and reflect from "within-without" in arriving at our own uniquely specific and specifically unique personal insights. I also trust that you will use your spiritual ingredients to fashion the daily bread needed for your lifelong nourishment towards maturity. Yet, I would feel lacking in achieving my purpose for this work if I failed to give to you what has been place upon my heart and spirit. Above all, I desire to give the best of what I have been blessed to intuitively realize, know, and understand. In writing much of this work, God has blessed me to apply much of the principles, precepts, laws, teachings, and reasoning processes as it relates to my own personal life experiences. However, I must admit that I am very much an ongoing 'work in progress' as well. In the course of my writings, I am very much the teacher and pupil as well!

Realizing, knowing, and understanding are all three very distinct and different perspectives. You may realize something and not know you realize it. You may realize something and not understand it. Or you may realize, know, and understand something without knowing how to use it. Ultimately, you will realize, know, and understand something and also have the maturity, wisdom, knowledge, and understanding on how it applies and how to activate its complete use in your life. Along the way in life's journey, you will find yourself at various crossroads in this process. There are several key things for you to do. You must be analytical, introspective use "within-without" reasoning, reflective – think back on past experiences and learn from them, and open enough to allow your spirit to receive guidance along the way. My first suggestion to knowing how to mature your infant, physically dominant self is to realize, know, and understand who you are physically.

Do you realize, know, and understand who you are physically? This may seem like a dumb question, but it is not. While we are all of the same basic physical makeup, (we all have arms, legs, feet, hands, eyes, ears, faces, internal organs, etc…), we are not all motivated and challenged by the same physical wants and needs. There is a finite number of physical wants and needs, (food, shelter, affection, nourishment, etc…) all men and women have. However, there are "uniquely specific" and "specifically unique" differences each and every individual has within their finite wants and needs. What motivates, inspires, and challenges me physically, while similar to other men, is uniquely, specifically individualized to me, and not like any other man ever created. What motivates, inspires, and challenges you physically? Identifying your uniquely specific wants and needs is the beginning of maturely developing. Through identifying and realizing your uniquely specific wants and needs, you can identify your strengths and weaknesses. Knowing your strengths and weaknesses allows you to establish foundation and boundaries for exploring in order to establish complete realization, knowledge, and understanding. It is important to analyze strengths independent of weaknesses and it is equally important to analyze strengths and weaknesses in conjunction with each other. Analyze in a complete and thorough way, or as the old saying goes; "Every which way but Sunday." This is a continual, ongoing process as is most of life's development. I am convinced the world would be a far better place if we all spent our time and energies in self-development of spirit, mind, and body. It is always far easier to look away from self and find fault and weaknesses in others and in the world around us, yet it is far more difficult to look inside at our own weaknesses.

If knowing, realizing, and understanding yourself physically is step one in bringing about maturity, then controlling your actions and reactions as a result of your knowing, realizing, and understanding is clearly step two. Control is a very powerful, yet elusive thing to achieve. Controlling actions and reactions require discipline, focus, practice, spiritual guidance, spiritual perspective, spiritual commitment, and spiritual awareness. In Chapter 1, I recall asking do you control your thoughts, or do your thoughts control you. I asked the question before for you to think about it but now I'd like to provide some insights from my thoughts.

Your thoughts control you; however, the outcome of your actions and reactions to your thoughts changes as you grow from physical orientation towards spiritual orientation. Why? The mind is the battleground, or forum, through which you are forced to act and react to life's thoughts, choices, and decisions, (see Chapter 1, Section 3 on, "Thoughts And Words Are Things" for reference). In growing from an infant, physically dominant mind into a mature, spiritually dominant mind, you shift from selfish actions and reactions to selfless actions and reactions to life's thoughts, choices, and decisions. Christ, again, serves as the model example because He consistently denied Himself all things in life physically in order to give Himself spiritually and completely for others. While He is the ultimate ideal we are aspiring towards, that does not mean we should not be selfish about some things. We should have the maturity to know what to be selfish about when it comes to physical things. Some things are obvious. We have to eat and clothe ourselves in a healthy, nourishing way, so we need to be very self-absorbed towards that end. It's the not so obvious physical things we need to be concerned about controlling. Here is my general rule about the not-so-obvious physical things. Ask yourself, does the outcome affect someone else in any way? If so, is that impact selfish towards my wants and needs or of mutual benefit to him as well? Or, is that impact selfless towards my wants and needs and purely beneficial to him? If you recall the Spiritual Law of Reciprocity, (Chapter 2, page 52), then you realize that selfless actions and reactions bring back EXPONENTIAL selfless actions, reactions, and blessings to you in your time of want and need. It is not luck or fate, but God's spiritual principle of Grace realized in your life when you practice selflessness on behalf of others.

Through asking these simple questions, you can gain perspective for controlling the not-so-obvious physical things that affect our actions and reactions. All actions in life's journey are processes that require trial and error. In your attempts to master realizing, knowing, and understanding your physical nature and controlling your actions and reactions, you will fail along the way. In fact, you may find that you often learn and gain far more from your failures than your successes because people tend to take their successes for granted. But failures remain strongly impressed on the memory. You will also succeed. I challenge you to introspect, reflect, and analyze your successes and failures. That way, you will acquire the wisdom, knowledge, understanding, and maturity to activate your actions and reactions with fullness of spirit, mind, and body.

Why is it that in life, we sometimes can know from a spiritually mature perspective what is right, yet not have the maturity of body and mind to always apply that which we know? Why is it that we can know and understand the proper spiritual law, precept, teaching, or principle as it applies to one situation we are dealing with, yet fail to realize the need to apply that same law, precept, teaching, or principle to another situation we encounter that it would work equally as well for? There is a clear answer for these questions. Our spiritual maturity and understanding is often well ahead of our physical and mental maturity and understanding. Think about it this way. When you are teaching children how to do something that is complicated to them, but simple to you, they often fail to recognize how to do what you have taught them consistently. That is because they have not had enough experience to know how to apply what you are teaching them to a variety of different situations. While you may have given them the proper training and instruction on what to do, as well as when to do it, and in what instances they need to do what you have taught them, they still fail to act or do what you have taught them consistently. However, they do act and do what they have been taught in some instances. They understand to some degree what you have taught them. There are several key reasons they are not fully aware. In comparison to them, your knowledge and understanding is based on your having experienced what you are teaching them over enough time for it to be simple to you. It was not always simple to you either. You had a learning curve as well that required your understanding when to apply what you were initially learning and to what situations it was applicable. At some point during your learning curve, you were also inconsistent in your understanding of when to act and when not to act. It is pretty certain that the person who taught you was surprised; or, if he was a good, sympathetic teacher, he understood, that he also went through the same process before it was easy for him as well. How does this analogy relate to our spirits being ahead of us physically and mentally? It does because once we become spiritually aware and begin to seek spiritual reorientation, we are inclined to seek spiritual insight and perspective. We are also open to hearing that little quiet, inner "Holy Spirit" voice that provides the proper insight, perspective, and guidance to life's actions and reactions. However, much like the child in the analogy, we are still on a learning curve. Sometimes we fail to recognize when to apply what we are spiritually aware of, or guided to. Also, remember, our physical nature is the infant part of ourselves and tends to act and respond based on selfish, physical wants and needs in spite of knowing and understanding what is spiritually proper. Our infant, physical self, much as a baby demands attention and focus, is quite good at convincing the mind to rationalize why the physical wants and needs are more important than acting and doing what is the Holy Spirit has led us to do. In time, as we continue to mature, we look back and realize that we have rationalized away the proper actions and reactions. In time, we do act and react in the proper way, not allowing our selfish, physical, infant self to force us to go against what we know and are led to that is spiritually proper.

Furthermore, as we progress in our spiritual development, we will often have full spiritual knowledge and understanding but still not have the physical and mental maturity to act on our knowledge and understanding. A child is rebellious in nature and requires mature, parental guidance and discipline to structure and correct his rebellious nature. Our physical, childish nature is also rebellious, even when we know what is right. The mind conforms to this dominant physical nature in the absence of mature guidance and discipline and is thus controlled by our physically rebellious nature. Have you ever observed a child do something wrong knowingly? Could you clearly see a guilty look on his face even as he continued to do it? Having said all of this, there is a key point I want make. Do not beat yourself up when you fail to act, react, or respond physically and mentally to what you know is spiritually right. Just keep trying! If you beat yourself up, you will get discouraged or defeated and stop trying. Gaining mature control and discipline over your physical actions and reactions takes time, patience, focus, and consistent, ongoing effort, and it will not come overnight. It is a lifelong pursuit! If you fail today, you can continue to strive for success tomorrow. Accept your failures and learn from them and continue to try to succeed. In time you will! Allow your failures to keep you humble. Continue seeking guidance and direction from God, Christ, and the Holy Spirit. It often takes our failures to realize we need help from sources far greater than us, which keeps us in a position of humility. Our failures also enable us to humbly help others overcome their failures in things we have already overcome successfully. By helping others we reciprocally position ourselves to receive the guidance and help we need with our own challenges.

In continuing with the thought process of leading you to new perspectives, let's focus on an old one, the existence of the devil. Often one cannot arrive at new perspectives without dissecting old ones. In dissecting old perspectives, we learn what we thought to be true is not wholly and absolutely true. In fact, there are many old perspectives that were once universally accepted as true, that when dissected, are now universally accepted as false. At one point, ancient civilizations thought the world was flat. They accepted this as a universal truth for many generations until African explorers, Spanish explorers, Scandinavian explorers, Asian explorers and other ancient explorers from various countries throughout the world circumnavigated the world and proved it was in fact round, and not flat.

Does the devil exist? He is certainly an old perspective that has existed in all cultures since the beginning of recorded time. One of my main reference points, the Holy Bible, speaks very clearly of his existence. Relating back to my initial story of Adam and Eve's fall from grace, the devil was represented as the serpent in the garden, (see Genesis, Chapter 3, verses 1 through 6). There are also countless other examples throughout the Bible pertaining to his existence. In addition to the Bible, all religious texts, cultures, and faiths recognize his existence. Are there new perspectives that are critical to your thoughts, insights, and understandings that merit dissecting our old perspectives of him? How do we identify how he impacts us in our aims at acquiring the keys to the sacred place we so passionately covet and desire?

I am certain that you know my pattern by now. Most of the questions I pose throughout this work are not merely rhetorical, but ones I have been led to provide my own insights and perspectives to. It is certainly very critical and essential to provide new perspectives on the existence of the devil and his impact on our spiritual reorientation to wholeness. Many of the old perspectives pertaining to the devil and his existence, warrant dissecting. As with other older perspectives, dissection allows for higher, absolute truths to come to light. Dissection also allows for the dismissal of old falsehoods that hinder gaining the insights, understandings, and maturity to continue progression to wholeness of spirit, mind, and body. Just as cultures the world over gained significant prosperity through traveling the seas to other foreign cultures to exchange their knowledge, traditions, unique commodities and goods, and customs, it is my hope that you shall prosper significantly through any new perspectives that increase your knowledge, insights, and understandings of the devil as it pertains to the questions I have posed. I know the concept of the devil is one of controversy. However, I have also discussed some other equally controversial topics already in this humble text. So this topic is also one I am not afraid to discuss. If nothing is ventured, nothing is gained! I am not afraid to venture with the hope that it leads to positive benefits, gains, insights, and perspectives to those seeking spiritual growth and clarity on their way towards spiritual fullness and completeness.

To the opening question of whether the devil exists, my response is yes, the devil exists! The devil, Satan, Lucifer, or any other number of names he is called, is one of the most misunderstood figures in our culture today. The new perspectives I want to provide is to point out some actual characteristics to identify him by. It is up to you to understand how he impacts you in your spiritual development and progression. Once you understand the characteristics to identify him by, then you can understand how to deal with him effectively.

Sports and games are ideal analogies to make my points clear. In most sports and games, the objective is to win. This objective is accomplished by defeating an opponent. In order to defeat the opponent, you must understand the opponent's strategy or game plan. You must also understand the opponent's strengths and weaknesses. With all of this knowledge, you must create a game plan of your own to enact, act, react, and execute that strategically leads to victory. A well strategized, executed game plan magnifies and capitalizes on your strengths while hiding and protecting your weaknesses.

A well strategized, executed game plan also magnifies and takes full advantage of your opponents' weaknesses and neutralizes or conquers their weaknesses.

What is the devil's game plan? How does he execute his game plan to succeed at keeping us from the keys to the "Sacred Place" we so desperately desire? Before talking abut his game plan and his execution for succeeding, I have been led to talk about two very common misconceptions about the devil. Misconception one: Satan's existence proves there is no God. I had a friend challenge my spiritual belief in God by asking this question: if God exists, why would He create a devil? Why does evil exist? My response to him was simply: how can we fully appreciate, know, realize, and understand the ultimate, awesome, Love and Goodness of God without an ultimate, bad evil to compare Him to? I also related the importance by discussing raising his children. I asked him how could his children know right without understanding wrong, good without bad, happiness without sadness, love without hate. The existence of the devil is part of God's plan. Evil and all evil forces only further validate God in that He can perform SUPREME GOOD and achieve GREAT WORKS in man and woman who are susceptible to doing evil and bad things in their journey through life.

One of the laws of physics states to every action, there is an opposite, opposing reaction. This physics principle, simply defined, refers to two concepts: duality and polarity. Duality refers to the male and female aspects of life. Adam and Eve are a good example of duality because in creating man, God also had to create a woman as a perfect mate, balance, and complement to man. Adam is also the perfect mate, balance, and complement to Eve and Eve is the perfect mate, balance, and complement to Adam. Polarity, (complete opposites), is also abundant in our physical world. Nature has an abundance of good examples: hot versus cold, winter versus summer, night versus day. These physical, scientific principles are also spiritual laws. Remember, Christ said, "As above, So below." God provides understanding, validation, and confirmation of many spiritual laws through physical, scientific principles so we can relate in the physical realm to Him. The value of the science of physics and other scientific studies is we can experiment, in the physical realm, to validate the theories and principles of our minds and spirits. Just as God thought, and then spoke, and it became, man and woman have the capacity to think of a concept, thing, or idea, and test that idea, thing, or concept through experimentation, and validate its truth.

On a much broader level, our efforts to use science to validate life in the physical sense through theorizing, then testing and experimenting on those theories should take us full circle in seeking to understand life from a full three dimensional, (spirit, mind, and body), perspective. One of the greatest scientific minds of the 20th century, Albert Einstein, confessed that the more he understood science, the more he realized that God existed. As with Einstein, we should realize the comparison because in applying scientific principles and experiments, we are bringing into physical realm the fruition of our thoughts and spirits. We are bringing into physical being that which started as a mere thought, just as God did in all of creation because He also began with Divine Thoughts. Hopefully, my point is clear. The fact that Satan exists does not mean God does not exist. In fact, Satan's existence, from the scientific principles of duality – good versus evil and polarity – diametrically opposing forces validates God's existence. Satan is not God's equal but, he represents the opposite end of God's love and goodness realized in the nature and essence of man and woman's spirit. Since God IS, WAS, and ALWAYS WILL BE, He is the original experimenter that conceived all that is, was, and ever will be, including Satan. God, the Original, Perfect Creator, defined all that He created in creating the experiment of all life, thus nothing falls outside of the bounds of His awesome creation. In defining all He created, He is master and supreme authority over His creation, just as the master scientist is master over his lab experiment. All scientific principles, like spiritual principles, have a purpose. Both are purposed for the understanding and edification of man and woman towards fully realized, (spirit, mind, and body), life as God originally intended.

The second big misconception today is: Satan's main plan of attack is through horror and fear. Our world today is visually overloaded. We have the Internet, movies, DVD technology, Cable

TV, satellite TV, ect... In ancient times, cultures relied on stories, oral legends, and books. Since we have so many visual outlets, books have become less important because everything can be created in visual form. In our present visual age, the misconception of Satan portrayed as an evil force that operates through horror and evil is vividly displayed. Many of our popular movies and books portray Satan as the ultimate evil leader that devours the souls of men and women through horrible experiences and legions of demonic forces. I am not saying that Satan does not have demonic forces. I am saying that horror is not Satan primary game plan. One of our earliest recorded biblical experiences makes my point very clearly. In Genesis, Chapter 3, verses 1-6, Eve first met Satan in the form of a serpent in the Garden of Eden. The Bible did not mention any horror or fear in this meeting. In fact, the serpent was described as being "beguiling" to Eve. Webster's Dictionary describes one who is beguiling as charming, not fearful. Another very significant reference in Webster's Dictionary describes a beguiling person as one who uses cunning and deception along with his charm. Eve had a discussion with Satan about eating the fruit from the Tree of the Knowledge of Good and Evil. So Satan did not use horror to force any acts from Eve. Satan's primary game plan was revealed in that first meeting. That plan is deception. Deception is an extremely powerful weapon. A master of deception achieves his deception so well that the one being deceived is not even aware of it. There is almost no way to overcome deception when you are not even aware of it. Eve was not even aware of Satan's deception until it was too late to change her mind about eating the fruit from the Tree of the Knowledge of Good and Evil. The deception was even deeper because not only did Satan convince Eve she and Adam would be "like God" he also knew that through deceiving Eve, he would get Adam to eat the fruit. Adam was his original target anyway since God gave the commandment to Adam not to eat of the fruit, not Eve. A master of deception also has a well-devised plan that is so subtly disguised that it cannot be discovered until it's too late to overcome.

If Satan's primary game plan is deception, what are his tactics for achieving his deception? His primary tactics are confusion, distraction, temptation, and using our physical fears and weaknesses to his advantage. There is another excellent biblical example of Satan attempting his plan of deception but he was identified and called a deceiver in this case. In the book of Matthew, Chapter 4, Satan approached Christ after he had fasted forty days and nights in the wilderness. The author of the story makes it clear that Christ was at his weakest point physically, having fasted for forty days when Satan approached. Satan first tried to use Christ's physical weakness as a tactic to deceive Him. Verse 3 states, "And the tempter came to him, he said, if thou be the Son of God, command these stones be made bread." Christ responded in verse 4 with the following comment: "It is written, man shall not live by bread alone, but by every word that proceedth out of the mouth of God." Next, Satan tried to use confusion as a tactic. Verse 5 states, "Then the devil taketh him up into the holy city, and setteth him on a pinnacle of the temple. And saith unto him, if thou be the Son of God, cast thyself down: for it is written, He shall give his angles charge concerning thee: and their hands they shall bear thee up, lest at any time thou dash they foot against a stone." Christ was not confused by Satan's attempt to use the Holy Scriptures to get him to act. Christ stated in verse

7, "It is written again, thou shalt not tempt the Lord thy God." Satan's last tactic was temptation. In Chapter 4, verses 8 and 9 states, "Then the devil taketh him up into an exceeding high mountain, and showeth him all the kingdoms of the world, and the glory of them. And saith unto him, all these things will I give thee, if thou wilt fall down and worship me." Christ was not fooled with Satan's temptation either. Christ states in verse 10, "Get thee hence Satan; for it is written, thou shalt worship the Lord they God, and Him only shalt thou serve."

These Biblical parables present some very important points for us to consider in understanding and recognizing Satan's game plan of deception. Important point number one: Satan has always used his game plan of deception to separate man and woman from God and full three dimensional existence, (spirit, mind, and body on one accord with God), as God intended. Satan was successful in taking the most precious gift Adam and Eve had, spiritual intimacy with

God away. He was also equally bold enough to challenge Christ, the Son of God, to try to take his spiritual intimacy with God away. So, Satan will most definitely challenge you and me.

Important point number two: Satan is persistent in his pursuit to achieve success with his plan. He had a three-phase approach with Christ, preying first on Christ's physical weakness because he realized Christ had just fasted for 40 days. The most obvious weakness Christ had at that point was hunger and lack of physical strength. When that tactic failed, he moved to the next phase, trying to confuse Christ with the scriptures to perform an act to prove He was the Son of God. When that tactic failed, he used his last tactic, temptation. Satan is a cunning and beguiling adversary and will use several approaches to get to us just as he did with Christ.

Important point number three: Satan seldom executes his plan in isolation because he knows deception works best when we are trying to deal with multiple challenges. Isn't it interesting that Satan approached Christ after He had fasted for forty days? Why didn't he approach Christ after Christ had performed one of His many miracles? Or as He was instructing the disciples in the many life lessons He did? Satan knew he had the advantage of approaching Christ at His weakest physically and mentally since Christ had just fasted. That gave Satan an advantage of not executing in isolation because Christ was not His usual, exceptionally strong, Self physically and mentally. When we are dealing with multiple challenges, we are spread so thinly that we can easily lose focus, get distracted, or not have our full energy to devote to any one challenge in the midst of dealing with several challenges. Christ succeeded in spite of His physical and mental weakness because His spiritual strength was what He relied upon most anyway. Christ knew His spiritual strength was the strongest part of His being and He also knew it could not be conquered in spite of His physical hunger and weakness. Is there a potential lesson in this for us? Yes, without any doubt, there is because just as Christ did, if we can still and contain our physical hungers and weaknesses and get to our spiritual strength, we too can succeed against Satan when he attacks us at our physically weakest point.

Important point number four: Satan knows the Holy Scriptures. However, Satan will use the Holy Scriptures out of context to confuse or deceive, not in the context of truth for spiritual growth and development. It is very important for us to know the scriptures and seek inner understanding from the Holy Spirit, Christ, and God to give us true understanding. It is equally important for us to put into action, in our day-to-day actions and reactions, our understanding of the principles of the scriptures to show the truth behind our words and deeds. Seeking to reason "within-without" will help tremendously as we strive to get spiritual guidance on the interpretation and understanding of spiritual texts and scriptures we encounter in our spiritual environments.

Important point number five: Since we are physically dominant and oriented since the original fall from grace, one of Satan's key tactics is to prey on our physical weaknesses and fears to successfully accomplish his game plan of deception. It is not by chance that the Biblical author mentioned Christ was hungry after fasting forty days and the tempter, (Satan), approached him. Just as Satan hoped to find Christ physically weak and vulnerable, he hopes to find us the same way. Is it likely that Satan will apply this tactic as his first strategy? Yes, it is! Consider sports and games as a comparison. A sound game plan in any sport uses an aggressive offensive attack. An aggressive offensive attack focuses on the obvious strengths of the person or team on offense while attacking the obvious weaknesses of the opponent at the same time. If the offensive attack fails, alternative offensive tactics are used and if they fail, alternative defensive plans are used. Satan was shrewd enough to know that his best offensive attack on Christ was physical hunger after Christ had fasted forty days. When he failed to get Christ to change the stones to bread as proof that He was the Son of God, he then moved to an alternative offensive attack to use scriptures to confuse Christ. When that failed also, Satan went on the defensive by portraying himself as lord over all the kingdoms of the world and asked Christ to worship him in exchange for all kingdoms of the world. Satan's last defensive attack failed and his plan of deception was defeated.

It makes sense that our physical weaknesses are Satan's first offensive point of attack. Our physically dominant orientation makes us easy prey for him to target, especially since he was successful in using it against Adam and Eve. Adam and Eve had no concern or interest in their physical needs, appearance, or desires until after eating the fruit of the Tree of Knowledge of Good and Evil. Genesis, Chapter 3, verse 7, states; "And the eyes of them both were opened, and they knew they were naked; and they sewed fig leaves together, and made themselves aprons." Since Satan's first plan of offensive attack is through preying on our physical orientation, we must continue to strive for spiritual maturity and reorientation to defeat this tactic. Just as Christ succeeded in not succumbing to his physical weakness and desire after fasting for forty days, we can also succeed as we continue to mature and become spiritually reoriented. It is only through our inner spiritual maturation and strength that we can overcome our physical and mental weaknesses. The spirit is the adult of our being, as the physical self is the child. The spirit nature tempers and balances physical and mental desires for wholeness of spirit, mind, and body without compromising our spiritual morals, values, and principles God gives us to live by. This is especially true as we progress in our spiritual orientation and development through seeking guidance from the Holy Spirit, Christ, and God along with our spiritual environment. We do not have to deny who we are physically, we just have to continue to mature fully, (spirit, mind, and body), so we understand what physical needs and desires are mutual to our needs spiritually and mentally as well, three dimensionally; spirit, mind, and body in that order. Putting it more simply, our physical needs and desires cannot be satisfied without considering how they affect our spiritual and mental needs. If our physical needs and desires violate our spiritual morals, precepts, and principles, we must consider that those desires are not good for us in total. At that point, we must reason "within-without" to find a way to fit those physical needs and desires into our spiritual orientation. In most cases, through reasoning "within-without" we can find common ground to meet our physical needs. If after reasoning we cannot find common ground, we must be mature and strong enough to let go of and not succumb to the physical want or need.

Using the comparison of the child to the physical nature let me give an example for clarity. Children want many things that are not good for them at the moment they want it. When parents take children to the grocery store, they want the candy most stores place near the register. Or, a child may want to eat only dessert at dinner or eat dessert before eating any other portions of dinner. It is the parent's responsibility to act as the adult to temper the child's desire for candy at the register, or feed him nourishing, balanced meals before allowing him dessert. The parent takes on the role of the mature spirit and Holy Spirit for the child. Because they must temper and put into perspective, by explaining to the child why getting candy at the register, or eating only dessert or dessert before other portions, is not nourishing for their physical and mental development. So in this example, since the child has a raw, inexperienced physical desire, absent of the ability to reason "within-without" the wise parent provides that guidance. In time, the child, having received that perspective from the parent, understands on his own why he should not have the candy at the register or eat only dessert or dessert without eating his other portions at dinner. In time, the child will have the same physical desire for the candy at the register, but will reason "within-without" through having learned from the parent, why he should choose not to ask for the candy. The child has matured in this instance and made a choice that is tempered through their own "within-without" reasoning and as a result makes a choice that best for him to develop physically and mentally. There is a clear progression in this process that comes through life experiences. As we mature spiritually, our physical and mental natures are tempered when we seek to reason "within-without." This occurs because we are forced to consider the what ifs and whys behind our physical and mental wants and desires and compare those to our spiritual environment, morals, precepts, and principles and to the leanings of the Holy Spirit, Christ, and God.

Let's examine Satan's tactics, (confusion, distraction, temptation, and using our physical fears and weaknesses), more closely.

Confusion is a very, very useful tactic in a world that continues to get increasingly more technologically complicated. We do not have the benefit of the full resources and knowledge of ancient history. Much has been destroyed, lost, and misinterpreted over time. However, it is at least safe for me to speak about today. It may be debatable that ancient man and woman had even more advanced technology in some cultures. The ancient Kemetian, (Egyptian), culture is a culture that comes to mind. After all, we still cannot, with all of today's modern technology, duplicate some of their advances, like construct pyramids like the great pyramid in Egypt. Based on the historical records we do have access to, it is probably safe to say their culture, as a whole, was not as technologically complicated as the one we now live in. In most ancient cultures, only the elite, wealthy, and royal people had access to technology while the majority of the general public was poor and did not have the means or access to the knowledge of the elite. In our world today, far more of the general population has access to technology and information through computers, televisions, magazines, and newspapers than ever before. Complexity leads to confusion. The more complicated worldwide society becomes, the more confusing it becomes to stay abreast of all of the information at our disposal. With this excessive overload of information, it becomes even more difficult to know what information is relevant from what is not.

How does all of this complexity impact us individually? Earlier, I mentioned the extreme visual nature of today's world. Just 100 mere years ago, it took months, years, and even decades for news to travel the globe. Today, news travels the entire globe in a matter of seconds! One hundred years ago, the primary means of receiving and accessing news was through printed media, (letters, newspapers, magazines, and books). Radios and televisions were in their infancy, and a limited media was accessible by a very small segment of the world's wealthy cultures. Now, news is relayed through printed media, via television, cable, satellite, radio, and the Internet to the majority of the world's population. These multiple, super speedy mediums increased the speed of our access to information from a snail's pace to warp speed on a space ship. Without question, we have far too much information, news, and resources to sort through to find simple, clear truth and understanding about life three dimensionally, (spirit, mind, and body). This does not seem to be a problem because it is a subtly deceiving world that we are born into so we are naturally comfortable and accustomed to it. It is a problem that becomes exponential in scope because it enables us to grow at warp speed into a wealth of physical information and become self-absorbed in all of this physical information in the absence of the same level of spiritual development. Since physical orientation is our natural orientation, it is very easy to feed our physical natures in a world of physical information overload. We also have far too many distractions that keep our focus on physical knowledge and information and off full development of spirit, mind and body.

Let me bring this point to a more personal level by using my own upbringing in my childhood spiritual environment. When I was young and growing up in the country, my parents were the primary source of knowledge for my development physically, mentally, and spiritually. What they taught me about life and understanding life wholly, and the development of my spiritual environment and mental development academically was much simpler for them to manage and control. We did not have a wealth of outside resources, (computers, the Internet, cable, etc…) at our fingertips. I was not more strongly influenced by the outside world with all of the excessive information and distractions that children today have exposure to. I was far more concerned with what my parents thought and not nearly as concerned with what my peers thought. Times were simpler. I did question my development in my childhood upbringing. I just did not have nearly as many outside sources to compound and confuse my parental guidance. So there were far fewer opportunities for me to get confused and lost amongst too much information coming from too many directions and sources as there are today.

Another good comparison of how complexity leads to confusion is the interpretations of the Holy Bible. At one point in time, there was an original Bible. This original Bible was written and interpreted in the dominant language of the time, Hebrew. Over the centuries that followed its original divine writing, it has been translated into other diverse languages. It has even been re-interpreted into languages that have far less comparative words and meanings so some of its original interpretation has been lost in translation. Archeologists are constantly finding ancient documents, such as the Rosetta Stone, to support or refute present interpretations. In the midst of all this complexity, comes confusion about which Bible to use as a source for true spiritual understanding. There is also complexity in how to interpret the scriptures. Should our understanding be purely literal for what they literally say? Or, should we seek a higher spiritual understanding beyond what is literally said? Does our understanding of the various higher levels of understandings broaden and deepen as we mature? If we consider the times and context in which the Holy Scriptures were written, we must consider that most ancient prophets were condemned for writing words of religious texts and often punished by death! I hope my point is clear. I have talked earlier about seeking the spirit of God, the Holy Spirit, and Christ behind the word so I think my perspective is clear. If not, let me make it clear. You should seek the higher spiritual understanding beyond what is literally said and that understanding broadens and deepens as you mature. However, I simply want you to realize that the power behind confusion extends even to our most sacred texts and teachings.

Confusion from another aspect is also a key tactic the devil uses to keep us unaware of our true, fully divine nature and power. Adam and Eve are a perfect example to illustrate my point. The devil was able to confuse them into thinking they would gain far more Godly attributes and power through eating of the Tree of Knowledge of Good and Evil. Satan knew all along that Adam and Eve had a very intimate, special relationship with God and that special relationship would be severed when Adam violated God's strictest commandment. Satan also knew that Adam and Eve were far more powerful and greater in their fully divine, original selves than they would be after their fall from grace. Let me make this issue even more personal for you. If Satan can keep you confused enough to view, pursue, and live life from a physically dominant perspective, then you will never fully realize the fullness of your greatest relationship and kindredness with God, (your spirit). You will fail to exercise the greatest portion of your being to become and realize the whole spirit, mind, and body God originally created you to be. If Satan is successful in keeping you in this state of focus, his battle is far easier. It is much, much easier to prey on your physical weaknesses in a world that is physically centered with all the trimmings, trappings, and visual enticements designed just to please selfish physical wants and needs.

Satan is the outside leader of the inner rebellion I discussed in Chapter 1 that must be addressed as we seek to move from physical orientation towards spiritual re-orientation. Satan is also the outside leader in a broader sense because he knows how to make the most of all the worldly trimmings, trappings, and enticements that attract and distract us away from spiritual development, focus, and nurturing in our efforts to become spiritually re-oriented. Satan is defined as the prince of this world by Christ in the Bible in the book of John, Chapter 12, verse 31: "Now is the judgement of this world; now shall the prince of this world be cast out." Satan is also identified in the same manner in the book of Ephesians, Chapter 2, verse 2:"Where in times past ye walked according to the course of this world, according to the prince of the power of the air, the spirit that now worketh in the children of disobedience." So, all the trimmings, trappings, and enticements of this world become powerful tools in Satan's arsenal to keep us confused. Added to our excessive amount of information, it is easy to see how confusion runs rampant in our world today.

It is important to make a critical point about the mind here. Just as the Holy Spirit speaks to our hearts and minds, our minds are also channels for other sources. Since the devil is a spirit, he also uses our minds to plant his seeds of confusion, distraction, physical weaknesses, etc… in executing his game plan of deception. Do you listen to and hear your thoughts when you are in a quiet, undistracted environment? Do you find yourself having a conversation in your mind sometimes? The phrase, "I was just talking to myself" is a very common one and talking to ourselves is a normal thing we do. Let me pose several very crucial questions for you to meditate on. Do you consider the source of your thoughts? Are your thoughts positive, negative, selfish, or selfless? Do the thoughts that cross your mind evoke feelings of physical desires and wants, anger, lust, greed, and envy? Or, do the thoughts that cross your mind evoke feelings of love, compassion, joy, happiness, peace, and giving? It is extremely important to realize that much of Satan's plan of attack is planted through our minds. A small, subtle, deceptive thought planted here and there, over the course of time, grows into a bigger, more dangerous one to overcome if we are not spiritually mature enough to challenge it and dismiss it from our minds.

In order to identify his tactics, we must understand and analyze what crosses our minds and from which source it is coming. Think of your mind this way; it is the control center where the decisions are made. Just as the central processing unit in a computer is the main engine that performs the operations of a computer; the mind is the central processing unit that governs our physical actions and reactions, spiritual actions, reactions, works, and deeds. So, whether you choose to do right or wrong, a selfish act or action, or a selfless act or action, the mind is the place where you ultimately began the thought process to make that choice and ultimately take that act or action. Can you see why the process of growth, change, and development towards complete spiritual reorientation is a significantly important process that is ongoing? It is because we do make some wrong choices and act and react improperly in the midst of the battlefront we are constantly engaged in. Through the convictions of the Holy Spirit, our own meditations, introspections, and reflections, we learn to correct our errors. It is okay to make some wrong choices and lose a temporary battle. It is even necessary in some cases for that to occur so we make the right choices and win the battle the next time. Without losing some of our battles, we have no opportunity to apply the tools necessary, (Holy Spirit convictions and urgings, introspection, and reflection), to acquire the wisdom, knowledge, and maturity to win those battles when they occur the next time. However, it is important that we continuously seek to win the battles and learn with each battle to make strides towards winning the next battle that occurs. Through this process comes the ability to win, mature, and spiritually reorient.

Along with using the tactic of confusion to keep you physically dominant, focused, and away from spiritual orientation, Satan also uses confusion to cloud issues related to spirituality. It is difficult to have definite convictions about our spiritual environment and the laws, precepts, principles, and morals we form if we are confused. Confusion has a way of causing us to doubt, waiver, and delay progressing towards any foundations, beliefs, actions, and reactions. As long as we remain confused, we are in a state of limbo and no progress is made. Or, worse can happen. We actually give up our efforts for trying to continue to grow spiritually. Or we become even more comfortable with our physically dominant nature and selfish ways. World complexity only heightens this tactic as a means of deception for Satan. It is your responsibility to seek clarity, wisdom, knowledge, and understanding as you continue your path towards spiritual development and maturity. You will never gain full understanding by intellectually trying to grasp the wealth of information, and misinformation, available in the world today. You can, through your continued spiritual reorientation, continue your progress. When things get overwhelmingly confusing, simply go back to a point of reference you are not confused on. For example, when we learn the various levels of mathematics, basic math, Algebra, Trigonometry, Calculus and so on, each step in our progression gets more challenging and can be confusing. The best way to continue learning Algebra after you have mastered basic math is to go back to basic principles when you are confused in a problem or concept you are trying to learn in Algebra. Going back and reviewing basic math principles achieves several very important purposes. It gives you confidence because you do know some math principles. It also allows you to review which of these basic principles may be important to understand and relate to the Algebra you are presently trying to learn. And it gives you the fortitude, renewed energy, and confidence to continue to learn the Algebra you may be struggling with. Having a common point of reference that you are not confused about gives you confidence and peace of mind. It also enables you to stay grounded in what you do know. Also, when put into a mature perspective through reflection and introspection, you also realize, at

179

some point, many of your common points were not always common points, but they became common points through your growth and maturation.

Along with going back to a point of common reference, it is equally important to simplify what you are confused about through prayer, introspection, and listening to the small quiet inner voice of the Holy Spirit for direction. Realize also that confusion is not always immediately overcome. Much like the math analogy I discussed earlier, progressing from a confusing issue is a process that takes time and patience. Confusion is essential for our growth and development. It is okay to have confusion on some things because that confusion keeps us humble and aware of the dependency we have on God's Omniscient Support and Grace to grow and gain understanding on the things we are confused about. Just be careful not to let confusion keep you off balance and out of focus, or stop you from striving to continue to grow. In fact, let it serve as the motivator to spur you to continue to grow. In times of confusion, it is imperative that you seek to balance and focus and realize that the confusion itself is a tactic used to keep you off track or away from seeking continued growth and development.

I hope by now you realize just how powerful the tactic of confusion can be in Satan's arsenal. It is one of his most potent weapons and is not to be underestimated. However, as with many of Satan's tactics, it can be overcome. To overcome confusion, it is essential to seek structure in your spiritual environment, apply ingredients from your daily bread, and govern, monitor, and evaluate your actions and reactions to life's day to-day issues. With structure, comes order. It takes hard work, discipline, and focus to develop structure. However, most of the work is in the process of developing the structure. Once you have developed the process, your task of overcoming confusion becomes much easier. Excelling at a particular sport is a perfect example. There is an old saying used by coaches, "Practice makes perfect." What separates star athletes from an ordinary athlete is hard work, discipline, and a willingness to practice harder, longer, and with more dedication in order to maximize their physical and mental talents to achieve. Another old saying among coaches is,

"How one practices is also how one performs in game situations." So, it is not a surprise that the star player excels when the game is on the line. That star player has practiced that situation, either through the practice scenarios the coach uses while practicing, or on his own time when he is putting in extra time to become the best. These same principles hold true for a collective team. Often, the team that structures its practices and prepares the most effectively to deal with game situations is also the team that wins consistently. Don't be afraid of putting in the time, discipline, focus, and work needed to structure your spiritual environment, apply the ingredients in your daily bread, and govern, monitor, and evaluate your actions and reactions to daily life issues. Through these essential skills, you will assure success in finding clarity, growth, and maturity over any confusion Satan attempts to bring your way.

Distractions in our lives today are a close relative to confusion. There is a very subtle difference between the two. Satan's goal, with the tactic of distraction, is to get you off track, out of focus, or unaware of your skills or strengths. Yes, confusion can lead to the same outcome. However, confusion is more mental in that we tend to get confused in our minds when trying to process and intellectualize spiritual things. Not all that is spiritual can be intellectualized and understood. In fact, much of what is spiritual requires your faith and trust in your leadings until you later see the outcome of the actions and reactions to those leadings. Or, that same faith is required to trust a spiritual law, precept, principle, or teaching when we first learn it but have not seen the application of that law, precept, principle, or teaching in our practical life experiences.

The parent, child relationship is a good comparison, as it has been throughout this work.

Parents establish and teach their children many rules that, to the child, do not make sense until they are older. For example, many parents teach their children not to play with strangers, especially adult strangers. That rule does not make sense to a 5 or 6 year old, whose whole focus at that age is to play games with anyone and everyone. As the child grows older, he learns of a friend or relative, or sees on the news a young child that was kidnapped, hurt, or injured by a stranger, and he realizes why his parents had the rule not to play with strangers. That 5 or 6 year old must have faith and trust, even though he may not understand the parent's rule, that his parent has an important reason for that rule and abide by the rule.

Another difference between confusion and distractions is confusion is more of an inner challenge. We also wrestle with our physically dominant nature, which can bring about confusion as we seek to reconcile our physical acts and actions to spiritual morals, precepts, and principles. Distractions tend to be more external in nature than confusion. Confusion often comes from an external source, (information overload, conflicting spiritual views as we seek different spiritual perspectives). But the actual struggle of overcoming confusion is within. Distractions are often external things: (stress on the job, problems with relationships, financial woes, and societal challenges), that keep you from focusing on your inner thoughts. The goal with distraction as a tactic is to get you so caught up in other outside factors that you do not take the time to think "within-without" or apply your spiritual ingredients, laws, precepts, and principles to daily life. Distractions are also often things beyond your personal control that you make personal issues. People cannot control when they may get a new boss that is difficult to work with. Yet, they must deal with the adjustments of learning what their new boss expects of them to perform their jobs successfully.

Just as distraction is a very important tactic used in a military battle or sporting event, it is also a very important tactic Satan uses against us. In a sporting event, if a team can keep its opponent distracted long enough, they can gain a decisive offensive advantage and crush the confidence of their opponent. Distractions are dangerous because they very sneakily consume your energy and focus far away from the whole balance of spirit, mind, and body you are seeking to achieve. Have you ever been merrily going along well balanced and happy with everything going great in your life until you encounter an issue outside of your control, such as a change to your job responsibilities, gets you off balance? All of a sudden, months have passed and you are stressed and totally engrossed in thinking about how this change has affected you in a bad way. You cannot sleep or rest well because you just can not seem to find an answer to overcome the stresses and problems with this new change. It is constantly on your mind and you can think of little else. The impact of the change affects your social, personal, and spiritual habits, focus, and enjoyment. This scenario, while not one caused by Satan, is a classic example of how distractions can get you off course in life. Satan's distraction tactics will be more specific to your own personal physical wants, desires, and weaknesses and will revolve around your inner struggles to conquer or overcome them. However, the outcome of getting off course for months, enduring stress and anxiety, and struggling constantly with trying to find solutions and answers to your problems caused by the distraction at hand are still much like the scenario above.

Before I tell you a simple answer that has best worked in my life, I'd like to offer my perspective of why Satan uses distractions. The art of warfare is a good concept to use to explain using distraction as a tactic. A smart military leader knows it is best to distract an enemy for several key reasons. One key reason is to keep the enemy from finding his own army's weaknesses. If he has a strong infantry and a weak naval force, he may use his infantry along with air support to distract the enemy naval troops approaching his navy. Another key reason is to keep his adversary away from his own strength to keep him from maximizing that strength or getting stronger. If the leader knows his enemy has an advantage in numbers, he may try to distract the enemy by rushing a large portion of his troops at one key area where the enemy has less troops to give the illusion that he actually has more troops than his enemy has. Or, if he knows the enemy has stronger cannons and guns, he may use a Guerilla squad or elite special forces unit to attack his enemy with the intent of destroying as many cannons and guns as he can to weaken the enemy's main strength.

How does this analogy relate to Satan using distraction as a tactic against us? It relates for many of the same key reasons. Satan uses distraction as a tactic to keep us from using our strengths. Our spiritual environment, laws, precepts, principles, teachings, ingredients of our daily bread, and guidance by the Holy Spirit are all key strengths Satan wants to keep us distracted from using. Satan also uses distraction to keep us from realizing his key weaknesses. His primary key weakness is he has no power or authority except his tools of suggestion, deception, distraction, and confusion. While they are powerful weapons, THEY ONLY WORK IF WE ALLOW THEM TO THROUGH OUR FAILURE TO USE OUR STRENGTHS!

Satan also uses distraction because he knows you are often very near growing to another level in your spiritual understanding and maturation. He uses distraction to keep you from using your talents, gifts, and ministry to help others. He uses distraction to keep you from focusing during times of progression. He uses distraction to keep you from recognizing your strongest spiritual strengths, talents, spiritual assets, and gifts in helping others. If he can successfully distract you during any of these times, he is winning small battles in his bigger war to conquer your continued growth toward full, Christ-realized maturity.

So, here are my suggestions to you. When you find you're getting caught up and distracted by the problems of the world or the problems of everyday existence, stop and take a deep breath. As you take that deep breath, stop and introspect, then think. Figure out if you are so engrossed with the situation that you are getting out of focus and balance. You have now identified that the tactic of distraction is being used against you. Once you are aware, you can begin to overcome it. What has worked absolutely best for me in conquering distractions is very simple. I let go and let God! Present, in intimate dialogue or prayer with, and to God, the issue. Then, release yourself of the responsibility of solving the distraction., seeking God's guidance, and leadings from the Holy Spirit on what actions and reactions you need to take relating to the distraction. Since many distractions are outside of your personal control anyway, you will have a very slim chance of overcoming it. By letting go and relinquishing it to God, you relieve the stress and burden of having to solve the problem. Now it is far easier to introspect and receive the direction and guidance you need from God and the Holy Spirit on the actions and reactions you need on a personal level to impact the distractions you are faced with. It then becomes easier to structure your approach to dealing with the distraction as well as determine which strengths, ingredients from your daily bread, laws, precepts, principles, and teachings are appropriate for you to use in your actions and reactions. The end result is a spiritually led, spiritually oriented approach to overcoming the distraction.

We often think we know how to solve our problems. However, all we have to rely on is the present and the past, and primarily the past. God has omniscient power and wisdom. He can see the past, present, and future. He has full "360 degree" life vision to address our problems and needs. A parent's ability, with his years of life's experiences and maturity, is a poor comparison, but an adequate one. A parent is much, much more capable of addressing a young child's problems and needs than the child is because the young child has not experienced dealing with a life issue the first time he encounters it. God, with His "360 degree" Omniscient Power and Wisdom, is completely and infinitely capable of solving our problems. There is no way He can fail! He also knows exactly how much to involve us in addressing the problem or distraction so we gain the full benefit of development, perspective, growth, and maturity out of the process. Letting go and letting God does not mean taking no action. It just means no action is taken without using the proper process of introspection, consultation with the Holy Spirit, and utilization of the proper ingredients of your daily bread to structure and plan your actions and reactions to assure they are in accordance with proper spiritual orientation. The problem with continued action without this proper structure, focus, and plan is continued action is based on the stresses and distractions that the distraction is designed to create. Continued action without a proper structure, focus, and plan, leads to a physical reaction. This leads to a reaction that is physically dominant without thinking about it spiritually. In dealing with our distractions, we must still do what is spiritually and morally right in the midst of our struggles. In fact, it is more important then, than ever to do what is spiritually right and moral because those times are a measure of how rooted, convicted, stable, mature, and strong we are in our spiritual orientation.

I once had a very difficult problem with a boss on my first job. I tried my best to get along with her. After trying to maintain my composure and doing all I could to avoid confrontations with her, I finally realized the boss was doing everything in her power to create conflicts and cause problems for me. I had almost come to my wits end and was totally frustrated and concerned about my job at this point. When I was talked with one of my co-workers, I realized he was also having a similar problem with our boss. After he and I discussed it, I realized the proper action to take was to let go and let God deal with it. I told him any time I encountered a problem that was bigger than my scope of resolve; I let go and gave it to God to solve. I must admit prior to realizing that I needed to let go and give this problem over to God, I had acted and reacted inappropriately out of personal anger and frustration. I had gotten caught up in the situation physically and emotionally and was acting and reacting to my physical and emotional responses in the absence of spiritual insight and reasoning. Yet, when I was speaking to my co-worker about his same challenges with our boss, I realized the answer to not only his problem, but mine as well. I decided immediately upon our discussion to let go and give the issue to God and when I did, I no longer stressed about how the boss treated me. I still had a spiritual and moral obligation not to act or react in violation of my spiritual principles. So I remained calm in times when the boss tried to provoke confrontation. I also did my work to the best of my ability and waited patiently for God to deal with the situation. Within two weeks, the boss came to a meeting and told the group that her husband had gotten a job transfer and they were moving to another part of the country! When the announcement was made, my co-worker looked immediately at me with amazement. I later reminded him that letting go and letting God always works when problems are bigger than us. LETTING GO AND LETTING GOD HAS NEVER FAILED ME! Often, it expedites the outcome of problems and issues I am dealing with. The toughest part of letting go and letting God is having the patience to await the final outcome. I can personally say the results I receive when I handle my distractions this way are far more blessed and successful than if I personally struggle, stress, and remain out of balance while trying to handle them myself. Try letting go and letting God the next time you encounter a difficult distraction or challenge in life that seems impossible and see what happens!

If confusion and distraction are not effective weapons against you, the devil will use one of his most effective tactics against you: temptation. Temptation works hand-in-hand with his strategies of confusion and distraction. He can confuse and distract you through temptation. If you are so focused on the temptation, you can very easily become confused and distracted away from other important things you should be focusing on. Referring back to when Satan tempted Christ on the mountain, (Matthew, Chapter 4, verses 8-9), Satan hoped through tempting Christ with all of the world's kingdoms to distract Him from fulfilling His destiny. If Christ had entertained the thought of ruling the worldly kingdoms Satan spoke of, He would have been distracted away from continuing His prayer and fasting in preparation for His final days before His crucifixion.

Satan can also just tempt you through preying on your physical weaknesses and fears. Remember, the skillful master of deception executes his tactics in a very subtle, almost invisible manner that makes it very difficult to recognize his deception unless you are sharply on guard for it. Make no mistake; the devil is a skillful master of deception since he is the originator of it. The goal of temptation is to entice you in order to gain a strong, decisive advantage or control. Why is it children seem compelled to do and want to do exactly the things their parents tell them not to do? Is it because the temptation and desire to do these things is far greater because children know the parents do not want them to do them? Is it far more exciting and enticing to the child as a result? Enticing becomes the key word to what makes temptation an effective tactic. In a world that is far, far more physically dominant, there are far, far more physically enticing attractions to meet our needs. However, most of these physically enticing attractions are not always best for us in a whole (spirit, mind, body) sense. Just as children are drawn to the very things their parents instruct them not to do, our childish, physically-selfish natures are often drawn to these worldly enticing attractions that satisfy and please us physically. These physically enticing worldly

187

attractions bring little to no benefit to us spiritually. Temptation becomes an easy tactic for Satan to employ because we are already naturally born to be inclined towards physical wants and desires. That natural inclination is multiplied by a world that is more physically dominant and focused than ever before with every possible visual image focused on displaying these enticements in full array to make them more attractive to us.

What lessons can we learn from Christ when Satan tempted Him after He had fasted for forty days in the wilderness? The first lesson we can learn is a lesson about how Satan works. Satan is clever enough to approach us with temptation at our time of greatest weakness. He approached Christ and encouraged Him to turn stones into bread knowing fully that Christ had not eaten in forty days! Satan knew that Christ was physically the hungriest He had ever been and thus at His weakest after fasting for forty days. The next lesson we learn is Satan also tempts us to act or react to things we desire through selfish, physical wants, purely for the benefit of those selfish, physical wants. Christ knew He was hungry. He could have acted or reacted purely based on that selfish physical want for hunger and changed the stones to bread if He desired to, had He been less than who He was. Many lesser men who were great men in the Bible acted on their own selfish temptations and thus failed to overcome them.

The next lesson we learn is the devil tempts us to act and react to things within our control. Christ knew, as Satan stated, that He was the Son of God. Christ was fully able to change the stones to bread if He wanted to. So the devil is clever to know if he preys on our biggest weaknesses, we have the control to act and react based on them. He will most often approach you when you are most vulnerable to a physically selfish weakness. He hopes he will get you to act or react to that physically selfish want or need without even considering any spiritual perspective, insight, or consequences. Ideally, he hopes you will act off the raw impulse behind the desire coupled with the weakness you have for what you desire. He also knows you have the free will to act and hopes you act impulsively without considering any spiritual perspective, insight, or guidance. The biggest reason temptation is such a challenging tactic to overcome is God has given us the free will to act independently. We have the authority to act freely, just as Adam and Eve did in the very beginning. We may also act rightly or wrongly, just as Adam and Eve did. Each wrong action takes us further from the "Sacred Place" we so desire just as it did for Adam and Eve. Ultimately, that is what Satan is striving for just as he achieved with Adam and Eve! The question you must ask is what is the motivating factor behind your actions? Is that motivating factor, or factors, whole of spirit, mind, and body? Or are the motivating factors enticing physical wants, desires, and needs absent of any spiritual perspective, insight and guidance?

The compelling question is how do you resist temptation? The answer is simple. Just as Christ did! You must be spiritually mature, and re-oriented enough, (spirit, mind, and body), to judge your physical wants, desires, and needs to make sure they are mutually aligned and beneficial to you wholly. When the devil approaches you to tempt you at your weakest point, (with your strongest and most selfish physical desire), take a split second, a moment, a minute, to pause and reason from "within-without" before acting. As you take that time to reason, you will incline your spirit to the wise counsel of the Holy Spirit, and draw from your spiritual daily bread what you need to remind you how to act and govern yourself according to what is best for you fully, (spirit, mind, and body), with regards to the temptation you are facing. A split second, a moment, and a minute of pause to introspect, reflect upon, and listen to that quiet inner voice is all that is needed in most instances to balance your acts and reactions to life's temptations wholly. Just as Christ did, you, too, will resist because you will realize the need to fulfill only physical wants, desires, and needs that do not conform to your spiritual orientation, and resist those that fulfill only physically selfish ends. Taking that split second or minute to pause and introspect and reflect is important and cannot be emphasized too much. Your chances of resisting the temptation are far greater if you take that time. Realize, however, that your childish, physically-selfish nature will be in rebellion against what is good for you wholly, (spirit, mind, and body). The childish, physically-selfish nature, being selfish towards its own wants and desires, will take that thought or suggestion of temptation planted by Satan and reason and rationalize why it is best and needed. So, don't act on your first thoughts around your temptations. Give yourself more time to introspect, reflect, and hear that little quiet, inner voice of the Holy Spirit before acting and reacting. In times of temptation, impulsiveness is a dangerous thing! So, take more time before acting. After you have taken the time and gained the introspection, reflection, perspective, and guidance wholly of spirit and mind, if it was a good thing to act or react to, it will still be good to act or react to. However, if you act or react out of immediate impulse and reflect, introspect, and seek spiritual consciousness later, you may find that act or reaction was wrong and then it is too late because you have already acted. There is another very important thing Christ did to overcome temptation. He used His knowledge of the Holy Scriptures, spiritual laws, precepts, and principles as His weapons of dialogue in conversing with the devil. He understood that speaking and knowing the truth behind the scriptures, spiritual laws, precepts, and principles would not allow Satan to distort the truth. The more you study and understand your spiritual environment, the Holy Scriptures, other spiritual texts, spiritual laws, precepts, and principles and focus on the continual wisdom, knowledge, understanding, and application of them, the stronger you will be in dismissing any distortions Satan tries to use against you.

Given that we are physical as part of our three dimensional wholeness of spirit, mind, and body, we will fail in our efforts to resist our physical temptations along the way. Do not be discouraged over failing to resist. Let your failures instead help you identify where you are most vulnerable to your physical wants and desires. If you know your own physical weaknesses and vulnerabilities, you will know better where Satan will plan to try tempting you. Seek to understand from a spiritual perspective how you should act and react to temptation. Realize that while you failed this time, you will succeed in time in conquering your vulnerabilities. Lose a battle today but keep fighting to win the war. Part of our ongoing maturation and evolution towards that "Sacred Place" comes through failing and losing battles along the way. Just remember to remind yourself what you learn through your failures and also remind yourself of the victories you achieve. That way, you will have the persistence, maturity, and confidence to continue to seek growth and stay the course.

How did Adam and Eve view themselves before their fall from grace? How did they see animals and plants they lived in harmony with before their fall? Was their view focused more on the spiritual essence and aura and less on their physical dimensions and characteristics? Let's make this introspection more personal. When you envision yourself without looking in a mirror, do you see yourself based on your physical, mental, and spiritual characteristics? Or do you view yourself purely through your physical characteristics? How do you view others? I realize I have already spent a great deal of time discussing some of our key physical weaknesses in Chapter 2. I simply want to encourage you to think about how you view yourself and others. As you do, analyze your image of yourself and others from a three-dimensional perspective, (spiritual, mental, and physical). Can you see yourself and others' characteristics in all ways? As always, it is more important to begin with you. Self-awareness and actualization of wholeness of spirit, mind, and body are the first critical steps. However, being able to look upon others beyond just their physical features helps improve your perception of them in other ways.

Let me see if I can be a little clearer using the car analogy I used in Chapter 1 regarding buying a car. When you buy a car, it is very important to know how well the inner workings, (engine, fuel injection, battery, horse power, etc…) operate in addition to how beautiful the paint job is and how plush the interior is. No matter how shiny and new the paint looks, it is not worth purchasing if the engine is blown. In order to understand a person's spiritual and mental character, it is necessary to seek to know them beyond their physical appearance. It is also necessary for you to know your own spiritual and mental character. How can you assess others without knowing yourself? How can you access others without knowing yourself?

Along with using the obvious sexual attractions men and women have for each other, Satan also uses physical beauty as a weakness against us. It is very easy to be blinded by a physically alluring mate of the opposite sex. We can become so blinded that we are too distracted to even assess them for what they offer spiritually and mentally. Since our physical natures are also selfish to their own ends, it reasons and rationalizes that it is okay to get by with all of the physical satisfaction and gratification being received from a physically alluring mate. Physical attraction and sexual attraction, much like the information overload I discussed earlier, are also greatly overexposed in the world today through television and print media. This feeds into a subtle mindset to view and focus on only physical appearance. Just remember, as with the automobile (the engine is far more important than the exterior appearance), it is more important to know the spiritual and mental character of mates, friends, and acquaintances than it is to find them physically pleasing. Otherwise, as with the automobile that has the beautiful paint job and blown engine, you are getting one-dimensional, physically attractive mates, friends, and acquaintances with no spiritual or mental substance. Don't be tricked by the exterior package; open yourself to your mates, friends, and acquaintances and show your full dimensions, (spirit, mind, and body) and seek to know theirs as well.

Were Adam and Eve physically perfect before their fall from grace? Or, were they still physically perfect after their fall, but felt less perfect having come into an awareness of their physical presence now dominant over their once balanced spirit, mind, and body? I realize my questions are somewhat leading. I hope you ponder over them nevertheless. The human form is one of the most perfectly formed creations in this vast expanse of creation God made. That was true from the very beginning. It is still true today. Adam and Eve were physically perfect before and after their fall from grace. Yet, after they had eaten of the Tree of the Knowledge of Good and Evil, they hid their physical form from God and each other. Why is that? Is it because they may have been led to believe they had physical weaknesses and flaws? Or, in their new physically dominant orientation, did they in some way realize how much less overall they had become? Or, did Satan realize from the very beginning that he could plant the seeds of insecurity within man and woman once he separated their special connection to God and reduced them to being physically dominant? It is likely that all of the above speculations are true. However, there is little doubt that my last rhetorical question is definitely true. Satan knew from the beginning of his game of deception, that once he reduced Adam and Eve to a physically dominant focus, he could create insecurities in them. Doesn't it stand to reason that Satan would know, first hand, how much less they were being removed from God's intimate presence since he also went through his own personal separation from God when He was removed from Heaven? Why do we all have insecurities about ourselves? A more important question to ask is why are we much more conscious of pointing out the insecurities of others in the world? Why do we thrive off the negative criticism and judgements of others? Does having a conscious perspective of someone else's insecurities in some way keep us from admitting and focusing on our own inner insecurities? Or does it only serve as a temporary distraction that masks us from facing ourselves fully? Before I answer, I challenge you to ask yourself and think what your own personal response is. Let me refer to my constant source for a perspective from God, the Bible. Genesis, Chapter 1, repeatedly states the following phrase: "And God saw everything that He made and behold it was very good," verses 25 and 31 end with this phrase. It is clear that God saw that Adam and Eve were very good as He did with all He created. If Adam and Eve were very good and pleasing to Him, He was perfectly satisfied with them in every way, including physically. So Adam and Eve did not change in their perfection of form God made, but their perception of their form was changed. Once Satan reduced them to being physically dominant with the absence of their intimate, spiritual relationship with God, he then convinced them they were far less than they were. Yes, Adam and Eve were far less in a whole, (spirit, mind, and body) sense just as Satan was in falling from Heaven and being part of God's Holy family. Yet, the deception that they were physically less led to the beginning seeds of insecurities within man and woman

193

was just that, a well conceived deception, by Satan. Adam and Eve were still the same physically as they were when God created them.

The beginning of our insecurities started there. Satan employed his deception well against Adam and Eve and he still uses it effectively today. It is a strategy, (preying on our inner insecurities), that has served him well. It worked so well against Adam and Eve because in their newfound awareness of their tremendous loss of spiritual orientation in their fall from grace, they realized how much weaker they were, being physically dominant, than their original complete, spirit, mind, and body selves, especially since they had an intimate connection to God in their original state. Therefore, it took very little to plant doubt about the possibility of physical weaknesses and insecurities to them. It continues to work well with us today, for the most part, for the same reason it worked against Adam and Eve. We are physically weak and vulnerable, just as Adam and Eve were after the fall in their separation from God and their individual loss of wholeness of perspective of spirit, mind, and body. We are born into physical existence, dominant physically and spiritually suppressed to grow into wholeness of spirit, mind, and body. Having physical weaknesses is okay. What is not okay is not accepting that we are, and were created, just as God intended from a physical standpoint; with certain weaknesses and vulnerabilities. Our physical weaknesses and vulnerabilities serve, if for no other purpose, to remind us that in God's absence, we are subject to failures, errors, and incompleteness of being. We are in our physical state our infancy with growth towards adults through becoming whole and reconnected to God through spiritual enlightenment, awakening, and re-orientation. Thus our physical weaknesses reinforce the need to acknowledge a Creator who is far greater than we are, God.

Satan was successful with creating insecurities in Adam and Eve also because he isolated them from their full selves, (spirit, mind, and body) to just one aspect or focus, their bodies. Relating to military strategy, if a battle is being fought with two enemies that have pistols, cruise missiles, and bombs, but one combatant can only use pistols, then it is no wonder that the combatant using only pistols is severely weaker and also well aware he is weaker. It would take very little for the other enemy to convince the one using pistols that he is very insecure in seeking victory. Just as Satan's goal was to isolate Adam and Eve from God, he also wants to isolate us from God and keep us physically dominant and focused in the absence of our wholeness of spirit and mind.

Thriving off the insecurities of others in the world, negative criticisms, and judgments of others, and having a conscious awareness of the insecurities of others are all powerful seeds of distraction Satan uses to keep us off the path towards spiritual reorientation. Planting seeds of our physical inadequacy is another tactic he uses well with the intent of deceiving us into feeling hopeless as the combatant going into battle with pistols against a foe with pistols, cruise missiles, and bombs. It is his hope that we will fail to realize how to activate and utilize our full arsenal, (spirit and mind to add the missiles and bombs) to complement our pistols, (physical state), through seeking spiritual reorientation. If he can keep you distracted and focused on the physical state of operating, he can maintain a superior position, because he is fighting you without your having the full three-dimensional power and maturity to fight with. Under those conditions, you continue, just as Adam and Eve and countless others in the Bible, to progress further and further away from that "Sacred Place" that brings intimate communication with God and wholeness of spirit, mind, and body as God intended for you. It is, therefore, critically important that you focus on YOUR OWN insecurities within. As you do, realize God made you physically weak and vulnerable, much as a baby is physically weak and vulnerable, so He can nourish and sustain you, just as a parent nourishes and sustains a baby, until you find your way back to the path to Him. Through seeking spiritual, mental, and physical maturation you grow into wholeness as the baby grows into wholeness from baby to child to adult. Allow your vulnerabilities to humble you into realizing the need for guidance and direction from that which is greater than you. You will maximize your spiritual environment, teachings, precepts, and principles as you grow into the fullness of spirit, mind, and body. So, instead of viewing your insecurities as weaknesses see them as a failsafe way of seeking spiritual reorientation. If you focus on spiritual reorientation, you will find that you will use your struggles to overcome your insecurities and they will serve as a positive benefit to others also facing and overcoming their own insecurities. It will make Satan's tactic of deceiving you to look at others' insecurities, criticisms, and judgments ineffective because you will have the love and compassion to help others as you seek to help yourself in overcoming your own insecurities. Your selfless spiritual growth and desires will fuel your progression and success through your daily battles and serve as an example of guidance for all others.

One essential theme that Christ attempted to convey consistently was compassion for others. He understood that having that compassion and love for others was a powerful positive force that allowed for the proper focus in dealing with the selfish physical nature of man and woman. He also knew that it is not possible for Satan to deceive and distract us with the negative energy that results from looking at others from a negative viewpoint. That same negative energy erodes your own positive self-energy that flows when there is love and compassion as a focal point. If you are self-absorbed with a positive, loving, compassionate focus for yourself and others, it is difficult for Satan's negative seeds of distraction to penetrate. Let me rephrase that. IT IS IMPOSSIBLE FOR SATAN'S NEGATIVE SEEDS TO PENETRATE YOU! When you focus with love and compassion for others and self, you are focusing through spiritual orientation, and spiritual orientation is as selfless as physical orientation is selfish. Christ is the perfect example of a spiritually oriented, mature person to follow. Focusing from a loving, compassionate viewpoint leaves no room or time for Satan's distractions to flourish.

Does Satan have any power over us? Did he have any power over Adam and Eve? If we look at the outcome of the choices of Adam and Eve, it is easy to conclude he did. He did not have any power over Adam and Eve that they did not give him through their free will to make wrong choices. He also does not have any power over us other than what we allow, just as Adam and Eve did, through our own free will to choose wrong over right. He does have artful deception and powers of persuasion through the art of deception. He uses his talent to deceive to the fullest. Satan knows he has no power over man and woman. Yet, he also knows he was successful in the very beginning in deceiving Adam and Eve into relinquishing their power to him in choosing, through their free will, to disobey God and choose wrongly. If Satan had power, would he need artful deception? Or, would he just exercise that power to his own full discretion? Wouldn't Adam and Eve have blindly obeyed Satan without question, if he had power? There is a big difference between power and influence. Satan had influence, through deception, over Adam and Eve. Adam and Eve had power. Adam and Eve had the power, just as we do, to choose right or wrong. Does Satan have power over us or influence? He only has influence if we allow him to influence our choices as he did Adams' and Eves'. Influence can be as valuable as power. There are countless examples throughout world history where kings of nations were influenced to fight wars by their wives or key advisors. Yes, the king has the power to act. But is he acting out of his own personal choice and conscience, or by the personal choice of his wife or advisor? If it is the wife's or advisor's choice through their influence upon the king, (who actually has the power to act), who truly has the power to act, the king, or the wife or advisor? Unless the king's choice, and the wife's or advisor's choice, is one and the same, the wife or advisor now has the power behind the action instead of the king. Can you see the subtle, deceptive danger here? It is very easy to be convinced, through someone else's influence, that his choice is your own if you are not carefully analyzing your choices. Always reflect, meditate, and introspect upon the influence of those around you and closest to you. Make sure their influence aligns with your spiritual orientation, precepts, principles, environment, and directions because it is very easy for Satan to use those in your immediate surroundings to impact your own free will to choose. It is also one of his greatest and most subtle tactics of deception to use.

Since Satan can be influential if allowed, it is your responsibility to question the choices that cross your mind. This is especially important for the choices that relate to physically oriented decisions. Remember that the mind is the medium through which Satan employs and plants his subtle, yet artful, tactics of deception and distraction.

Proper thinking, analyzing, and questioning from "within-without" will allow you to listen to that quiet Holy Spirit voice and seek continued guidance on your choices. You will also find the proper balance by comparing your thoughts on choices to your spiritual environment, precepts, and principles. Then, you are properly using your own power to continue your progression towards proper wholeness of spirit, mind, and body. Do not be discouraged if Satan deceives you into choosing wrongly. Learn from your wrong choices for the next time you have a choice to analyze and act on. Remember, Satan can only hope to influence you, but YOU and only YOU have the POWER!

I realize I have covered a lot once again. I promise that my intent is not to overload you, but to enlighten you with fresh perspectives, insights, and thoughts. Reflect on these "Spiritual Truisms."

Chapter 4 New Perspectives Spiritual Truisms:

- The physical self is the infant of our being. As with a baby, the physical self is selfishly absorbed on things that satisfy physical wants, needs, and desires.

- In order to have a full, three-dimensional balanced life, we must also seek to fulfill spiritual and mental needs in addition to seeking satisfaction of physical needs.

- Balance your physical wants, needs, and desires with your spiritual laws, morals, precepts, and principles. That way your actions and reactions to life will be more spiritually oriented and selfless. They will be wholly, (spirit, mind, and body), satisfying to you and others.

- Realize that the mind is a bridge, (and conveyor) between the physical and spiritual self. It is very, very important to examine the thoughts that enter your mind and determine the basis of their origins and focus. Are those thoughts of a selfish physical nature and where did they originate? Or, are those thoughts selfless, loving, and compassionate towards you and others?

- Your thoughts ultimately control you. It is important to make sure that thoughts you act on and react to are in alignment and agreement with your spiritual laws, morals, precepts, and principles because your actions and reactions to your thoughts ultimately reflect you to others. Are you reflecting a full, wholly realized, spirit, mind, and body person as Christ did, or a partly realized, physically focused, person to others? If your physical actions and reactions are properly aligned, you are properly spiritually oriented and whole, (spirit, mind, and body), as God intended.

- Gaining maturity of the infant physical self requires thinking and reasoning from "within-without." You must look inside and seek perspective from that quiet, inner Holy Spirit voice along with applying your spiritual daily bread ingredients to find the proper perspective and balance.

- Seek to realize, know, and understand where you are in your physical maturity and development. What motivates you physically? What are your physical strengths and weaknesses? How can you learn from your failures to grow? What can you learn from your successes?

- Once you realize, know, and understand your physical motivations, strengths and weaknesses, controlling your actions and reactions is the next critical step. Mastering this control is an ongoing, developmental process.

- Gaining control over your actions and reactions is a very powerful, and often elusive, process that takes focus, discipline, and constant practice. Do not get discouraged when you fail. Analyze your failures from "within-without" and seek guidance and understanding from the Holy Spirit. If you analyze your failures in this manner, they will become one of your greatest resources for successfully overcoming future failures. Use your successes to gain strength and encouragement for continued growth.

- Do not allow Satan to distract you by deceiving you into focusing on the negative distractions, criticisms, and judgments of others. Instead focus on you and your own development. You will be of great benefit to others through your example by dealing with your own self-development and an example for them to follow.

- The devil does exist. His primary purpose is not to create horror and fear, but to deceive through confusion, distraction, and temptation.

- The devil's existence does not prove the absence of God. In fact, his existence confirms the ABSOLUTE existence and DOMINION of God. Without Satan, how could we ever fully appreciate the Supreme Love, Goodness, Compassion, Joy, Grace, and Strength of God?

- Satan has always used his game plan of deception to separate man and woman from God and full, three-dimensional existence of spirit, mind, and body and one-accordance with God, as God intended.

- Since we are physically dominant and oriented since our original fall from grace, one of Satan's key tactics is to prey on our "perceived" physical weaknesses and fears. That plan of attack was the original plan he used successfully against Adam and Eve. It was also one of his first plans of attack against Christ. But it failed!

- The devil is persistent in employing his tactics to achieve success in his plan to deceive you. He will use more than one strategy to make sure you are battling on several fronts. If one tactic fails, he will readily employ another tactic. He also knows the Holy Scriptures but will use them out of context to confuse you. It is his hope that you will fail to study, know, understand, and seek spiritual guidance in understanding them so he has an advantage.

- It is important that you study, know, understand, and seek knowledge and wisdom of the Holy Spiritual texts, spiritual laws, precepts, and principles so Satan cannot deceive you through changing the truth.

- Seeking spiritual reorientation and maturity is a successful tactic for overcoming the devil's attacks on your physical orientation. Through spiritual reorientation and maturity comes the ability to properly align, weigh, and balance your physical nature. Christ was spiritually mature and oriented and successfully defeated the devil on every occasion. So can you if you pattern yourself accordingly after Christ!

- Satan's tactics of confusion and distraction are very closely related. Confusion is more internal, (as you are processing the thoughts that enter your mind), and Satan plants the thoughts to bring your confusion. For example, Satan may try to distort your understanding of the Holy Scriptures with some intellectual or scientific perspective that is contrary to your spiritual understanding. Distractions are more external, (in your day to day physical environment and beyond your personal control). You may be distracted by a problem on the job or from a crisis with a family member. Each, confusion and distractions, are designed to keep you from focusing on the development of your full divine nature and proper orientation and wholeness, (spirit, mind, and body).

- If you are confused and distracted, you will be too absorbed in that confusion and distraction to focus on wholeness of spirit, mind, and body. You will be physically focused and susceptible to your physically selfish nature in making choices and decisions absent of the balance of your spiritual insight, perspective, and guidance.

- Satan's ultimate aim is to keep you so confused and distracted that you act purely from a physical nature absent of your full three dimensional self, just as Adam and Eve did. Then you are operating from an immature, physically dominant nature and spiritually powerless.

- To overcome confusion, it is essential to seek structure in your spiritual environment, use the proper ingredients of your daily bread, use introspection, and reasoning behind your actions and reactions to life's daily issues. With structure, introspection, and reasoning, comes order and balance.

- Consider the source of the thoughts that cross your mind. It is very important to realize that external things in your physical environment trigger most of the thoughts that enter your mind. So, it is essentially important to meditate and reflect from 'within-without" on your thoughts before determining and acting upon them.

- It is important to realize that much of Satan's plan of attack is planted through our minds. In order to identify his tactics, we must be able to understand and analyze what crosses our minds and from which source it is coming. Think of your mind this way; it is the control center where the decisions are processed. So whether you choose right or wrong, the mind is the place that ultimately leads to your proper or improper action or reaction.

- When distractions are not within your ability to solve them, "Let go and let God." This will release you of the burden of worrying and prevent you from being distracted from your continual growth and maturity. It is also a reflection of your faith that God is able to resolve all challenges and issues in your life. Just remember, often YOU are in God's way in your efforts to solve issues outside of your control and are hindering God's blessings to deliver you. Also, remember to have the maturity and patience to allow whatever time it takes to solve your issues and challenges. As my Mama always reminded me, "Our time is not always God's time." God knows the proper and right time to solve our issues and challenges so we get the full benefit from their resolution.

- The quiet, inner voice of the Holy Spirit is forever present to be that inner voice of reason as long as you are willing to be still and quiet yourself and listen. It is up to you to accept the convictions, perspective, and guidance that is provided from the Holy Spirit.

- The devil's plan with his tactic of temptation is to get you to act or react to your physical impulses without introspection and spiritual reasoning.

- He will approach at the time of your weakest physical vulnerability to that which you are tempted by, (just as he did with Christ offering him bread after He had fasted forty days).

- DO NOT react and respond to your physical impulses without taking time to reflect, introspect, analyze, and seek spiritual counsel from the Holy Spirit. By waiting to react and respond, you allow yourself time to balance physical impulses with spiritual orientation and maturity.

- Do not get discouraged by failing to resist. Let your failures help you identify where you are most vulnerable to your physical wants and desires. Seek to understand from a spiritual perspective how you should have acted and reacted to the temptation. Realize that while you failed this time, you can and WILL succeed in time in conquering your vulnerabilities. Lose a battle today, but keep fighting and win the war!

- Satan has NO POWER over us except the power we yield to him through our free will to choose. He uses his game plan of deception through the tactics of confusion, distraction, and temptation to influence us to yield OUR power to him. God gave us the authority from the very beginning to control our free will and power to make choices.

- Accept YOUR POWER and seek to understand how the devil seeks to influence and usurp and control your power. As you continue to understand his tactics and game plan, you will continue to mature towards full spiritual re-orientation and, ultimately successfully remain in control over your will not be influenced, just as Christ did.

New perspectives are essential for growth and change. New perspectives are essential for maturity. It is certainly my fervent prayer that these new perspectives I have expressed for your consideration will bring the growth, change, and maturity you are seeking. Use the questions below to identify your most profound new perspectives from this chapter.

Question(s) 1:
How does knowing that the physical self is the infant of three dimensional self, (spirit, mind, and body), change how you view yourself? How will you change your approach to development fully?
Thoughts, Insights, and Reflections

Question(s) 1 Thoughts, Insights, and Reflections

Question(s) 2:

How has the new perspectives from this chapter changed your understanding of who the devil is? How does he impact your development into wholeness of spirit, mind, and body and what key tactics does he use, (confusion, distraction, temptation, using your physical fears and weaknesses), most effectively against you? How will you overcome them?

Thoughts, Insights, and Reflections

Question(s) 2 – Thoughts, Insights, and Reflections

Question(s) 3:

What personal physical wants, desires, needs, and weaknesses does Satan use to influence you to keep you from your spiritual growth, development, and maturation? How can you learn from Christ, your spiritual environment, spiritual texts and sources, and other spiritual mentors to overcome these wants, desires, needs, and weaknesses to conquer his influence?

Thoughts, Insights, and Reflections

Question(s) 3 – Thoughts, Insights, and Reflections

Question(s) 4:
What other personal perspectives and understandings have you gained from this chapter? What other spiritual texts and resources can you use to further enhance your knowledge?
Thoughts, Insights, and Reflections

Question(s) 4 – Thoughts, Insights, and Reflections

Chapter 5 Continued Maturation

Mama always told me that with each generation, we get weaker, but wiser. Over the years, as I have grown from childhood to adulthood, I have grown in my understanding of how each generation gets weaker, but wiser. It stands to reason that Adam and Eve would have been the absolute strongest people God ever made. In their original creation, God made them fully complete (spirit, mind, and body), and very much in the image of Him, the Holy Spirit, and Christ. Since all men and women who have followed Adam and Eve have been born physically dominant and spiritually dormant, there is no way any man or woman born after Adam and Eve could have been as strong. Christ is the only exception to this rule. Looking at it from a more contemporary perspective, my brothers, sisters, and I are not as physically strong as our parents were. Our parents worked much harder physically, toiling long days in the fields throughout their lives. They were thus hardened and strengthened through their strenuous physical lifestyle. As children, we also worked in the fields, but on a much more limited basis. We are wiser because our parents allowed us to receive a lot more education than they had. Most of us received some formal training after high school whereas our parents did not even complete a high school education.

It is very logical from a spiritual perspective that we continue to become weaker, but wiser with the passing of time since Adam and Eve were created. It is even logical that our physical strength, as a whole, is less because technology now allows machines to do much of the manual labor humans once had to do just a few decades ago. It is also logical that we are intellectually smarter because there are more opportunities than ever before to access knowledge that heightens our intellect. Here is a question for your consideration in light of our newfound intellectual wisdom. If humans have grown wiser, why have the keys to the "Sacred Place" we seek become more elusive to locate? Isn't it logical to think if we are intellectually wiser, we should have much better wisdom, knowledge, and understanding to successfully identify the keys and unlock the "Sacred Place" we so desperately seek? I am certain that by now you are accustomed to me providing the views and perspectives I have been led to convey. If not, please continue to indulge me. I hope you continue to gain from what I have been led to relate. I ask for your patience a little longer with the hope that what I have related has been simple and clear. Yet, I realize grasping new views and perspectives takes time to digest and can be complicated. If my path has been a little roundabout at times to make my point, I trust that the point was made. I would much rather be more thorough in my explanations than too brief because I want to make sure I provide as broad a perspective as I possibly can.

One of the most significant keys that we MUST find lies within the many, various spiritual texts God has created through men and women throughout time in various cultures that point the way. It is very important to understand that many spiritual texts have more than one meaning. As we grow and mature, our insight grows to broader and deeper understandings. Without getting too in depth, because delving deeper on this issue is for another work another time, I want to restate that many ancient spiritual scholars, writers, leaders, and prophets had to write in parables, symbolisms, and riddles to convey what they were divinely led to write. They were often banished from their countries, or killed for conveying divinely led texts in a clear, easy to understand manner. Military coding used during warfare is a good comparison. In order to prevent the danger of the information falling into enemy hands, a smart army intelligence organization creates top secret coding to communicate battle plans in a language only they can interpret. If the messenger carrying the secret coding is caught, the enemy tortures him to get access to the information he is holding. If the messenger fails to reveal his information, he is killed. He is often killed if he reveals his information as well! If the secret coding is deciphered, the army loses valuable knowledge on their strategic plans that could result in the loss of the battle and ultimately the war.

As with the army messenger, many ancient spiritual writers, scholars, prophets, and leaders had to write in a way that still allowed those seeking spiritual truth to find it in the midst of the parable, symbol, or riddle. If many spiritual texts have more than one meaning, how does God know if we will receive all the meanings? God knows that those who seek to understand will analyze, introspect, seek spiritual counsel, meditate, and interact with others to understand spiritual text. In time, as they grow and mature, they will uncover the full perspectives, insights, understandings, and meanings behind the hidden text. While writing in secret codes was the norm, there are exceptions. Not all ancient spiritual writers, scholars, leaders, and prophets had to write in secret codes. In those cultures where they were allowed free expression of spiritual truth, men and women have been able to have more balance of spirit, mind, and body and do great things for their society and the world as a whole. The reason spiritual truth has been such a threat is simple. In a world that is physically dominant, spiritual truth is the only thing that will bring into full perspective and reality the balance of man and woman, (spirit, mind, and body) as God intended. This restoration of balance to full, three-dimensional self is contrary to the physically dominant nature we are born into. Whether the rebellion between our physically dominant world and the spirit is within man and woman, or inspired by the great influencer, (Satan), the end result is the same. Many world leaders throughout the history of the world, have knowingly, or unknowingly, (through being influenced by the devil), fought against divine spiritual truth for fear of losing physical control, or political and economic power and resources over their people once spiritual truth is brought to light amongst the masses. The book of Ephesians, Chapter 6, verse 12, makes this point clear with the following scriptures, "For we wrestle not against flesh and blood, but against principalities, against powers, against the rulers of darkness of this world, against spiritual wickedness in high places."

What other multiple meanings are there behind man and woman being weaker, but wiser? There are several additional perspectives in addition to the ones I have already mentioned. Man and woman have most definitely been spiritually weaker since Adam and Eve chose to separate themselves from God and fully balanced and mature, (spirit, mind, and body) orientation, and chose a physically dominant existence. In becoming spiritually weaker, Adam and Eve became carnally and physically wiser because they then became aware of their physical bodies. That physical body became overwhelmingly their primary reality over seeing themselves as "a spirit in a body" as they did before their fall from grace. They took upon physically stronger traits, characteristics, behaviors, responsibilities, wants, and desires after their choice. Adam and Eve became immediately aware of their physical nakedness after their choice whereas prior to their choice, they never even realized they were physically naked in the midst of their "spiritually dominant and clothed," total, three-dimensional selves. The Holy Bible makes this point in Genesis, Chapter 1, verse 16, because after eating of the Tree of the Knowledge of Good and Evil, Adam and Eve covered themselves with fig leaves to hide their physical nakedness. God gave Adam the responsibility of having to work, sweat, and toil for his sustenance until he died as an added physical responsibility after his fall, (see Genesis, Chapter 1, verse 17). Eve was given the responsibility of bearing sorrow and pain in having children, desiring her husband, and submitting to her husband after her fall, (see Genesis, Chapter 1, verse 16). Adam and Eve became clearly spiritually weaker because they were forced to accept physically stronger traits, characteristics, behaviors, responsibilities, wants, and desires after their choice. They were most definitely weaker in a very, very critical way that man and woman have been since that fateful fall. Their perspective shifted from spiritual orientation to physical orientation, focusing on physical traits, characteristics, behaviors, responsibilities, wants, and desires.

How else can the statement weaker but wiser be viewed? Over the history of time that man and woman have struggled with locating the keys to the "sacred place" between them and God, they have grown wiser in understanding their failures, challenges, and shortcomings. Prior to the coming of Christ, spiritual writers, scholars, leaders, and prophets foretold of His coming to provide an "absolute, ideal standard" to prove it was possible to restore wholeness and fullness of spirit, mind, and body to man and woman. These ancient authors also told stories, legends, and parables identifying many of the issues, challenges, and shortcomings man and woman are faced with in restoring that wholeness. Christ fulfilled His life's prophecies and provided the "absolute ideal" and validated that it is possible to restore full three-dimensional wholeness through His life. We are most certainly now wiser, having had Christ's life story and ideal example to evaluate, introspect upon, seek to understand, obtain spiritual insight and counsel from, and pattern our own lives after.

The main purpose of this chapter is about continued maturation. WISDOM, KNOWLEDGE, and Understanding COMBINED, will lead to continued maturation. It is my hope, and prayer, that you will gain continued wisdom, knowledge, and understanding combined, based on the beginnings, foundation, daily bread, and new perspectives provided thus far that will enable you to uncover the full depth and breadth of the spiritual texts for your continued growth. Each step is a progression towards full completion of spiritual orientation and completeness of three-dimensional self, (spirit, mind, and body) that God intended us all to be. It is also through spiritual reorientation and development that we acquire the keys and also the wisdom, knowledge, and understanding of how to use these keys to renew the "Sacred Place" we are seeking between us and God.

What is maturation? Webster's Dictionary defines maturation as follows: "The emergence of personal characteristics and behavioral phenomena through growth processes." What exactly does that mean in the context of seeking and acquiring the keys to the "Sacred Place" we are seeking? Maturation, in its simplest form, is a natural thing that occurs with time. Maturation, in its most complex and complete form, requires focus, nurturing, effort, and guidance from an internal and external perspective. Maturation, in its most complex and complete form, also includes growth of our spirits and minds as well as physical growth. Isn't it reasonable that since we are now physically dominant, we will more naturally grow physically and that is the simplest type of growth? We will all mature in the simplest way from childhood through adulthood by maintaining the simple, basic physical needs of food, clothing, and shelter. Whether we mature "simply" or "completely" is the important thought we need to consider. Simple, physical, natural maturation is "letting life live you." Complex, complete maturation is "living life" wholly, (spirit, mind, and body). The primary difference between the two is how actively we choose to engage in this awesome process called life. In the simple mindset of "let life live you," people develop their basic, physical wants, desires, and needs. At this most basic level, people also react to life entirely based on their physical wants, desires, and needs. By contrast, one who seeks to mature completely and chooses to "live life," develops an active, proactive approach to life and development. This active, proactive approach enables one to encompass whole development of spirit, mind, and body in dealing with life's ongoing daily progression.

A good real world analogy to relate the difference between the two is performing a job. In most jobs, there are a series of tasks or processes that must be performed. Most jobs are challenging because most jobs in today's complex industrial and technological world we live in involve a large variety of diverse tasks that require an equally large variety of job skills. In addition, many of these tasks require performing multiple tasks at the same time. There are also varying levels of tasks, some primary job functions and others secondary, maybe even tertiary job functions. All of these varying levels of job functions are essential to completing the work assignment. As a result, the individual must prioritize his job tasks, perform a variety of different tasks, and perform multiple tasks all at the same time. Most jobs require good planning, organization, experience, time management, flexibility to changes, and people management skills. One who allows himself to simply mature naturally in their jobs is a person who often lets the job "live him" and thus reacts to his job based on what the job dictates. He constantly fight fires because he has no sense of understanding which of his job tasks are primary, secondary, or tertiary. He also has no sense of understanding how to prioritize, plan, organize, multi-task, delegate or involve others needed to complete his job. That is why constant firefights are his normal mode of operation. He does not run his job. His job runs him!

By contrast, one who is completely mature in his job "lives his job," and runs his job through proper, proactive processes. He seldom fights fires because through proper understanding of major and minor tasks, efficient planning, organization, timely actions and reactions to unexpected changes, and successful people management skills, he smoothly performs all job functions. When occasional fires do arise, he is prepared to minimize any problems because he is knowledgeable and prepared to handle them proactively with the least amount of strain to work processes. A person who is simply mature not only fights fires, but also often fights the same fires repeatedly without putting any thought, time, or energy into finding ways to prevent the same fires from repeating. A completely mature person fights fires too but also takes time to analyze and understand the cause of the fire. If the same fire occurs again, he is prepared to put it out and eventually extinguish it to prevent it from reoccurring. A completely mature person may continue to fight fires but he will also continue to be proactive and active in finding solutions to extinguish them. A simply mature person may spend his entire career fighting the same reoccurring fires. A completely mature person evolves to higher job levels and promotions through conquering and extinguishing the fires in his path.

Hopefully, this job analogy makes some simple, distinct points about the difference between simple maturity and complete maturity. Simple maturity is one dimensional, physical. Complete maturity is three dimensional, (spirit, mind, and body). Maturation in its simplest form is dangerous to us because it is a physically dominant perspective that causes us to act and react through our physical natures in progressing through life. It is also subject to influences outside our own inner spiritual counsel and guidance, reasoning, introspection, and environment. While there may be a very, very small chance that full maturity can occur naturally under these conditions, there is a far, far greater chance it will NEVER bring you into full balance of self, (spirit, mind, and body). Your physically dominant will and the influences outside in the world are all in strong opposition to inner spiritual development and balance. There is a small chance that in spite of the odds, you will still grow to understand and acquire complete maturation of spirit, mind, and body. After all, God is Gracious and Loving enough to allow anything to be possible. What you must ask yourself is, are you willing to gamble with such small odds that you will be successful through simple, natural, physically dominant living to mature wholly? Are you willing to take an active part in assuring you will completely mature? My hope is the LATTER!

The question of simple, natural maturation has been asked for you to consider. Working a job comparing a simply mature perspective to a completely mature perspective has been examined. I trust that you are asking and answering your own questions about where you are in the process of maturation, as am I. Let's continue to provide even more perspective. Simple, natural maturation, as defined by Webster's Dictionary, speaks of purely physical processes and characteristics. Complete maturation is far more than just physical because it includes the spiritual and mental processes and characteristics as well. You definitely have a basis of understanding, through realizing you are three-dimensional, seeking to define and understand your spiritual environment, knowing your spiritual laws, precepts and principles, understanding your daily bread recipe along with its ingredients, and seeking continued perspectives on how to seek continued maturation. All of these important keys are essential for continued maturation. Continued maturation, like most things in life, is an ongoing, continual, and continuous process that occurs moment to moment, experience to experience, day to day. Continued maturation is a process that requires, above all, personal desire, "within-without" reasoning, focus, nurturing, and guidance from spiritual counsel, mentors, texts, and daily practical application. You must use all of these key tools, along with your acquired wisdom, knowledge, and understanding available to accomplish continued maturation.

Another major key to the "Sacred Place" that is vital for continued maturation is self-analysis. There are many major differences between man and woman and God. One of the most clearly distinctive differences is we only have the ability to analyze our life's experiences during and after they have occurred. God, being Omnipotent and All-Knowing, is not bound by our physical laws of space and time and has total, Perfect Wisdom, Knowledge, and Understanding of our past, present, and future. Once Adam and Eve ate of the tree of the Knowledge of Good and Evil, God the Father, Christ the Son, and the Holy Spirit immediately banished them from the Garden of Eden, (see scriptural reference in Genesis, Chapter 1, verse 22). This banishment was essential because Adam and Eve's new physically dominant natures and perspectives were far less mature than they were when they were fully three-dimensional (spirit, mind, and body) as they were originally created. So God knew they did not have the maturity of full self to act responsibly and react to life on earth in their newfound state of perspective. God was exercising good parenting over his children (Adam and Eve) by forbidding them to eat of the tree of life and become immortal like Him, Christ, and the Holy Spirit. As children, we often think we are mature and big enough to handle things well before we can. Most young teenagers think they are mature enough to drive and get licensed by the time they are 14 years old because they may be physically large and physically developed enough. Parents, having the benefit of years of driving experience, understand that while 14 year olds may be physically large enough, but they are not cautious enough, attentive enough to other drivers, and respectful enough of the danger of driving a car at high speeds can cause. There are occasional exceptions because some 14 year olds are mature enough to drive a car with the caution, attention, and respect of its dangers. The majority of 14 year olds, however, are not mature enough and not ready to be given free reign without parental guidance. Allowing them that free reign could be life threatening to them and others. This analogy pales in comparison to God having Omniscient Knowledge of our lives. The analogy does illustrate a very important point. God, like all loving, compassionate, caring parents has the proper Experience, Wisdom, Knowledge, and Understanding tempered with His love to know what is best for us. Parents, having years and years of driving experience, possess good insights on what they know their 14 year old children will need to know to start driving. Parents can even reflect back and recall when they first started driving at a young age. Unlike God, parents do not have the omniscient power to know with certainty what their children will experience before it occurs. God knew that Adam and Eve, in their new physically dominant natures, were not mature enough to remain in the Garden of Eden and have access to the Tree of Life. They had to start the growth and maturation process again and this was a new beginning from physical dominance to full, three-dimensional (spirit, mind, body) dominance before being maturely complete as they were originally.

While God knows all and everything, finite to infinite, beginning to end, we are confined to a physical world that is bound by space and time. We truly only have the "NOW." I know that sounds strange. I'll explain what I mean. Being physically dominant, yet a spirit in a body and mind that comprises our whole self, we are still only capable of realizing our life experiences, from birth to death, in the present, and recalling the past. We never get a future in the true sense in that as time moves forward, (the only direction time can move in our physical realm), that which would be the future, becomes the present. As the present, (now) passes, it becomes the past. Is that clear or confusing? Take some time to think on it, meditate on it and reflect from "within-without" on it. One thing is certain. Once you understand that you have only the "NOW" each and every second, minute, hour, day, week, month, year, and decade of your "NOW" should be realized as what it truly is: a precious gift from God to grow back towards the original, three-dimensional (spirit, mind, and body) self He created you to be. Combine that with the knowledge that only God is truly ALL-KNOWING of all that WAS, IS, and EVER WILL BE and then you should grasp just how important it is to understand your continued development and maturity.

Although we are confined to the now and the past, we acquire wisdom, knowledge, and understanding through analysis, reflection, and introspection. This wisdom, knowledge, and understanding help us shape and mold our futures in a positive, mature way. As you reason and analyze your now and past, you begin to understand how your choices, actions, and reactions led to the outcomes, (good or bad), that resulted from those choices, actions, and reactions. If the outcomes are bad, then you know you must seek a different choice, action, or reaction to get a different, more positive outcome. Your awareness of the process of analysis, reflection, and introspection and the need to choose a different choice, action, or reaction is the beginning of acquiring the wisdom, knowledge, and understanding needed to grow and mature. This wisdom, knowledge, and understanding is then grown and expanded as you continue to analyze, reason from "within-without," seek spiritual counsel and guidance from your spiritual environment and the Holy Spirit, and apply your daily bread recipes to bring about choices, actions, and reactions that are balanced and properly spiritually-oriented. The result is new and better choices. Once you have arrived at knowing a new and better choice through this process, you must then apply, act or react, upon your new choice to see if it brings the good, positive outcome you desire. This process is an ongoing, continuously repeated cycle that eventually leads to positive outcomes in the end. The reason it is an ongoing process is because, unlike God, we do not always know if our new choice, action, or reaction will bring the positive desired outcome until we see it occur. Once it has occurred, we must then review the outcome to be certain it produced the result we expected and hoped it would. It is also ongoing because the process is very dynamic. Our new choice, action, or reaction may bring about a positive outcome in one situation and a negative outcome in another similar situation. Each and every situation in life is "uniquely specific" and "specifically unique" and must be a part of the process of continuous analysis on its own special merit.

The beginning of our spiritual reorientation starts the process of restoring our full, three-dimensional, (spirit, mind, and body), natures and is the next important step for continued maturation. Once this process begins, we have a decisive advantage for continued, complete maturation. In fact, our capacity to mature fully is very limited until we begin to spiritually reorient ourselves because we fail to consistently analyze and reason with the benefit of spiritual consciousness and counsel. Without the benefit of spiritual consciousness and counsel, (the Holy Spirit, spiritual mentors, Holy texts, Christ's model example), our reasoning is subject to and dominated by our physical natures and perspectives. Why is that so? There are several perspectives I'd like to share. The first perspective has been a consistent and prevalent theme throughout this book. In being born into a physical world, with a physical focus being the dominant focus, the view is one of exterior, (outer, physical things), not inner, (invisible spiritual things), such as love and compassion for others. We are programmed to view with the eyes of the physical body, (not the inner eye of the heart and spirit), which whispers to us in its soft, quiet, compassionate voice to view from "within-without." The broadest, most complete view is STILL from within when you have a spiritual perspective that allows you to look from "within-without" because your natural, outer physical view is complimented from the inner spirit that tempers and balances your perspective beyond just physical wants, desires, and needs.

The next perspective is particularly significant to our world we live in today. Since we are now a part of a world that is more physically visible than ever before, it is increasingly more difficult to stop and seek inner vision of the heart and spirit. We find it increasingly difficult to still ourselves in the midst of all the noise and chaos to even hear that quiet, inner voice of the spirit to provide "within-without" reasoning and perspective. It is not by chance that the world offers an abundance of physically attractive distractions designed to absorb us to view absent of spiritual insight and perspective. The great deceiver, Satan, has always known that distracting man and woman through the physical view would divert their focus from the greatest voice of reason, the spirit within, through whom they were capable of seeking the proper perspective and conviction. The devil's goal, (just as it was with Adam and Eve), is to get us so wrapped up into viewing life physically that we fail to listen to, and awaken, the spiritual viewpoint within us. That way, we impulsively choose to act and react based purely on physical wants, desires, and needs, (our lowest, most basic level of need). If you are wondering if physically focused vision relates to being judgmental, critical, and focused on others instead of yourself, I'll tell you, it clearly does! Our instinctive, physical wants, desires, and needs, are just as selfishly animalistic as the physical instincts animals exhibit in their efforts to survive. With animals, their need to survive means they must focus instinctively on preying on other weaker animals for their survival. Humans react much like animals in a physical sense, in the absence of the balance of spiritual perspective and the proper mental perspective, and focus on others, and how they can fulfill and meet our own selfish needs. That focus becomes one of judging what others have to offer for our own gain without any thought to that other person's needs.

Today's television and news media has made great entertainment out of all the sensational events occurring in the world today. It seems that the more sensationally violent, sexual, or negative news content is, the better it is received. It is no surprise that is true because all of these things, (violence, sex, and negative drama), are appealing and exciting to our physical natures. I challenge you not to let the world deceive you into getting so wrapped up in this so called "entertainment" with all of its perverse physically dominant views that you fail to stop and reason "within-without" with a clear, mature spiritually and mentally balanced conscience to relate to how you choose to act and react to the world around you. Instead, ask yourself how you can be of positive benefit to others who are caught up in seeing the world through physically focused lenses. Can you show them a different choice, action, or reaction in how you deal with them to broaden their view? What you will find if you do is they will be intrigued about why your approach is so different from the worldly approach they are used to. Moreover, they will be drawn to understand how you arrived at such a different perspective than what they are so physically accustomed to seeing. In time, they may even begin to listen and reason from "within-without" and seek to understand their choices, actions, and reactions from a more whole and complete, (spirit, mind, and body), perspective as well. As they evolve through seeking to understand their spiritual environment, using their spiritual daily bread, seeking the wise counsel of the Holy Spirit and inclining their hearts to hearing His quiet, inner voice of conviction and reason along with other spiritual mentors and guidance, they will begin the journey of restoring spiritual reorientation and fullness of self, (spirit, mind, and body). If your choice, action, and reaction that you provided leads to this awesome outcome, then it becomes their greatest gift from you!

There are several detrimental aspects to this whole vicious cycle of thinking, acting, and reacting from a pure physically led perspective. Just like physical vision, which looks away from the inner you; focusing on, judging, and criticizing others for your own physical wants, desires, and needs, keeps you looking away from your own choices, actions, and reactions. It also exhausts a lot of time that could be spent on introspection and self improvement. Thinking about your own choices, actions, and reactions from "within-without" forces you to incline your heart, mind, and spirit to your spiritual environment, daily bread, and wise, appropriate spiritual counsel so your choices, actions, and reactions are spiritually focused, balanced, and oriented.

Remember this small but important fact. The mind is the forum, conduit, and center where we process the thoughts that lead to our choices to act and react to life's decisions. If the mind is oriented and influenced by physical wants, desires, and needs, resulting actions and reactions are decided based on those wants, desires, and needs. Just as it is possible to analyze the now with the complete maturity of spirit, mind, and body, it is also possible to analyze the now based entirely on our physically dominant natures with those wants, desires, and needs dictating our choices, actions, and reactions.

Is it still possible to make choices, act, and react in a spiritually proper way even when we are physically dominant? Yes, it is. My response is based on several observations. First of all, although we are born into the flesh and die in the spirit, being born into this world, we are still made in God's image just as Adam and Eve were from the very beginning. That spirit within us is dormant but it is still within us! While physically dominant, we are primarily subject to physical orientation, and we begin the process of spiritual rebirth and awakening through our spiritual environment as we grow from infancy towards childhood to adulthood. There is a spiritual "conscience" and "voice" within us that whispers to our physically dominant natures what is spiritually proper and right in our choices, actions, and reactions. However, let me remind you of my earlier discussions in chapter one regarding the small, inner, quiet voice of the Holy Spirit. Realize that that small, inner, quiet voice is speaking in the midst of our loud, physically overbearing voice that dominates our mind's thoughts. When you combine that loud, physically overbearing voice with a world that is also physically loud, visually loud, and geared to attract and appeal to our physical wants, desires, and needs, then it is very easy to see why we often fail to hear that small, quiet, inner voice that is guiding us towards wise spiritual counsel. When we still ourselves in the midst of all this physical dominance and noise, God created us to hear that small, quiet, inner Holy Spirit voice naturally and temper our choices, actions, and outcomes through that voice. We can only consistently listen and hear as we continue to become spiritually oriented and away from our original physically oriented natures.

I do feel there is a very important reason we occasionally make the right spiritual choices, actions, and reactions in spite of our physically dominant natures. The reason is simple. When we do reflect upon and analyze those proper spiritual actions and reactions in the midst of our physically dominant natures, we realize there is a part of us within, (our spirits), that is nourished, fulfilled, and pleased. We gain an inner joy, happiness, and peace unlike any other feeling we are capable of experiencing physically or mentally from those proper spiritual choices, actions, and reactions. That very first proper spiritual choice, action, or reaction to the counsel of that small, quiet, inner voice of the Holy Spirit is the beginning of our awareness of the last and most significant part of our being and likeness to God, (our spirits). No physical or mental wants, desires, or needs can replace that yearning and feeling. Once you begin to acknowledge that quiet, inner, Holy Spirit consciousness, it is up to you to hear and seek to understand it amongst all of the noise of your physical nature and the world. It is also up to you to begin to understand and analyze your spiritual foundation, environment, mentors and counsel, and daily bread recipes in starting your journey towards wholeness. Once you begin, the journey is a lifelong process.

Vicarious learning is another essential key to continued, maturation. Being the youngest of seven children, I have benefited tremendously from my older brothers and sisters. I only had to watch the choices, actions, and reactions they made and think about them to learn without having to make those same choices. Or, in some cases, I would make the same choices. That is vicarious learning. Taking the analogy further, if my older brothers did something that led to them getting a whipping from Mama, I knew not to do that. If they did something that got praises and rewards from Mama, then of course, I wanted to be smart enough to do it so I could also be praised and rewarded. Being the youngest, my praises and rewards were usually larger and better than theirs because Mama did not expect me to be as smart or mature as they were because they were older and had more experience and responsibility. If there is one major mistake men and women have made since Adam and Eve's original fall from grace, it is their failure to learn vicariously from their ancestors. I have always been an avid student of history and culture. When I was young, I had a thirst for the history of all human cultures with a special interest in Native American and African American cultures. As I grew older and learned all I could about Native American and African American cultures, my interest expanded to African cultures, European cultures, and other world cultures. As I continued to mature spiritually, I began to reason from "within-without" and ask why I had such a strong interest in history and culture. The inner response I received was: in all of the history of human existence, our greatest and most lasting achievements and successes have come when we were properly aligned and focused with God. That is true of any and all cultures that have achieved great things. The common thread to abundant, prosperous, fruitful life WAS, IS, and ALWAYS WILL BE a renewed connection of spirit, mind, and body wholeness between humankind to God. If we understand this "Spiritual Truism," then we can vicariously analyze the cultures that have successfully achieved great things, and, by contrast, the cultures that have failed miserably. Then, we can seek to understand and apply the principles behind their successes and eliminate the principles behind their failures. In my own very personal and intimate relationship with God, I find that He is very much the PERFECT parent, just as Mama was. He always rewards me for doing the right things far more than He allows me to be punished for doing the wrong things I do in life. Yet, right and wrong choices, actions, and reactions always lead to rewards and successes, or punishments and suffering, as they have since the beginning of our existence.

Vicarious learning is more of an inner, "within-without" reasoning process. Your primary goal and focus should be to compare others choices, actions, reactions, and outcomes to your own, NOT to condemn or criticize others. Be careful not to judge others' actions along the way. In fact, always show sympathy, compassion, and understanding to others and offer the benefit of your perspective, good choices, actions, and reactions if others seek and need it. The purpose of analyzing other's choices, actions, reactions, and outcomes is not to belittle or put them down, but to improve your own choices, actions, reactions, and outcomes.

Another very positive outcome in this process is you can be a role model to others in the choices, actions, and reactions you make. Since your positive choices, actions, and reactions lead to positive outcomes, they learn through analyzing your outcomes, how to make positive choices as well. Others are ALWAYS watching the choices, actions, and reactions you make in life. Ultimately, vicarious learning leads to wisdom beyond your years because you acquire knowledge and understanding without having to spend the time going through the situation to gain that important insight, knowledge, and understanding. You can apply that knowledge and understanding as necessary to help you avoid problems and challenges you see others fall into. By the same token, if it a positive action or choice, you can use it to further your growth and maturation at a faster pace. The outcome will always be positive with this more whole, complete way of reasoning because you either learn vicariously to make better decisions for your own experiences or you serve as a positive role model for others facing similar situations who need to learn how to apply spiritually led, focused, and oriented reasoning to their own experiences.

There is a tremendous difference between judging and criticizing others and serving as a positive influence and example to others through the choices you make once "within-without" reasoning is applied. Christ is the model and most absolute, ideal example of setting the proper example through His choices, actions, and reactions. Yet, He did not judge and criticize the masses like the religious powers of His times did. Instead, He showed through His own practical, everyday life experiences and related through parables and analogies to the masses the proper way to approach life's issues. He applied the proper "within-without" reasoning and took it even further by providing real life day to day examples to the Holy Scriptures to make them real and understandable. He also led by example out of love and compassion for all, not out of judgment and condemnation. If you lead others through your choices, actions, and reactions, lead by example out of compassion and love, just as Christ did. Whether you realize it or not, your choices, actions, and reactions lead others anyway. The question is, are you leading them in the way you desire?

Humility is also one of the most valuable keys to life and continued maturity. However, humility is one of the most difficult traits to focus on and master. Part of our physical, human natures is to become prideful and arrogant when we learn something new. We also tend to become narrow-minded for some reason as we learn more. We fail to realize that in all of God's Infinite Wisdom, Knowledge, and Capacity, we can never, ever even scratch the surface of all there is to know in our physical and mental capacity. How could man and woman, with a finite physical capacity and form, grasp all of the Infinite Wisdom and Knowledge of God, Who is ALL EVERYTHING, (physically, mentally, and spiritually)? When you ask the question and put it into the proper, ABSOLUTE context it deserves to be placed, you should realize the need for humility.

What is essential for us to know in order to live as God intended? Is it even essential to know everything? While I cannot ask all of the thought provoking questions that have crossed my heart, mind, and spirit over my life, nor can I answer all of them, I can provide the insight and conclusions I have been blessed to reach. One very significant insight is the more I learn, the more I realize I do not know and how vast the difference is between God's Knowledge and Wisdom is and my own. This is a very significant point to me because it keeps me grounded and humble enough in knowing I do not need to know everything when I have a relationship with God, Who is ALL-KNOWING about everything that IS, WAS and EVER WILL BE. It is also that same insight that gives me the faith to trust that God, my Parent, as any good parent does, imparts and shares what knowledge and wisdom I need to know as I progress through this awesome journey of life at the exact point and place WHEN AND WHERE I need it. HE, and ONLY HE, knows the proper time, order, and season I will need to know what is essential to where I am in my growth to that "Sacred Place" between Him and me that I am striving to get back to. My own personal faith and trust is an essential must in this whole process. It is through having this faith and trust that I remain humbly patient in seeking to know, understand, and accept each new daily life experience aimed "specifically unique" and "uniquely specific" at me as a learning tool to my continued spiritual growth, reorientation, and development.

Humility is difficult to maintain because it is a lot like that quiet, inner spirit. It requires meekness that goes against our physical natures. That's why our physical characteristics such as pride, arrogance, and narrow-mindedness become dangerous foes. Any aspect of our being, our inner spirit for example, that is gentle, quiet, and meek tends to get lost to our loud, more aggressive physically dominant natures which we naturally evolve towards as we grow from child to adult. Our combined intellectual development along with our physically loud and dominant development is another hindrance and threat to humility in the context of spiritual growth. Our world today, without question, is intellectually overloaded. We have computers, colleges and universities all over the world, major scientific centers, technological machinery, and advances unlike any we have been able to verify from most ancient cultures of the past. We are most certainly more intellectually arrogant, prideful, and narrow-minded in our self appointed authority on all we know now more than ever before. Humility requires, (above everything else), an open mindedness to the reality that one must constantly seek to know more. At the same time one must have the maturity to realize that one will never know all there is to know from a physical, intellectual, and mental standpoint. The physical self has a limited, finite capacity. The very part of us that is capable of grasping all that there is our spirits within. Once the inner spirit within us is properly re-oriented, developed, and matured, then and only then, do we have the capacity for the infinite wisdom, knowledge, and understanding at our disposal through our relationship with God, Christ, and the Holy Spirit. It takes a great deal of maturity and inner focus to control our physical and intellectual pride and arrogance because those characteristics are such a natural, innate part of our physical orientation as we grow through physical life. Physical and intellectual growth and development are far more natural in our world that is physically and intellectually dominant. Having this knowledge and understanding challenges you to be aware and conscious of your physical and intellectual pride and arrogance. As you are, you will properly focus and put into perspective when you are allowing those characteristics to stifle your humility. By properly focusing and putting into perspective those characteristics, you will keep an open mind, heart, and spirit to learn more. You will stay humble enough to realize the need to seek insight, perspective, and counsel from that which is greater than yourself, (the Holy Spirit, Christ, God, your spiritual environment, mentors, laws, precepts, spiritual texts, and principles).

Each and every occasion we encounter others and experience life's experiences is an opportunity to learn more. Even when we are teaching others, we learn as well as long as we are open to receive the insights and perspectives that students bring in their efforts to learn. Christ was a living example of open minded humility. Although He was all knowing, and realized in His Spirit who He was, He still chose to seek to learn all He could about the spiritual teachings of all cultures during His life. He knew He had to understand, from a physical and mental perspective, all of the world's spiritual knowledge so He could properly relate to, appreciate, and understand how men and women viewed life since their fall from grace. He also knew He had to do so to fulfill the prophecies of His life. If we take that same perspective of being open to others' spiritual perspectives and principles, we will further broaden and enhance our own perspectives and principles while also showing them the truth, essence, and value behind our own. Stop looking for what is wrong with others' perspectives and principles when they are not exactly the same as yours. Instead, look for the common thread between the two and then see if you can find an even broader perspective of your own from theirs. If their perspective is totally opposite from yours, that does not make your perspectives and principles any less valid.

The next equally important key for continued maturation is practical application. Practical application is the choices, actions, and reactions put into active use to life's experiences and instances. It differs from vicarious learning because what is learned is based on an actual choice, action, or reaction and the outcome that results from that actual choice, action, or reaction. Let me put it another way for further clarity. A woman can vicariously learn, by watching her best friend have a baby; that having a baby is a difficult, painful process. She can even gain further vicarious knowledge through talking with her friend about the process of having a baby. However, she will not truly gain actual, practical application and know how difficult and painful having a baby is until she actually has her own and endures the labor pains and other aches and pains that accompany having a baby. Vicarious learning is very valuable in shaping the choices and decisions we make. But, we must still choose to act, not act, react or not react, in order to apply what we learn practically. Practical application, in the context of continued maturation, is simply exercising our "free will" to choose our action or reaction to life's choices and experiences balanced with, and tempered by a whole, three-dimensional perspective, (spirit, mind, and body). These practical application choices ultimately define our properly ordered and complete, (spirit, mind, and body), or improperly ordered and less than complete, (body and mind, or body, mind, and maybe spirit) actions, choices and reactions. The single, most distinct difference between man and woman and all other life forms on earth, (animals, vegetables, and minerals), is our unique ability, through practical application to life's experiences, to choose freely. Nature has a clearly defined, instinctive pattern. Animals follow natural, instinctive laws of behavior to survive. There are distinctive seasons; winter, spring, summer, and fall. The earth follows a distinctive orbit through space. You can be sure of this: our unique ability, through practical application, to choose freely sets us apart and makes us God-like because we freely choose to shape our life's course, pattern, and direction through this practical application and freedom of choice. The Bible makes this point very clearly and shows that God, Christ, and the Holy Spirit exercised that same practical application and will to choose. In Genesis throughout the creation and origins of earth, animal life, and man and woman, two small, but very powerful words validate their practical application and free will to choose, "Let Us."

"Let Us" precedes everything that was created in the Heavens and earth. In making day to day choices in life, we also exercise our powers to choose freely. It was established from the very creation of man and woman that they would have the free will to choose as God, Christ, and the Holy Spirit did.

Even before Adam and Eve fell from grace, God gave them the authority and dominion over all of life on earth. Genesis, Chapter 1, verses 27 and 28 states, "So God created man in his own image, in the image of God created he him, male and female created he them. And God blessed them and God said unto them, Be fruitful and multiply, and replenish the earth, and subdue it; and have dominion over the fish of the sea, and over the fowl of the air, and over every living thing that moveth upon the earth." God also told them about the Tree of the Knowledge of Good and Evil and advised them not to eat of it. (see Genesis, Chapter 2, verse 17). However, God did not take away their authority to choose to disobey His commandment to eat of the forbidden fruit. They, at the very beginning, had the ability to apply their free will practically and choose freely to disobey God and ultimately did.

The ability we have to choose the direction, course, and outcome of our lives freely is our most special, unique gift from God. Whether you realize it or not, yesterday's and today's choices very much determine the future outcomes of your tomorrows. Practical daily application takes on a far greater significance when you realize that each action, reaction, or inaction affects the future outcomes in your life. Have you ever looked back over your life at a choice you did not make and wonder how your life would have been different if you had made that choice? Let me give you my own personal example. I was one of the star players on our high school basketball team. After we won the state championship, a scout for one of the local, very well respected colleges approached me and asked me to play in a high school all star game with two of the other top guards in the state. I acknowledged him and even expressed an interest in playing. But, I never followed up with him afterwards and did not play in the game. At the completion of my senior year, I had dreams of playing basketball at one of the ACC powerhouse schools like Wake Forest or UNC Chapel Hill. I did not even think twice about following up with the scout from that local college, since it was not an ACC school. Ultimately, none of the ACC schools I dreamed of playing for recruited me to play for them. I ended up going to another school and did not even get the chance to play basketball there either. The school I attended offered me an academic scholarship and only an opportunity to try making the basketball team as a walk on. Consequently, I chose not to even play college basketball. Periodically, I think back on the opportunity I had to follow up with the scout for the local college, but did not act on. I wonder how differently my life would have been if I had chosen to follow up with him and play in that all star game. I wonder what would have happened if I would have chosen, instead, to play for his college and wonder how differently my college career athletically and academically would have been. Yet, I still realize that I chose not to pursue that path and it was totally my choice that determined the outcomes that followed. I now realize afterwards that this opportunity may have been my best opportunity to use my basketball talents and take them as far as they would take me. In a way, I will always wonder how far I could have taken my basketball talents since I did not pursue that path and ended up not playing on the college level at all.

What are the benefits of introspecting, reflecting, and reasoning from "within-without" on past choices? The benefits are increased wisdom, knowledge, and understanding that increase maturation towards complete maturation. A number of years have passed since I left high school. In introspecting, reflecting, and reasoning from "within-without" on this choice, I know my decision not to play in that all star game, or pursue that local, well respected college, led me towards focusing on academic development instead of athletic development. I may have had a very, very small chance to become a professional athlete but the odds were far, far greater that I would not have. I played the position of guard, and at that time the NBA was patterning their guards after the most successful guard of the time, Magic Johnson. Magic Johnson was a very tall guard, being 6' 8" tall. I was only 6' 1" tall. I also practiced with the basketball players at the college I attended and realized the players on the team were much stronger than I was. I was equally as athletic in all other respects. My high school program did not focus on weight training for basketball players. I did not have the opportunity to attend basketball camps like a lot of the players on the college team did since they were young. Fortunately, I had obtained an academic scholarship that required me to maintain a 3.0 grade point average in order to keep my scholarship. I was serious enough about obtaining a college degree to realize it was risky to play college ball as a walk on because I had to maintain a 3.0 or better grade point average. As I have reflected over this choice, I know with certainty I made a wise decision not to play given the circumstances because my college education has been far more valuable to me than pursuing playing basketball with the limited potential of where my basketball career could have taken me under the conditions I had to choose from. I now clearly have that wisdom, knowledge, and understanding, through introspecting, reflecting, and reasoning "within-without" that I made the right choice in this instance. However, there are other instances where I realize I made wrong choices and suffered through the outcomes that resulted from those wrong choices. It is critical to understand that it is not whether your choices, actions, and reactions are right or wrong. What is most important is that you look back, reflect, introspect, and reason from "within-without" about those choices, actions, and reactions and acquire continued wisdom, knowledge, and understanding for future choices, actions, and reactions based on your past outcomes.

Obtaining complete maturation in life may seem impossible since we are so physically oriented, dominant and surrounded by a physically dominant world. However, Christ proved it is not impossible to obtain complete maturation! Just as Christ did, we must be diligent in seeking the highest truth behind spiritual texts, learning vicariously from others' experiences, being humble enough to have the willingness to continue to learn, applying proactively the proper practical applications in the choices, actions and reactions to life's day-to-day issues, and reasoning "within-without" to introspect, reflect, and analyze each and every experience we have on a daily basis. If we are diligent, earnest, and humble enough to actively try to implement these important spiritual principles and keys in our lives, we will see continual growth in our ongoing maturation towards spiritual reorientation and wholeness.

Continued maturation is an everyday, ongoing process. Let me leave you with these Spiritual Truisims in closing.

Chapter 5 Continued Maturation Spiritual Truisms:

- Spiritual texts have more than one meaning. God knows that those who seek to understand will analyze, introspect, seek spiritual counsel, meditate, and interact with others to understand. Our understanding and knowledge of the various meanings become more complete as we mature, (much like our understanding broadens as we grow from infant to child to adult). In time, as we diligently seek to understand we will uncover the full perspectives, insights, and meanings specific to our own unique spiritual needs.

- The spiritual truth behind spiritual texts has always been a threat to the physical dominance of the world. Spiritual truth is the only thing that will bring into full perspective and awareness the balance of man and woman, (spirit, mind, and body) as God intended us. Restoring full, three dimensional balance is contrary to the physically dominant nature we are born into.

- Webster's Dictionary defines maturation as: "The emergence of personal characteristics and behavioral phenomena through growth processes."

- Maturation, in its simplest form, is physical maturation and is dangerous to us. It is dangerous to us because it is physically dominant in perspective and focus and causes us to act and react to our physical wants, desires, and needs in life without the benefit of spiritual and mental balance and wholeness.

- Maturation, in its more complete form, also includes growth of our spirits and minds, balanced with physical growth and development.

- Whether we mature simply or completely is based on whether we "live life" to experience the wholeness of our being, (spirit, mind, and body), or let life "live us" through just living to experience the physical in life after physical wants, desires, and needs.

- We must choose to act, react, and be proactive to life as life's events, circumstances, and situations present themselves. Or, we end up, through our inaction, always reacting to life's events, circumstances, and situations based on our physical response to life or the influence of other things outside of our full spirit, mind, and body capacity.

- Complete maturation is a process that requires, above all things, personal desire, inner, introspective thinking – "within-without" reasoning focus, nurturing, guidance, and conviction from spiritual counsel, mentors, texts, and practical daily application.

- Analysis is one of the essential key skills for continued maturation.

- One of the most clearly distinctive differences between man and woman and God Almighty is we only have the ability to analyze with total, clear wisdom, knowledge, and understanding our life's experiences during and after they have occurred. God knows our past, present, and future.

- As you reason, introspect, and analyze your now and past, you will begin to understand how your choices, actions, and reactions led to the outcomes, (good or bad), that resulted.

- You can use your increasing wisdom, knowledge, and understanding gained through your reasoning, introspection, and analysis to shape and prepare your choices, actions, and reactions of your future.

- Your awareness of the process of analysis and the need to choose a different choice, action, or reaction is the first step in acquiring wisdom, knowledge, and understanding.

- Yes, it is still possible to make choices, act, and react in a spiritually proper way even when we are physically dominant. Those times when we do is God graciously showing us what we are capable of and also God's way of showing us we are more than just physical.

- While we are primarily born into and subject to physical orientation, we begin the process of spiritual rebirth and awakening through our spiritual environment as we grow from infancy towards adulthood. So, there is a spiritual conscience and voice within that whispers to our physically dominant natures what is spiritually proper and right in our choices, actions, and reactions.

- When we do introspect, reflect, analyze, reason and apply the proper spiritual actions and reactions, we realize there is a part of us, (our spirits), that yearns to exist and complete our wholeness.

- We gain an inner joy, happiness, peace, and fulfillment unlike any other feeling we are capable of experiencing, (physically and mentally) from proper spiritual actions and reactions. God created that yearning to lead man and woman back to wholeness and away from the physically dominant nature Adam and Eve chose.

- That very first proper choice, action, or reaction to the small, quiet, Holy Spirit inner voice speaking to us is the beginning of our awareness of the last and most significant part of our being

238

and likeness to God, our spirits. No mental or physical wants, desires, or needs can replace that part of our being.

- Humility is one of the essential keys to continued maturation. Yet it is one of the most difficult traits to keep focused on.

- The more we learn, the more we should realize how much we do not know and further appreciate the vast and infinite distance between God's knowledge and our own.

- Humility requires an open mindedness to the reality that one must constantly seek to know more and also be open minded enough to realize that one will never know all there is from a purely mental, physical, and spiritual standpoint. Based on our uniquely specific and specifically unique needs, there is a finite amount of knowledge we each must attain to fulfill our wholeness and purpose for life.

- Once our inner-spirit within us is properly mature and re-oriented, then and only then, do we have the capacity and access to the full, infinite wisdom and knowledge of God, Christ, and the Holy Spirit. It is important that we seek and acquire access to that wisdom and knowledge specific to our own intimate needs and purposes.

- Be aware and conscious of your physical, mental, and intellectual pride and arrogance. As you are, you will properly focus and put into perspective when you are allowing those traits to stifle your humility. You will keep an open mind, heart, and spirit to learn and be of use to others' learning.

- Christ was a living example of open-minded humility. Although He was all-knowing, (and realized in His Spirit He was all-knowing), He still chose to seek to learn all He could about the spiritual teachings of all cultures during His life.

- Practical application is another very important key for continued maturation.

- Practical application, in the context of continued maturation, is simply exercising our free wills to choose to act, or react, to life's choices and experiences in a manner that is properly balanced, aligned, and oriented fully, (spirit, mind, and body). These choices, actions, and reactions ultimately define our complete, or less than complete development through life.

- To think about, (from "within-without"), your own choices, actions, and reactions is an inner view of how you are living life. It forces you to incline your heart and spirit to your spiritual environment, wise spiritual counsel and conviction, and daily bread ingredients so your choices, actions, and reactions are spiritually focused, oriented, and whole.

- There is a big difference between judging and criticizing others and serving as a positive influence to others through the choices you make once you properly reason from "within-without."

- If you lead others through your choices, actions, and reactions, lead by example out of love and compassion, (just as Christ did), not out of judgment and criticism.

If you are blessed to live a long, normal life, continued maturation will occur in your life. The question you must ask is will you mature in your most simple physically dominant form or will you mature wholly and completely, spirit, mind, and body? It is my hope that you will take charge of your maturation to assure it is whole and complete! It is my prayer that the substance of this chapter will give you invaluable insights and perspectives that will enable you to actively and proactively "live life" and mature to your fullest potential and capacity! **Use the questions below for your own personal insights and reflections.**

Question(s) 1:

What important spiritual texts do you rely on to seek spiritual knowledge, wisdom, and understanding? Are there higher truths beyond your present understandings and perspectives and further questions you have yet to answer?

Thoughts, Insights, and Reflections

Question(s) 1 Thoughts, Insights, and Reflections

Question(s) 2:

Are there fundamental, key points of references within your current wisdom, knowledge, and understanding that will give you further understanding and clarity of the spiritual texts you presently rely on for spiritual guidance and direction? Can you outline and define these key points of references below and use them as a foundation to seek higher, absolute truths?

Thoughts, Insights, and Reflections

Question(s) 2 Thoughts, Insights, and Reflections

Question(s) 3:

What critical keys identified in this chapter, (self analysis, initial spiritual reorientation, vicarious learning, humility, and practical application) are most important for your present active complete maturation? Can you define how these keys are important to your present maturation towards complete maturation? How can you use these critical keys to better understand others?

Thoughts, Insights, and Reflections

Question(s) 3 Thoughts, Insights, and Reflections

Question(s) 4:
What other personal perspectives and understandings have you gained from this chapter? What other spiritual texts and resources can you use to further enhance your knowledge?

Thoughts, Insights, and Reflections

Question(s) 4 Thoughts, Insights, and Reflections

Chapter 6 Christ Mindedness

When I began this quest of conveying the insights, understandings, and perspectives God placed on my spirit, I had no idea where it would lead. However, I did realize and know one thing with certainty: these insights, understandings, and perspectives are just a beginning. As this humble work began to unfold and take shape, God also helped me realize that the level of knowledge, wisdom, and understanding He was conveying through me is fundamental and elementary. Make no mistake, fundamental, elementary knowledge, wisdom, and understanding is very significant! No matter how intellectual, theoretical, scientific, philosophical, or profound a subject is, it must start with a fundamental, elementary foundation of perspective and insight. True knowledge, wisdom, and understanding are no different and start with simple, fundamental foundations and principles. Christ stated in the Holy Scriptures in the book of Mark, Chapter 10, verse 15; "I tell you the truth, anyone who will not receive the kingdom of God like a little child will never enter it." Children are wide eyed, open-minded, innocent, and curious to learn new things. Children see the simple truths of things in life that adults often complicate. Children also accept the simple truths of life because they are still innocent and have not been tainted and corrupted by their selfish physical wants, desires, and needs or the outside influences of the world with all of its material and physical trappings designed to distract us away from simple, spiritual truths.

The further in time man and woman has progressed away from their original fall from grace, the more complex, confused, and shrouded in mystic, intrigue, political, social, cultural, and intellectual babble the way became! The way back to the special, "Sacred Place" and the keys we so covet to find it, became very, very complicated long, long ago. Hopefully, these simple, elementary perspectives will bring

249

some simplicity and clarity of thought, insight, and understanding for you. If you have gained fundamental, elementary understanding, wisdom, knowledge, and spiritual reorientation through this work, then you are at the BEGINNING of your growth towards full spirit, mind, and body completeness.

When Adam and Eve made their choice to eat of the fruit from the Tree of Knowledge of Good and Evil, they had a shift in consciousness and awareness from spiritual orientation to physical orientation. They, at that point, stopped viewing themselves as spiritual beings with a body, and began to view themselves as physical beings with a spirit within. This shift began the outer, physically focused view instead of their previous, natural, inner, spiritually focused view of life and the world around them. In making that shift, they predetermined the consciousness of all men and women after them. While we do not have the choice of entering into the world spiritually fully conscious as Adam and Eve did, (because Adam and Eve relinquished that right for us with their choice), we do have a choice to RENEW spiritually oriented consciousness. God has always left a way for us to seek Him and renew our spiritually oriented consciousness through our own free will as we grow and experience life. Christ was the first person born into the world with a physical body and full spiritual consciousness and orientation. Throughout the legends and prophesies of Christ's coming before He arrived, great, learned, spiritual leaders and prophets spoke of, and knew He would come into the world just as He did with His full spiritual consciousness and orientation.

Christ mindedness is a perspective shift from physical orientation to spiritual orientation. The significance of Christ fulfilling His works and being whole is significant because God provided A MOST significant key, (Christ as a model), to the world through divinely inspired leaders, prophets, and writers to prove the possibility of restoring the proper spiritual orientation and consciousness for man and woman to aspire to. Thus, Christ was just as significant as a model example, from the first divinely inspired writings ever written about Him, as He was during His life, and as He is also even today: long after His life and fulfillment of His life's purpose. There are many essential keys for us to find to that "Sacred Place" we long for between us and God that I have been led to share throughout this humble work. Hopefully, you have acquired many of those keys for your further development. Among all of them, Christ, (as the model of complete wholeness of spirit, mind, and body) is A MASTER KEY of all these!

In spite of the numerous physical and worldly challenges we face today, it is significant for us to realize how privileged and blessed we are to have the full history of Christ's life as a model example. Until Christ's birth, men and women had to rely on their legends of prophesy in the Holy Bible, other divinely inspired texts, and spiritual leadings from their spiritual environment, mentors and teachers, and God, that Christ would one day come into existence to prove we could renew ourselves to wholeness and the full spiritual orientation we lost through Adam and Eve. Can you imagine how difficult it must have been for men and women prior to Christ's existence to seek spiritual orientation and wholeness with just the promise that Christ would one day come to provide the ideal example for them to follow? From a practical, active standpoint, it is certainly far more likely we can achieve something if we have a complete, historical example to follow and pattern ourselves after. Can we achieve that same thing if we are the first one attempting to do it with nothing to follow as an example? How much more difficult is it in that instance? Here is a simple, practical example. I can tell you a legend or story on how to fly a plane; however, I know the legend and story of flying a plane, but I have actually never flown a plane before. While I know the legend and story of flying a plane, and there are countless other legends and stories of flying planes, no one has ever flown a plane before. You can try flying a plane from my legend. Will you succeed and practically master flying a plane just from the story? Will you fail totally? Now, let's take the same challenge, flying a plane, with the benefit of a practical example to follow. Instead of telling you a legend or story on flying a plane, I take you to an accomplished flight school. At the flight school, flying planes has been mastered through thoroughly documenting all of the practical steps, skills, talents, and tools needed to successfully fly a plane from countless successful flights. There are instructors who specialize in teaching the art of flying planes, and they instruct on all levels; from first time, novice pilots, to seasoned, experienced, top notch pilots. Will having a flight school with all of the experience, knowledge, teaching, and actual, practical hands on instruction to draw from increase your chances of success? I think you get the picture. Christ was significant to men and women before He came because He was the promise of hope that was motivation for them to aspire towards restoring wholeness and spiritual orientation. He is far more significant to you and me because we now know of His life and have a PERFECT, IDEAL example to follow in our quest to attain wholeness, (spirit, mind, and body) and restore that "Sacred Place" between us and God we desire. If we seek to know intimately "Who," "What," and "Why" Christ was, we have a perfect training plan to follow.

Understanding that "Christ Mindedness" is a perspective shift of consciousness and focus from physical to spiritual is just the beginning: but it is a vitally critical beginning! I realize I have made some bold contentions throughout this book by God's leading and see no reason I should avoid continuing to do so. Sometimes, it takes a bold, shocking revelation to shock one's consciousness into shifting their thoughts about things to a whole new perspective. Some bold contentions ring spiritually true once processed and considered from deep within. Yet, bold contentions often become the topic of debate for intellectually-minded naysayers who prefer accepting the false notion that they can mentally and physically reason away spiritual truths and in some way change its reality. Spiritual truth is beyond intellectual reasoning and change. It is not bound by the logic and interpretations of men and women, but is bound to the core of Divine Principles and Universal Truths of a much higher, absolute source, God. In order to reason and accept spiritual truths fully, one must seek to know from "within-without" and also seek to align that truth with the proper sources of reference, (the Holy Spirit, the Bible and other divine spiritual texts, their spiritual environment, teachings, and leadings). All of this must be tempered and combined with the faith and trust of knowing and accepting that spiritual truth is rooted in the aspect of our existence that is foreign and uniquely different from our physical and mental natures and capacities. And that it is also closest to God in characteristics and resemblance because it is our spirits within us.

I realize I have asked a lot of you by challenging you to reflect, introspect, and think of life from a totally new perspective throughout this work. However, of all that I have asked, there is one simple, yet important thing I have requested and required from you since the very beginning: your trust. Just trust me enough to seek to validate the truth because if you seek truth earnestly, you SHALL FIND it. If you look "within-without," you will begin to process and understand the truths in your spiritual environment. It will start to cry out to you. At first, the cry may be a soft whisper in the conscious of your hearts', minds', and spirits' ear. In time, it will ring out loudly and clearly as you begin to adjust your heart, mind, and spirit and still yourself enough to hear it. As naturally as a baby knows its mothers voice, our spirits within us knows the voice of God's Divine Principles and Universal Truths once we hear them.

Having qualified the need for bold contentions, I want to make one about Christ in the context of how He is represented. Before I do, let me tell you why. It is vitally essential to understand Christ in your present spiritual environment along with what He stands for and represents. Once you have a thorough grasp of Him in your spiritual environment, it is equally vital to branch out and seek information, knowledge, and perspective from others to further enhance your perspective of Him. In the context of becoming Christ Minded, one of the most vital things we must be willing to do is expand our wisdom, knowledge, and understanding beyond where we are presently in order to continue our growth and development. My bold contention with respect to Christ is we must be willing to seek to understand Him from as many perspectives outside of our own spiritual environment and understanding as we can. Becoming Christ Minded is advancing from our childlike, adolescent, narrow state of just accepting our spiritual environment perspectives in total, to becoming an adult, and opening our hearts and minds, through introspection, reflection, and seeking the wise counsel of the Holy

Spirit, to expand beyond to others' perspectives to further broaden, enhance, and deepen our understanding and maturity. Christ did just that Himself throughout His life.

Hopefully, I have given you clear reasons why I am offering a bold contention about Christ and how He is represented. Consequently, I shall move forward with my contentions and ask that you are open enough to introspect, reflect, and seek your own wise counsel to my contentions. The ideal and image of Christ, the person, is represented in all cultures that have existed throughout the ages of time. It does not matter whether the name of Christ is Yasshua, (as it was in the ancient Hebrew language), or Jehovah, or Osirus, or some other name. It does not matter what Christ's name is in Chinese, Portuguese, German, Russian, Spanish, Polish, French, Italian, the many, many diverse languages of Africa, or any other world languages or ancient languages time has long forgotten. What does matter is that the SPIRITUAL TRUTH of the ideal of the person of Christ is known in all cultures of our existence! That has been a spiritual truth since that fateful fall from grace Adam and Eve suffered from the very beginning. It is time for us to stop trying to confine this important, foundational, key, universal truth to the primary language of the present day, English, in the midst of the many languages of all times. By accepting such a narrow, myopic intellectual viewpoint, we allow Satan to alienate us from other world interpretations and views that could very much broaden our wisdom, knowledge, and understanding of Christ in His entirety.

Let me explain why taking such a narrow, myopic view is dangerous. I am not certain how many languages have existed since the beginning of time. It is safe to say there have been literally hundreds of thousands of them. The question you must ask is this, what has been lost to our interpretation, perspective, and understanding due to our efforts to communicate through different languages? I am sure most of us, as young children in elementary school, have participated in the childhood experiment to illustrate the difficulty of communication, by starting a phrase on one side of the room and passing it on to the next student, and the next, until everyone in the room has passed it from the first student to the last. By the time the phrase gets to the last student, it is completely different from the phrase that was passed from the first student. This little childhood experiment is a simple, but clear illustration on the difficulty of languages. It is very easy to lose the full scope, perspective, and understanding in translation from one language to another. Without being open-minded enough to consider the scope, perspective, and understandings of other languages and cultures, can we be certain we have the full scope, perspective, and understanding God intended? Is it possible there are bits and pieces of God's greater whole scattered amongst all of the various languages and cultures that have existed since our beginning? Let's bring this thought process a little more current. Since we have no way of fully knowing what has been lost in the thousands upon thousands of ancient languages that have been discarded by current languages, can we at least be open-minded and mature enough to seek a broader understanding of the current languages and cultures that presently exist? My response is; yes, it is imperative, essential, and necessary if we hope to know as much as we desire, because I am convinced that every language and culture has vital and essential interpretations, perspectives, and viewpoints that enhance the part to further complete the wholeness of all that God intends us to understand. I am not suggesting we each need to go out and take extensive classes on Chinese, Portuguese, German, Russian, Spanish, Polish, French, Italian, the many, many diverse languages of Africa. I am asking that you at least be open to learning the key interpretations, perspectives, and viewpoints of others' languages that God brings into your path that are different from your own. If God brings others from other languages, cultures, and environments that are different from your own, there is something within their viewpoint that He has for you to further enhance and broaden your own, and vice versa.

Here is a simple, specific perspective to make my point clear. There should be no reason a devout Christian cannot learn from a devout Muslim and there should be no reason a devout Muslim cannot learn from a devout Christian. The question each must ask is this; how can I become closer, more complete, and serve God better in my own "uniquely specific" and "specifically unique" faith from what I learn from my Christian, or Muslim brother?

On a more general and broader level, think of it this way. One who is considered an "expert" on a subject is one who knows every possible thought, ideal, point of reference, historical viewpoint, piece of knowledge, and cultural insight on that subject. How can we be experts on "Spiritual Truth" as it relates to Christ without opening our perspective to others outside our own narrow scope? We cannot! We must be willing to seek and hear all that we can from every walk of life and every culture from every walk of life that we encounter along life's journey. As we do, we must reason, process, and think "within-without" what we understand with each new source of knowledge and reference outside our own. As we do, we will realize other points of knowledge and references do not have to take away, or lessen, our own knowledge and perspective. Instead they enhance our own when we are mature enough and open-minded enough to seek a different perspective than our own. Unless we are mature and open-minded, we get caught up in the same age old trap the devil often uses to deceive us: intellectualizing and assuming from a narrow position, that our knowledge is the only knowledge that is right, and that matters. With a narrow, intellectual, physically dominant, arrogant perspective, we fail to open ourselves to seek whatever further knowledge we could gain to make our perspective more whole and complete. I encourage you to FIRST seek to understand Christ in your own culture, spiritual context, environment, and spiritual texts. Then seek to understand the nature of Christ through others who are from different cultures, spiritual environments, and points of reference. If you do, you will only add to your full and complete understanding of Him. It will also confirm God's universal truth of why Christ was purposed to exist. Christ proves this point in His life. Christ chose to study religion from all cultures around the world during His life. He did so because He understood that the universality of God's sovereign, divine laws, precepts, and principles would reflect consistently in all cultures who were seeking to apply and live by them. He also understood those common, divine truths crossed all languages, customs, and traditions. It is truly time for us to open our perspectives to the Holy Bible and other divine texts towards this same perspective shift. That way, we can draw from other spiritually inspired writings and texts to enhance, not take away, from its divine validity.

Can you imagine how awesome it must have been for Christ to be born with a spiritually whole, mature consciousness? In Chapter one, I mentioned we die in the spirit and are born into the flesh as we enter this world. I hope you have meditated on what dying in the spirit and being born in the flesh means. Just in case you have not, let me provide my own perspective for your consideration. Before man and woman are born into the physical realm, they are part of a universal spiritual realm that is infinitely present. Since God the Spirit WAS, IS, and ALWAYS WILL BE, that spiritual realm existed before God created any and all that was spoken and became physically into being. Genesis, Chapter 1, verses 1 and 2 validate this fact and state, "In the beginning, God created the heaven and earth. And the earth was without form, and void; and darkness was upon the face of the deep. And the spirit of God moved upon the face of the waters." It is that eternal, ethereal, and infinite spiritual realm of God from the very beginning that all that we know of as life in the physical sense, all of every man and woman that has been, or will be born into life, comes from. After Adam and Eve's fall from grace, man and woman lost, (through becoming physically focused and dominant), their awareness and conscious connection to that eternal, ethereal, infinite spirit realm of God. That is how when we are born into the physical realm, we die in the spirit, (we lose the original spiritual connection and awareness of that infinite connection as we become physically formed). As we grow and develop through this life, we must re-discover that aspect of who we are. Christ never lost that connection and aspect of who He was when He was born into the physical realm. His awareness was one critical key to His fulfillment of life in providing the perfect example for us to follow.

Since one of my most important resources for clarity has been providing natural, practical analogies to make my point, I'll see if I can provide one to make this clear. The world's greatest geniuses knew at an early age what they were born to accomplish in life. They had a unique awareness of their purpose and maximized their talents to fulfill that purpose. Being a student of African culture, I'd like to select as my first example, Imhotep. Imhotep was Kemetian, (known today as Egyptian). Imhotep is considered by many historians as one of the world's first geniuses, (see as a reference, World's Great Men of Color, Volume 1, page 38; Author: J.

A. Rogers). He was chief advisor to Pharoah Zoser. He was also the chief architect, head physician, royal priest, master builder, philosopher, and scholar. He is credited with building the world's first pyramid, the step pyramid of Saqqarah. This outstanding architectural achievement spawned the beginning of the pyramids, one of the world's most fascinating structures ever built. He also diagnosed and treated more than 200 illnesses of his time and wrote numerous volumes of books on medicine, science, architecture, and philosophy. While much of Imhotep's awesome legacy has been lost over time, he is spoken of extensively in Kemetian hieroglyphics that have survived on their ancient monuments. For comparison, let's take a more contemporary example of our times, Dr. Albert Einstein. Dr Einstein, by most modern scientific accounts, is the most significant genius of science whose theories on Physics has forever changed the technological understanding of the world as we know it. When he created and wrote the Theory of Relativity, he realized the awesome power behind the world's smallest molecule, the atom. He made the following quote to President Harry Truman about atomic power and the potential of the atomic bomb, "I do not know with what weapons World War III will be fought, but World War IV will be fought with sticks and stones." Please refer to "The Culture of Einstein" by Alex Johnson for reference. Dr. Einstein's theories about the laws of Physics and space are still being validated and continue to be the foundational theory that shapes our understanding of this vast universe and the physical laws and principles that govern it. He attributed his foundation of his principles to his deep reflection and understanding of spirituality. These two great geniuses are two examples of men who maximized their mental and physical potential and capacity and achieved great things as a result. There are countless other examples of other great accomplishments of men and women the world over. My point in providing these two great examples is a simple one. True, innate awareness of one's purpose and capacity, (be it physical, mental, or spiritual), allows one to fully use that capacity to do great things. Just as Christ has true full awareness of His spiritual consciousness and achieved an ideal standard for us to follow, we each have that same capacity as we seek to fully understand our own God given capacity. Christ Himself said that those who followed after Him have the capacity to do far greater things than He did. Let me give you another question to consider. Is it possible, through acquiring full spiritual wholeness and maturity, to get far more mental and physical capacity out of life? Are Imhotep and Einstein examples of the far greater works Christ spoke of? Do I need to answer these questions? I'll remain consistent and do so. Yes, they are! Imhotep and Einstein are two examples among many people who maximized their mental and physical capacity through developing themselves to full spiritual maturity.

Just in case I have not given you enough food for thought, I feel led to go further with the concept of maximizing our full, untapped potential. Medical scientists and physicians estimate that the average human uses less than five percent of his brain's capacity. As our modern, 21st century technology continues to improve the advancement of science; our understanding of the workings of the human body continues to improve. Most scientists today believe we only use such a limited portion of our brains because that portion is the active, cognitive portion, functioning and processing at a given time to achieve what our physical bodies require at that given moment. For example, if you are at work analyzing a problem, your brain is actively engaging that part of itself, (the frontal lobe), that deals with problem solving. That would be the percentage of the brain that is active if your brain were scanned with an MRI, (magnetic resonance imaging), scanner. Scientists now share the common belief that there is another portion of our brains within the remaining ninety five percent that is not actively engaged that is still functioning on a less active level. While you are focusing on analyzing your problem at work, your body still continues to breathe, your heart continues to beat, your eyes, ears, and nose continue to perform their various bodily functions. These autonomic, natural functions are still controlled by a less active part of your brain. The percentage of brain capacity being used for these autonomic body functions is under debate. Even with all of our modern technology, scientists still have difficulty determining how much of the brain's capacity we currently use. Scientist do have a much better feel for the awesome power of the brain and realize that even simple multi-tasking functions that infants can perform naturally are far more complicated to program into our most complex computers. A 2 year old can coordinate movements in the form of crawling and walking but our most advanced computers, with the most intricate, detailed programming are still not capable of simulating those simple childlike movements. My intention is not to provide an exacting scientific lesson on the brain because I am not medically qualified to do so. My real intention is to get you to realize how awesomely powerful and complex our brains are. Here is the question I want you to ponder. If our awesomely powerful brains are only being used at a minimum of five percent by most estimates, how much more awesome power are we failing to realize with the remaining ninety five percent? Here are even more important questions for you to consider. Are there much greater, higher levels of cognitive abilities we fail to access because they can only be reached through becoming fully whole, balanced, and mature of spirit, mind, and body? If there are far greater mental and cognitive abilities we are capable of, what can we learn from the lives of geniuses like Imhotep and Albert Einstein? What can we learn from Christ's life as an example of that capacity? Yes, I firmly believe Imhotep and Albert Einstein provide a glimpse of a far greater use of their mental and cognitive capacities through their achievements. Christ is still the most ideal, model example, and proves through all of the wondrous miracles He performed during His life this important truism. Hopefully, these humble insights I have been guided to share will ignite within you the desire to seek and reach greater cognitive heights within as you strive to restore wholeness of spirit, mind, and body during your life's journey.

Christ being born in full awareness of His spiritual consciousness is an awesome thing. He knew right away He was properly oriented, spirit, mind, and body. Christ never viewed Himself as a body dominated by physical wants, desires, and needs, and knew He was a Spiritual manifestation and representation of God Almighty with a mind and a body. Even as a small child, He was focused, interested, and sought after spiritual knowledge, perspectives, and teachings. He spent a great deal of His childhood astounding great spiritual leaders of His times with His profound wisdom, knowledge, insight, and understanding. In the Bible in the book of Luke, Chapter 2, verses 46 and 47 it states, "And it came to pass, that after three days, they found him in the temple sitting in the midst of doctors, both hearing and asking them questions. And all that heard him were astonished at his understanding and answers." These verses make reference to Christ the child being in the midst of the great doctors and learned men of His time seeking and also imparting great knowledge and understanding. This is significant because it is clear that Christ the child had more maturity and wholeness of spirit, mind, and body as a young child than the most learned doctors and learned spiritual leaders of His times. Can you imagine how much more advanced in His wisdom, knowledge, and understanding, even as a young child, He was? Christ's spiritually conscious awareness allowed Him to live three-dimensionally. He was complete with the proper order, maturity, and balance of spirit, mind, and body. He was whole and complete at the beginning of His life, throughout His life. He did not start life as every man and woman has since Adam and Eve's fall from grace with a physically dominant focus, susceptible to all of the physically selfish wants, desires, and needs suppressing His spiritual nature. Instead, He had awareness of His physical and mental self with all of the strengths, weaknesses, and capacities of each, controlled by His spiritually mature and enlightened consciousness of God and His relationship and oneness to God and the Holy Spirit.

From an athletic comparison, NBA legend Michael Jordan is a good person to draw an analogy from to make my point. Michael Jordan was far, far superior to his peers on the basketball court. He still remains as the standard to which all other NBA guards, players, and winners are compared to. Jordan knew his athletic talents, strengths, and weaknesses far better than his opponents.

If an opponent singled out a weakness for a particular game and attempted to exploit it to defeat him, he worked incessantly to overcome that weakness, so no other opponent could exploit it the next time. He was a whole, complete player with the most athletic talent, the strongest will and desire to win, the most competitive drive to succeed, and the most drive to maximize all of his skills to win. He not only knew his own game better than anyone else, but he also knew his competitors better than anyone, and knew their best strengths and worst weaknesses. He used his knowledge of his own innate talents, his tremendous ability to think and execute at a consistently high level, his knowledge of his competitors' strengths and weaknesses, and lastly his competitive zeal to win and be the best, to compete at a much higher level than anyone ever has. Many very successful NBA players go their entire careers playing only to their strengths and are very successful without ever working on their weaknesses or seeking to understand the strengths and weaknesses of their opponents. Other players are successful without having the desire, drive, and work ethic to maximize all of their physical talents and abilities, or become the best as he did. Michael Jordan represents an ideal model for future young players in that he sought to be as whole mentally and physically as he could be to be the best.

With respect to the spiritual orientation and wholeness we are seeking, Christ is clearly the ideal for us to follow because He had the maturity to understand fully who He was three dimensionally, (spirit, mind, and body). He had to know His complete physical and mental strengths and weaknesses in order to relate to what men and women face in being born physically oriented. However, He had the maturity to understand how to keep spiritually focused, driven, controlled, and practically applied His maturity and knowledge to His daily life experiences to provide the ideal example for us to pattern ourselves after. Since we are born into the physical and die in the spirit at birth, we have to relearn through our spiritual awakening, development, and reorientation what Christ knew from the very beginning. His ideal and perfect mastery of spiritually governing his physical and mental capacities is not only a model for us, it is also the PROOF we need that it is possible! In order for the student to become the master, he must have a perfect standard to follow. Since we are not born, as Christ was, with full, mature spiritual consciousness, we must work, like Michael Jordan did, at overcoming our physical and mental weaknesses once we begin our spiritual reorientation from physical dominance to spiritual focus.

There is a very popular saying that was originally credited to Mao Zedong, one of China's prominent leaders of the early 20th century; "Mind over matter." This saying was also popular in the 60's and 70's and speaks to the power we have within us once our minds and wills are properly focused and applied. A properly focused and applied mind can overcome any physical obstacle, challenge, limitation, and restriction to accomplish what it is set upon. Let me offer for you a new saying that will further fine tune this perspective, "Spirit over mind over matter." Hopefully you are progressing along the continuum of spiritual orientation and can see the tremendous power and value to "Spirit over mind over matter." I'll offer my usual insights on what I have been led to share. Once you temper your mental thoughts with the spiritual laws, precepts, principles, recipes, and leadings as you progress through life, your actions, decisions, and choices will be mature, whole, complete, and fulfilling to you spiritually, mentally and physically. If you recall that I spoke of the mind being the conduit for actions and reactions to life's choices, then, you will also recall that if you are physically focused, then the dominant thoughts that prevail in your mind will be towards selfish physical wants, desires, and needs. With a "Spirit over mind over matter" approach, you now temper those thoughts with all of the essential spiritual laws, precepts, principles, recipes, and leadings to make certain your actions and reactions are mature, whole, and complete to you spiritually, mentally, and physically. How will this make your life's actions, decisions, and choices more satisfying, fulfilling, and complete? It will in that you are now living three-dimensionally and nourishing your whole self, (spirit, mind, and body). You will certainly find inner peace, happiness, joy, fulfillment, and contentment in your decisions, choices, actions, and reactions and how they affect everyone you meet and greet along life's journey.

However, the outcome of this three-dimensional nourishment is far, far greater than that! Let me again call upon your memory regarding my discussion on the physical self versus the spiritual self. Remember, the physical self is as selfish as the spiritual self is selfless. So, when you allow yourself to fulfill your physically dominant wants and needs, it is often singularly focused on you and your wants, desires, and needs. Don't forget to factor in the outside influence of the Devil and his whole aim to use his influence of the world with all of its physically appealing trappings. Most often, our efforts to seek physically dominant wants and needs come at the expense of others. This creates a vicious cycle because just as we seek to satisfy our own selfish physical wants, desires, and needs, others who are also physically dominant do the exact same thing to us in return, (the spiritual law of reciprocity is in effect here). The moral of this scenario is simple. We may satisfy our own selfish physical wants, desires, and needs today at the expense of others, but we will be the victims of someone else, (through the spiritual law of reciprocity), tomorrow doing the exact same thing to us. There is one added input pertaining to reciprocity I'd like to add. The reciprocity is usually exponential in either direction, good or bad. If you hurt or harm others through your selfish desires to fulfill your physical wants, desires, and needs; you can rest assured that the returned hurt, harm, and pain will be exponentially greater when it comes back to you! It has been my own personal experience that when I have applied the proper spiritual laws, precepts, recipes, and teachings to give of myself to help others selflessly, the returning good things have been far more exponential. God, as the proud parent to His children would far rather reward our rights than punish our wrongs. I challenge you to put it to the test for yourself and see what happens.

Christ was a Master of using His spiritual consciousness, power, maturity, and understanding over matter. It is clear from His story that He applied the proper spiritual laws, precepts, principles, and recipes over His mind, body, and all external physical and mental challenges He faced. Think about it for a second -"Spirit over mind over matter." "Spirit over mind over matter" is the original equation God applied from the foundation of creation. In the beginning, all that God formed into matter was ordered into creation, (heaven, stars, planets, earth, man, woman, nature, and animals), by the "Spirit," (God, Christ, and the Holy Spirit) calling that matter into existence. Scientifically, the process of "Spirit over mind over matter" is defined as the Big Bang theory. Some scientists who are scientific purists believe that all of life originated from a colossal big bang at the beginning of time. They have elaborate models and equations detailing and explaining how carbon, hydrogen, nitrogen, oxygen, dust particles, and a host of other trace chemical elements formed into a large ball of fire and chemicals under tremendous heat and stress. Ultimately this large ball exploded and from that cataclysmic explosion, life began. The most important, yet simple question, these learned scientists cannot answer is one a simple preschool child would ask. How did it all begin? Who created the chemicals, formed all of them into a ball of fire, and created the heat and pressure that caused it to explode? Scientists are as perplexed as the doctors and learned leaders were when Christ the child asked questions in the temple when you ask them these simple questions.

Getting back to the perspective of "Spirit over mind over matter" as the original equation, let me offer another dayto-day example to emphasize the point. An inventor first births an idea in his head before it is ever physically created. In birthing that idea, he goes through a series of mental analyses in his own mind about the specific details, concepts, and workings of that idea. The idea may form from his awareness of a need for something that is useful or needed to improve of fill a need he has. It does not matter why the inventor births the idea. What does matter is just as God thought first of all He created, the inventor, (like God), originally thought of his idea before attempting to create it. So this idea was first just a thought, thing, or concept, (remember thoughts are things), that does not even exist as we know existence, (in a physical sense), until it is physically made. Once the inventor begins to construct the idea on paper or computer, and later builds a prototype or model, he makes it into a physical thing. When the final idea is completed, it has become a physical, tangible invention created for whatever purpose it was designed. Whether the inventor realizes it or not, he has applied the principle of "spirit over mind over matter" just as God does. The final invention was called or created from that which was not, (it was originally just a mere thought or concept), into its final form. In the simplest sense, that is how "Spirit over mind over matter" works.

There are still more aspects to "Spirit over mind over matter" I need to explain. If you recall in Chapter One, (Principle three), I talked about how thoughts, words, and expressions are things. Christ understood the significance of how thoughts, words, and expressions are things and their significance in the concept of "Spirit over mind over matter." He knew, as a Master would, that His thoughts, words, and expressions are things that exist in the spiritual realm until called into the physical realm. One clear, practical example among many in the Bible is the numerous occasions He turned water into wine. Christ was present at the beginning of all that was created. So He knew how to express His words to make or create whatever He desired, such as changing water into wine.

In a more practical daily life experience, how is "Spirit over mind over matter" applicable to you? Have you ever thought of someone during the day that you have not heard from in a long time and within a short while received a call, email, or saw them face-to-face soon afterwards? If so, your thoughts of that person became, and called that person into your presence. When you heard from them or saw them, I am sure your comment was, "I was just thinking about you earlier today or this week." Now comes a more important question that you may have even been asking when you read about thoughts, words, and expressions being things in Chapter One. Why can't we make our thoughts, words, and expressions manifest all the time as God does? My response is a simple, straightforward one. The reason we can not is we are not fully mature when we are physically dominant and led to seek after our physical wants, desires, and needs. We begin to see, as we grow and mature towards spiritual orientation, the relationship between our thoughts, words, expressions, and actual manifestations regarding them as we grow. In fact, we may very possibly begin to see the correlation while we are physically dominant in nature. It is important to realize that our thoughts, words, and expressions are powerful resources. Any powerful resource can be a tremendous asset, (when properly used), or a tremendous danger, (when used improperly). An adult who has been properly trained to use a gun knows a gun is useful for hunting and protecting him from danger. A child can take that same gun and point it at another child and kill them while playing because they are not mature enough to understand how dangerous it is until it is too late. If we are not maturing towards spiritual reorientation, the danger in understanding that our thought, words, and expressions are things is we can choose to use the power behind those thoughts, words, and things to satisfy physical wants, desires, and needs. Christ chose what He said very carefully! It is also clear He chose His thoughts very carefully as well based on what He said. He also chose how He said things very carefully. He acknowledged the power of God the Father and the Holy Spirit and sought their power, guidance, grace, and insight through prayer because He realized the need to stay connected and balanced as a physical man in a physical world. He always applied "Spirit over mind over matter" with His thoughts, words, expressions, and actions.

This new perspective shift to "Spirit over mind over matter" is another important key to the "Sacred Place" you are seeking. Now that you have another new perspective to include in your progression, how do you pattern after Christ to reach wholeness? First of all, recognize that awareness of a new perspective is another beginning point. I realize you must feel as if there are many beginning points as you progress through this book! I agree, there are many new beginning points as we grow and evolve through life. Do not get discouraged by new beginning points, but accept them each and realize without new beginning points, there is no progression from where you are.

One of the mistakes we make as adults in life is to make the assumption that we reach a point where we don't need to continue to grow. Since life is a dynamic, ever-changing process, how can we ever think we can reach a point where there is no need to grow and change? If we do, do we in essence stand still? Do we go backwards, or are we left behind as the changes around us occur? Is part of life's journey about how we grow and adapt along the way? I hope you are introspecting and answering these questions because they are not rhetorical ones. Three simple words convey my response, YES to all of the above! We stand still, go backwards, or are left behind if we fail to seize each new beginning as an opportunity for further progression and development. That beginning point, combined with the many, many other insights and perspectives I hope you have gotten through reading this humble work, should be the beginning of a perspective shift to change the way you think and approach your thoughts, actions, reactions, and decisions in dealing with everyday life choices. As with many other beginnings you have arrived at, it will take time, practice, patience, successes, and even failures, to grow and progress into your new mindset and perspective shift.

One of the major, key challenges we must face in making our perspective shift to "Spirit over mind over matter" is our physical emotions. Everyone is emotionally sensitive to something. Everyone has insecurities about some aspect of their person, (be it a physical attribute such as height, weight, or facial features), or a mental aspect, (they may feel less intelligent, or not as talented in some way as someone else). It is those emotional sensitivities and insecurities that trigger our emotional response and reactions to life that become a negative barrier that gets us out of focus and balance and drains our energy towards the positive, productive perspective shift of "Spirit over mind over matter." Just as positive thoughts, words, and expressions produce positive outcomes, negative thoughts, words, and expressions produce negative outcomes.

So you may say, think, or express something based on your own emotional sensitivity and insecurity that becomes negative or harmful for you and others. Or, you may say, think, and express something based on your emotional sensitivity and insecurity that you fully intend to cause harm and it does just that: causes harm. Again, I remind you to keep the law of reciprocity, (what you do comes back in return exponentially), in mind. How can you overcome and properly manage your actions, reactions, and decisions when your emotional sensitivities and insecurities are triggered?

The absolute best way to answer that question is to go back to our model source, Christ. How did Christ respond to things people did that affected Him emotionally? One of the most powerful examples of His response in the Bible is in the book of Luke, Chapter 23, verse 34. Christ made one simple, yet profound statement in this verse, "Father forgive them, for they know not what they do." Christ sought forgiveness against the Romans and Jews who had just persecuted and crucified Him on the cross! Christ chose to return love and kindness to those who tried to hurt Him because He knew He had to set the perfect example of how to react to His feelings when people hurt Him so others would have the proper perspective on how to deal with the same instances in their lives. Christ, being mature and whole, (spirit, mind, and body), recognized that beyond His own personal negative emotion and pain, was the true nature of Who He was, and also what He wanted to give to others with His thoughts, words, and expressions – Love. What do you think the reciprocal return is for you when you respond, as Christ did, to negative emotions with a positive thought, word, or expression for the person who hurt you? I can speak from personal experience. When I have chosen to apply positive thoughts, words, and expressions or prayed for forgiveness for someone else who created negative emotions and hurt me, I have always been blessed with good things in return for me and the other person. Often, I have found that the other person came back to me later and confessed he did something wrong out of his own selfish wants, desires, and needs or because of his envy or jealousy of me. He learned, through how I responded to him, that he was wrong and chose to change not only his view of me to one that gained their highest respect, but he also changed his view of himself in making choices, and how those choices affect others. The true essence of the love Christ displayed is tested MOST when we must give it when someone gives us the exact opposite and causes pain. When you can give that love back through your positive thought, word, expression, or prayer, your positive exponential return is always guaranteed. Often, that positive impact will also change the very person or persons who selfishly caused you pain as well.

On the other hand, I have also experienced the negative reciprocity of thinking, saying, or expressing something harmful to someone who hurt me only to have that pain return more severely to me through other later experiences. It truly does work both ways. Trust me on that! It is okay to mess up and react wrongly as long as you seek to learn from your mistakes and seek to change for future situations. Our wrongs and errors are far more memorable because generally the exponential outcome is far greater. Make certain that you introspect, ("within-without" analysis), seek spiritual counsel and conviction in analyzing your thoughts, words, expressions, actions, and reactions and you will have success in applying "Spirit over mind over matter" to both good and bad experiences in your life.

There is another very subtle, but dangerous aspect in dealing with negative emotional reactions you must consider. Controlling your physical impulse to act or react immediately to the situation is significant. Have you ever watched a child throw a temper tantrum? As an adult, you realize just how silly it looks whereas the child does not realize it. It only looks silly to us as adults because we have learned to control and manage our feelings not to overreact for being denied something we want. Negative emotions trigger the temper tantrum in us as adults and while we may not scream, cry, and kick on the floor. We do have a tendency to speak immediately, think, or express immediately without thinking and reasoning, about what we are speaking, thinking, or expressing. A pause for introspective reasoning is a critical MUST that we need to include in our reaction. If we can pause long enough to process out thoughts without reacting immediately, we can balance and temper our initial physical response with the proper spiritual perspective, counsel, conviction, and the proper morals, laws, precepts, and principles and respond as we should. Those initial impulses are not wholly how we feel, but are just a reaction at that instant when we are hurt. I am an easy going person by nature. Most people who know me would say that I am a laid back person. If someone says or does something to hurt or anger me, I am not easy going at that instant. If I allow myself to act or react at that instant, I would do something totally against my normal character and nature. I would regret my action later because after I had time to introspect, seek spiritual perspective and conviction, and compare my reaction to my morals, laws, precepts, and principles, I would clearly realize my reaction was not true to who I am in total, (spirit, mind, and body). One of the first things you must do to check your physical impulse to act is remind yourself that you are far more than just your initial physical emotional response. You also have a spirit with a mind to function and process how you want to act, react, and respond based on your whole complete self. It is difficult to pause and process your thoughts, words, and expressions when someone causes you negative emotional feelings. It is possible to do with time, patience, and practice, and one really great thing is the more you do it, the more natural it becomes for you to do. Christ, the Master, always took time to think about what and how He said things to make sure they were spiritually aligned with His counsel, (God and the Holy Spirit), morals, laws, precepts, and principles. He knew in order for His life to properly reflect His full complete self, (spirit, mind, and body),

He had to always use "Spirit over mind over matter" to the fullest extent.

Spirit over matter is essentially governing one's mind and body through wise spiritual counsel, leading, morals, laws, precepts, daily bread, and continued growth and maturation through introspection and reflection of life's day-to-day actions, reactions, choices, and decisions. We do not have the luxury of being divinely mature as Christ was but we must evolve towards that maturity using Christ as a model example to pattern ourselves after. If you are governing your mind through "Spirit over mind over matter," then it is okay to have mind over matter because your mind is properly spiritually grounded, oriented, and focused.

While all of the principles that speak to the essence of Christ are invaluable to your spiritual reorientation, evolving from "mind over matter" to "Spirit over mind over matter" is a foundational, core principle that is an essential principle to build all of the other valuable ones upon. With the proper perspective and "mindset shift," everything else becomes easier and clearer to understand. Through shifting your perspective from "mind over matter" to "Spirit over mind over matter" you actually make a major transition from a childlike, physically oriented nature to a mature adult, spiritually-oriented nature that is the essential foundation for all of the various tools, keys, and perspectives discussed throughout this humble work. Think of it this way. There are clearly critical stages of development in life. We generally, readily know these important critical stages from a physical standpoint (from infant to teenager to adult, etc...); however, seldom do we realize critical spiritual stages of development. Without any doubt this important, critical shift will ultimately accelerate your growth and development and lead to Christ Mindedness and wholeness.

I'm going ask another very important question. How do you discern or distinguish wise spiritual counsel from the Holy Spirit from other thoughts that cross your mind? It is important to consider this question because having the proper spiritual counsel is the foundation of putting our morals, laws, precepts, and daily bread into place and perspective as we move from physical dominance to spiritual reorientation. It is also a very important question because it has been one that man and woman have struggled with since that original, fateful fall from grace. Just as the Holy Spirit speaks and whispers to our conscious minds, so does Satan. Since Satan's primary game plan is to deceive, he most certainly uses his deception to mask his presence and voice. Satan was once the principle Arch angel prior to being kicked out of Heaven. He knows the scriptures and uses his knowledge to speak using scriptural references to mislead us. Once you combine Satan's deceptive tactics with our physically dominant, selfish desires that dictate our own thoughts in our minds, it is easy to see that our mind is cluttered with many diverse thoughts all at one time.

With all of this mental clutter converging and overlapping continuously and simultaneously, it is easy to see why it is extremely, extremely important to be disciplined, focused, and concentrated on discerning the voice of the Holy Spirit. Bear in mind that the Holy Spirit speaks in a quiet, soft, meek way, and will not seek to dominate your physical leadings or free will. One important key to discerning the quiet, soft, meek voice of the Holy Spirit is to realize His counsel and leading reminds you of the laws, precepts, and principles of your spiritual environment and daily bread to guide you in your choices, actions, and reactions. Another important key to discerning the Holy

Spirit's voice is to compare if the thoughts and suggestions you are receiving are ringing true spiritually. The best way to answer this crucially important question is to refer to the Master, Christ, as the model to follow. There are several key fundamental things Christ did continually and consistently throughout His life. His continual, consistent habits produced continual, consistent results. One of these key, fundamental things Christ did was to isolate Himself from everything as often as He could. Christ knew and recognized the importance of isolating Himself in times when He wanted and needed to meditate, fast, pray, and listen to the wise counsel of the Holy Spirit and God. Christ knew He did not need any outside, worldly physical distractions or outside influences from others around Him to take His focus off stilling His spirit, mind, and body enough to introspect, listen, analyze, and discern the wise counsel He was seeking.

I realize we now live in a world that does not value isolation, solitude and quietness. I also realize that constant, loud, overbearing noise is the normal environment most people in the world are accustomed to because the majority of the world population lives in or around large urban cities. There may have never been a time in the history of humankind that is more flooded with noise as the world is now. So, noise is definitely now the norm. I grew up in a rural, country area of South Carolina. I can still appreciate isolation, solitude, and quietness. There is a certain physical and mental stimulation to a bustling, noisy urban environment; however, it is very, very easy to get so caught up in the noise, hustle, and bustle that you fail to focus on thinking "within-without." So, the transition to thinking backwards, thinking "without-within," is a very subtle, natural thing that can occur.

I have talked at length about "within-without" thinking but I did not provide a lot of perspective on "without-within" thinking. One very easy and simple analogy to offer has been an indirect theme or focus thus far thinking led by physically dominant wants and needs. If we went from babies to childhood to adulthood programmed to satisfy physical wants, desires, and needs only, our physical bodies would dictate the thoughts that control our actions, reactions, choices, and decisions to life. On a more specific and simple level, we would eat, drink, satisfy sexual needs, and pursue social activities that are purely pleasing and sustaining of our physical bodies. Our minds as the conduit of active thought, would only process thoughts triggered by our physical bodies in times of want or need for any of these various physical things to sustain us physically. In other words, when our bodies become physiologically hungry for food, our sole mental thought would pertain to eating to fill that hunger; when we become young adults and start experiencing sexual attraction, our bodies would trigger our sexual urges and our thought would be on finding a sexually attractive mate to fulfill those urges with.

Another ideal example of "without-within" thinking is training an animal that is bred for a specific intent, for example, training a hunting dog. Hunting dogs are trained from the time they are very young pups to pursue a specific prey. An owner of hunting dogs knows the proper techniques and rituals to use in training his specific breed of dog to get them to understand how to pursue the prey they are supposed to hunt. As the puppy becomes a dog, it naturally pursues the prey it was trained to pursue because it has been programmed and conditioned through constant and consistent techniques and rituals to pursue this prey since it was small. As an adult dog, it will now instinctively pursue that prey without fail and will pursue that prey for the rest of his life.

As humans, it is probably easier now than ever before to lead a physically dominant life. My earlier analogy of progressing from baby to teenager to adult living to sustain and satisfy only physical wants, desires, and needs matches well to the physically dominant world we now live in. Without question, to live, function, and seek choices, actions, and reactions only to physical needs clearly leads to reasoning "without-within" in that the physical nature is the controlling nature without allowing any inner introspection, perspective, and conviction of the spirit and any other spiritual counsel, principles, morals, and precepts. When our selfish, physically dominant natures are combined with the influences of external worldly factors, a very dangerous situation is at hand because these external worldly factors further influence an already selfish physical nature to make the "without" reasoning even more complete. There are a lot of examples of outside worldly factors I could use as examples that we are conditioned to but the best one is the television. Many of our thoughts about politics, religion, other cultures of the world, and even very personal habits like deciding what foods we eat and what clothes we wear are influenced by what we see on television. It is not my perspective that television has no purpose. It is okay to enjoy television. Actually, the television can provide enjoyment, knowledge, and information that is pertinent for your growth and maturation. It is not okay to accept blindly as fact and truth everything you observe on television without analyzing and questioning it for yourself. It is very, very important to seek entertainment, knowledge, and information from other outside sources to validate the entertainment, knowledge, and information you are getting from the television is credible and beneficial to you in a positive, constructive, fully developmental way, (spirit, mind, and body). Be certain to seek to understand and analyze the message or platform behind the programs you watch to make sure they are in agreement with the morals, standards, laws, precepts, and principles you stand for. At the very least, qualify what you watch as purely entertainment, or something of substance. By qualifying what you watch, you maintain the proper perspective of control on how it affects you as opposed to allowing what you watch to subtly, (or directly), impact your thinking, reasoning, and beliefs.

Thinking from "without-within," as opposed to thinking "within-without" is actually far less thinking on your own individual basis, and far more acting and reacting based on the impacts and effects of outside worldly influences in making life's choices. In our present world of clutter and noise, this way of thinking is also a distracted, disjointed, unfocused way of thinking. Most of us have heard the expression, "I just need to clear my head for a second." Did that expression come from the tremendous burdens our minds carry in all of the noise and clutter of the world today? It is very difficult, (if not nearly impossible), to focus and think clearly when you are distracted by too many noises and things going on around you at one time. Whether that noise is the subtly distracting noise of some form of entertainment that you are obsessed with, like a professional sporting event, or a really loud distracting noise, like a police siren blaring late at night, you still get out of focus in either case from it. It is also important to realize that our physical natures respond to these external noises and distractions purely through our impulse and instinctive natures to react. Another way to define noise in this context is anything that gets you so physically engrossed into one of your physical wants, desires, and needs that you act and react purely on those physical impulses and fail to analyze, reason, and introspect to gain a whole perspective and view, (think with the inclusion of spiritual counsel, morals, precepts, and principles to temper your actions and reactions). I'll close my explanation of the dangers of "without-within" thinking with one reminder. One of Satan's primary tools of deception is distraction. If Satan can offer a physically pleasing noise or distraction to keep you off focus, out of focus, reacting, and acting purely to your physical impulses, he has gained the control through influencing you to think "without-within". When you are thinking this way and in essence "thinking backwards," you are so out of focus and balance that you will not hear the Holy Spirit to even discern His voice and leading.

Just as Christ did, one of the first basic things you must do to hear the Holy Spirit is to still, isolate, and quiet yourself enough to listen for Him. Everyone needs a place and space they can go to for solitude, isolation, and quietness. Finding and taking the space to force yourself to think and listen to your own thoughts allows you to begin the process of analyzing those thoughts. As you begin to process and analyze those thoughts, you also begin to find the point of reference where they originate and are tied to. One simple way to think of your thoughts is to think of them as a library of different reference books on different topics. You are the resource librarian that is responsible for pulling those thoughts for their respective needs, and you are also responsible for putting those books of thoughts back on the proper shelves. Now you can begin to ask yourself some important introspective questions to begin the process of reasoning "within-without." Think of the process of reasoning "within-without" as cataloguing your reference books. Did that thought originate from a physical shelf, an outside worldly shelf, or a spiritual shelf? Before cataloguing and replacing that thought on its appropriate shelf, consider what substance it contains, what should be retained, and where it should be retained to further your growth and development. As you begin the process of cataloguing, compare the thoughts that appear to be spiritual with your spiritual environment, morals, laws, precepts, foundation, daily bread, and counsel from the Holy Spirit. Are they consistent or inconsistent to these important comparisons? If they are not, there is a very strong possibility that Satan may be trying to approach you through the disguise of spirituality to confuse you from reaching a new point of spiritual growth, awareness, or development. If the thought is consistent, place it where it aligns in your spiritual perspective, insight and understanding, and apply it accordingly. If the thought is consistent and you are not certain how it fits yet, store it for future use, (archive it), and retrieve it when you realize where it does fit. It is equally important, (in fact, it may even be more important), to put your physical and outside worldly thoughts through the same process of reasoning. The governing principle in how those thoughts should be considered is simple. How do they align with my spiritual environment, morals, laws, precepts, principles, foundation, daily bread, and spiritual counsel? If they do not align with these important criteria, chances are you do not need to act or react quickly or store them for present or future use. If they do, it is okay to act, react, and store them accordingly for future use and need.

Now that you have quieted yourself enough to hear, analyze, reference, and catalogue your thoughts, you begin to find the voice of the Holy Spirit. The Holy Spirit is bound above all else, by TRUTH. You will begin to see the pattern of truth resonate when He speaks in that quiet, still voice of reason within you. Your spiritual conscience will recognize that truth and know the rightness of it when you hear it, (just as a child knows it has done wrong when a parent tells him). Another distinguishing aspect to the voice of the Holy Spirit is His voice will lead you towards selfless acts of the spirit, (having compassion and love through your actions and reactions to others, giving selflessly to others in need, conforming to spiritual principles, morals, precepts, and convictions for wrong doings). In time, you will begin to distinguish His voice clearly from all other thoughts and expressions that converge in your mind.

Does prayer, meditation, and fasting help us in having a discerning heart, mind, and ear to the Holy Spirit? Yes, they most definitely do! Christ used them continually and continuously so it is clear these are very important essential keys. Prayer, meditation, and fasting are important and essential because they force us to suppress our dominant physical natures when all else fails. Our physical bodies are so dominant and demanding in our need to physically exist and survive. We have a unique and delicate balance to maintain in that we must preserve the physical body in order to live life as we know it in this world. Since preserving and sustaining our physical bodies is such a prevailing, natural, ongoing part of life, it is very difficult to force that significant, natural physical nature to take a back seat to our inner spiritual natures as we begin the process of spiritual reorientation. Even after we begin the process of spiritual reorientation, suppressing our natural physical wants, desires, and needs is still our most difficult task and one I am convinced we must constantly battle with throughout our lives. A simple way to think of it is thinking of breaking a bad habit. A bad habit may only take a little while to form, but can take years and years to break and overcome. As you attempt to overcome it, it has become such a natural part of your behavior that you are not even consciously aware of it. As you become conscious that you are doing it, you then realize the bad habit formed partially because you want to do it. After you conquer or contain the desire to want to do it, you still have to struggle with stopping it because a part of you selfishly received some pleasure or benefit from doing it. Ultimately, you will reach a point where you have the conscious awareness of it, the will power to fight against it, and the diminishing selfish desire no longer to do it and begin to stop doing it. It may take you years and years to break it but it may have taken only several weeks to form the habit in the first place. This example is a very simple comparison of physical dominance. Physical dominance is far, far more difficult to overcome because unlike the bad habit, we must still maintain a physical existence to exist mentally and spiritually. We do not have the option of getting rid of our physical selves entirely because we still must sustain life physically as a temple for our spirits and minds to reside in. Through the proper spiritual reorientation, we must maturely determine, contain, order, and balance those physical wants, desires, and needs with our spiritual principles, morals, precepts, foundation, daily bread, and counsel so they keep us healthy and completely balanced of spirit, mind, and body. Given that we are so naturally physical in a physical world, we sometimes need an extra jolt to shock us into suppressing our physical selves when all else fails, and praying, meditating, and fasting are very powerful tools that provide that jolt we need. In order to overcome a bad habit, it takes consistent, continual focus. It also takes consistent and continual prayer, meditation, and fasting as a part of our lifelong discipline because we will always have the physical nature to contend with. In time, these important tools become such a natural part of our discipline and habit that we find it far easier to continue our transition from physical orientation to spiritual orientation. Praying, fasting, and meditating are sustenance for our spiritual nourishment much like our physical bodies need food, exercise, rest, and shelter for physical nourishment and good health. Through praying, fasting and meditating, we prepare our minds and bodies and properly position them to be open to spiritual perspectives, understanding, and counsel. Our minds begin to get sorted and cleared of all the clutter and noise so we can hear clearly and distinctly. Our bodies become conditioned to defer from focusing on noisy, demanding physical wants, desires, and needs to allow us to pursue inner spirit needs. Just as Christ did, we can train our minds and bodies through using these valuable tools. These valuable tools are important keys in our progression from physical dominance to Christ mindedness.

I realize I have only provided a small, very specific perspective of what Christ Mindedness is. However, I hope in providing this perspective, you more clearly have an awareness of what you must do to reflect that same wholeness of spirit, mind, and body Christ did through His life. It is also my hope that you realize that Christ mindedness is a discipline and way of life that we can each pattern our ongoing growth and development after. Christ used some distinct, specific tools that are certainly keys that are essential to finding that "Sacred Place" between us and God. True to form, I will summarize the main truisms from this chapter for your review.

Chapter 6 CHRISTMINDEDNESS Spiritual Truisms:

- Christ was the first person born into the world with a physical body with full spiritual consciousness and orientation.

- Christ mindedness is a shift in perspective from physical orientation to spiritual orientation.

- The significance of Christ fulfilling His works and being whole is significant because God provided the first significant key, (Christ as a model), to the world through divinely inspired leaders, prophets, and writers to prove the possibility of restoring the proper spiritual orientation and consciousness for man and woman to aspire after.

- Spiritual truth is beyond intellectual reasoning and change. It is not bound by the logic and interpretations of men and women, but is bound to the core of Divine Principles and Universal Truths of a much higher source, God.

- As naturally as a baby knows its mothers voice, our spirits within us know the voice of God's Divine Principles and Universal Truths once we hear them.

- The ideal and image of Christ, the person, is represented in all cultures that have existed throughout the ages of time.

- I encourage you first to seek to understand Christ in your own culture, spiritual context, environment, and spiritual texts. Then seek to understand the nature of Christ through others who are from different cultures, spiritual environments, and points of reference. If you do, you will only add to your full and complete understanding of Him.

- Christ chose to study religion from all cultures around the world during His life. He did so because He understood that the universality of God's sovereign, Divine Laws, Precepts, and Principles would reflect consistently in all cultures seeking to apply and live by them.

- It is truly time for us to open our perspectives to the Holy Bible and other divine texts towards this same perspective shift. That way, we can draw from other spiritually in spired writings and texts to enhance, not take away, from its divine validity.

- True, innate awareness of one's purpose and capacity, (be it physical, mental, or spiritual), allows one to use that capacity to do great things fully. Just as Christ has true, full awareness of His spiritual consciousness and achieved an ideal standard for us to follow, we each have that same capacity as we seek to understand our own "uniquely specific" and "specifically unique" God given capacity fully.

- Christ never viewed Himself as a body dominated by physical wants, desires, and needs and knew He was a Spiritual manifestation and representation of God Almighty with a mind and a body.

- Christ's spiritually conscious awareness allowed Him to live three dimensionally whole with the proper order, maturity, and balance, (spirit, mind, and body). He was whole and complete at the beginning of His life, throughout His life.

- Christ's ideal and perfect mastery of spiritually governing his physical and mental capacities is not only a model for us, it is also the PROOF we need that it is possible!

- Adopting a "Spirit over mind over matter" perspective is the most essential mindset to achieving Christ mindedness.

- With a "Spirit over mind over matter" approach, you now temper your thoughts with all of the essential spiritual laws, precepts, principles, recipes, and leadings to make certain your actions and reactions are mature, whole, and complete to you spiritually, mentally, and physically.

- "Spirit over mind over matter" is the original equation God applied from the foundation of creation. In the beginning, all that God formed into matter was ordered into creation, (heaven, stars, planets, earth, man, woman, nature, and animals), by the "Spirit," (God, Christ, and the Holy Spirit) calling that matter into existence.

- Christ chose what He said very carefully. It is also clear He chose carefully His thoughts as well based on what He said. He also chose how He said things very carefully. He acknowledged the power of God the Father and the Holy Spirit and sought their power, guidance, grace, and insight through prayer because He realized the need to stay connected and balanced as a physical man in a physical world.

- Christ always applied the principle of "Spirit over mind over matter" to His thoughts, words, expressions, and actions.

- This new perspective shift to "Spirit over mind over matter" is another important key to that "Sacred Place" we are seeking.

- One of the major, key challenges we must face in making our perspective shift to "Spirit over mind over matter" is our physical emotions.

- The proper way to respond to emotional pain and hurt others cause you is to give back positive words, thoughts, expressions, prayer, and love. If you respond that way, you will always be certain to avoid allowing your physical reactions to distract you from applying the proper "Spirit over mind over matter". Your positive response will yield exponential positive results for you and others as well.

- Controlling your physical impulse to act or immediately react to a painful or negative situation is significant.

- A pause for introspective reasoning is a critical must that you need to include in your reaction. If you can pause long enough to process without reacting immediately, you can balance and temper your initial physical response with the proper spiritual perspective, counsel, conviction, and the proper morals, laws, precepts, and principles to respond as you should.

- Christ knew in order for His life to reflect His full, complete self properly, (spirit, mind, and body) that He had to always use "Spirit over mind over matter" to the fullest extent.

- It is very important to know how to discern the wise counsel, conviction, and leadings of the Holy Spirit as you seek to progress from physical orientation to spiritual orientation.

- The proper way to think is from "within-without" because by thinking this way, you include and balance your thoughts, words, expressions, and actions with the proper spiritual perspectives, orientation, morals, laws, principles, precepts, and counsel.

- Thinking "without-within" is a physically dominant way of thinking and is "backward thinking."

- Think of the process of reasoning "within-without" as cataloguing your reference books. Did your thought originate from a physical shelf, an outside worldly shelf, or a spiritual shelf?

- As you begin the process of cataloguing, compare the thoughts that appear to be spiritual with your spiritual environment, morals, laws, precepts, foundation, daily bread, and counsel from the Holy Spirit. Are they consistent or inconsistent to these important comparisons?

- The Holy Spirit is bound, above all else, by TRUTH. You will begin to see the pattern of truth resonate when He speaks in His quiet, still voice of reason within you. Your spiritual conscience will recognize that truth and know the rightness of it when you hear it, (just as a child knows it has done wrong when his parents tell him).

- Another distinguishing aspect to the voice of the Holy Spirit is His voice will lead you towards selfless acts of the spirit, having compassion and love through your actions and reactions to others, giving selflessly to others in need, conforming to spiritual principles, morals, laws, precepts, and convictions for wrong doings.

- Praying, meditating and fasting are important and essential tools because they force us to suppress our dominant physical natures when all else fails.

- Isolating yourself, praying, meditating, and fasting are all very important tools that will allow you to focus away from your physical dominance and still yourself to listening, hearing, and discerning the Holy Spirit. It is especially more important to isolate yourself in the world we are in today that is dominated by noise and distractions more than ever before.

- Praying, fasting, and meditating are sustenance for our spiritual nourishment much like our physical bodies need food, exercise, rest, and shelter for physical nourishment and good health. Through praying, fasting, and meditating, we prepare our minds and bodies and properly position them to be open to spiritual perspectives, understanding and counsel.

"Christ Mindedness" is clearly a discipline and way of life. At the foundation of this discipline and way of life is a critical shift from child to adult by shifting from "mind over matter" to "Spirit over mind over matter." The simple insights and perspectives in this chapter are by no means meant to provide a complete, thorough assessment of the person of Christ. Instead, they are meant to provide basic, foundational insights and perspectives to open your own perspective of Christ based on your personal spiritual environment, spiritual texts, and teachings of Him. Use the questions below to assist your transition from "mind over matter" to "Spirit over mind over matter" and continued development toward "Christ Mindedness" and wholeness.

Question 1:

What does the image of "Christ Mindedness" convey to you now that you have been given these humble insights and perspectives to expand your thoughts of Him?

Thoughts, Insights, and Reflections

Question 1 – Thoughts, Insights, and Reflections

Question(s) 2:

What key characteristics, qualities, and traits did Christ exemplify that enabled Him to provide the ideal, model example of wholeness of spirit, mind, and body for us to follow? What can you learn in your own personal spiritual development and reorientation from Him?

Thoughts, Insights, and Reflections

Question(s) 2 – Thoughts, Insights, and Reflections

Question(s) 3:
Why is the perspective shift from "mind over matter" to "Spirit over mind over matter" a key, foundational, critical transition in your maturation from childhood, physical dominance to adulthood and spiritual reorientation? What specific insights, perspectives, and understandings can you draw from Christ's model, life example?
Thoughts, Insights, and Reflections

Question(s) 3 – Thoughts, Insights, and Reflections

Question(s) 4:

What other personal insights, observations, introspections, and perspectives have you learned from this chapter that will assist in your continued spiritual reorientation and development? What key tools from this chapter are most valuable to you and why?

Question(s) 4 Thoughts, Insights, and Reflections

Question(s) 4 – Thoughts, Insights, and Reflections

The Sacred Place Revealed

Chapter 7

One of my own personal responsibilities in approaching the conclusion of this work is to "empty out" what has been put in so I can now be filled with a newer, higher level of insight. I already know and am graciously, humbly excited that if I seek, study, and strive, that God will fill me with more for my continued progression. So, I truly hope you have been uniquely, specifically, and individually blessed with newfound, fundamental understanding, wisdom, knowledge, and spiritual reorientation through this work so far. I also ask for your collective continued prayers and patient support for any future works to come!

Writing and expressing this book has been a profoundly awesome experience. I have been writing short stories and poetry for some time. Yet, I must admit that no other work I have written to date comes remotely close to this experience. In all of my other works, I was the creator. I thought of the story, in the same ancient, time honored tradition of other writers before me. Or, I was inspired to relate a story someone shared that I felt was worthy of inspiring others, or could be useful to others. I then formulated what I wanted to express, developed the context of emotions and images I wanted to generate in the minds of the readers, and created a specific plot or moral I wanted the reader to conclude. I view writing much like a painting in that the intent is to create a visual image of the experience through the story in the mind of the reader. It is also much like a painting in that each reader's visual, mental, and emotional perspective is unique to them based on their own specific perspective. This writing has been like no other writing I have ever done in any respect. As I sat down and began writing, what was written poured through me. Each time I write, it pours through me. It spills out and over and flows freely, each respective thought and perspective flowing openly, naturally, and freely. I know what I am writing. I even understand what I am writing. What I have not known is how it would flow, nor have I had any control over how it flowed. Yet, I can honestly say, as I review it, it flows. Interestingly, each time I stop and start writing again, I am able to pick up where I left off, in spite of my not having any particular outline, structure, or plan until I sit down to write. With this work, I see myself less of an author in my traditional understanding of authors and what I have done in writing in the past. I see myself more as a humbled messenger, a vessel that has been blessed to be filled with all of what has been conveyed. My own unique, personal purpose was to pour it out for consumption for all that is thirsty for the nourishment within its truths. Yet I know I was purposed and prepared through my own "specifically unique" and "uniquely specific" tiny life experiences to be of use in this profoundly awesome process. This work is also different from any of my other writing because each person who thirsts for the substance of its nourishment will receive specifically that nourishment they uniquely need. This work has a "Divinely Universal Truth" that speaks the same message to all that are drawn to it. Yet, it is much like the painting I spoke of earlier because that "Divinely Universal Truth" is very much "specifically unique" and "uniquely specific" to each and every person according to their purposed need of spiritual growth, insight, perspective, and reorientation.

Let me give a more specific analogy of this work compared to my other writing. With my earlier writings, readers tend to draw a much narrower perspective, conclusion, and moral, like one would though viewing a painting done in black and white on a flat, one-dimensional perspective. Each reader may see the same painting, but have a slightly different interpretation of it based on where their eyes are drawn to on the painting. With this work, readers will view the picture in all its full, brilliant, radiant colors with a wide-eyed, panoramic, three-dimensional perspective. They will see the full three-dimensional, profound wholeness of the painting, as if they are standing in the midst of a live scene, and at the same time, be drawn to the "uniquely specific" and "specifically unique" beauty of the area of the painting aimed at the "eye" of their spiritual attraction and need. I trust and know you will be drawn to the truth of this work that you are seeking that is individually specific and specifically individual to you. I also know and trust you will know the truth behind what it shares because that truth is in your spirit and confirmed through your own personal and special spiritual bond to God. I also trust and know you will thirst for more, just as I do!

Of all the questions I have posed throughout this humble, reflective, introspective work, the last one I will ask and answer is the culmination of all the thoughts, insights, analogies, and perspectives I have been blessed and led to share. It is my fervent hope and prayer that God has used me as an able and ample vessel to pour out the essential foundational and elementary "keys" that are essential to finding the "Sacred Place" we so earnestly have sought since the beginnings of time. Far greater spiritual minds, prophets, leaders, teachers, and mentors than I have sought to discover and provide the keys to solving this wondrous and awesome experience we call "life." Far greater spiritual minds, prophets, leaders, teachers, and mentors than I have also provided an abundant wealth of profound insights, perspectives, spiritual works and texts, and even doctrines and teachings; that have become institutions of the highest level and standard to the age old question and questions of identifying and defining this wondrous experience called life. From another viewpoint, these same mystical questions have been pondered through science, technology, intellectual and philosophical reasoning, mathematics, physics, and any other way known to man. In the midst of all of this overwhelming pondering, knowledge, profound insight, perspective, spiritual teaching, and doctrines, I was personally led by God to one simple and profound truth. My purpose for this humble work He chose to bring through me was to bring about a simple, foundational understanding of some of the basic, essential keys to restoring life fully: spirit, mind, and body. In presenting those basic, simple, foundational keys, I have also been charged with one defining purpose in the midst of all other purposes. That one important, defining purpose is not the key! I am certain you are surprised with this revelation, but it is true!

I hope this surprising revelation has gotten your full, undivided attention. I have most certainly been led to share with you what the one key, defining purpose for this work is. However, just as I have been led to share simple insights, how's, why's, and what's throughout this work, I must now continue on to do the same thing for the sake of fulfilling the intent of being thorough and clear to assure I am giving all that is within me for your benefit and good. Make no mistake; all of the various, multiple foundational keys are significant and important keys for your self awareness, actualization, understanding, definition, and spiritual reorientation. Each chapter, ideally, contains very important building blocks, components, pieces, and perspectives to help you from an elementary and foundational perspective do self-analysis, evaluation, identification, and revelation of who you are and how you were formed and conceived wholly and fully when God created you; and set you apart as special amongst all of His awesome and wondrous creations. Each chapter is a progression from one stage to the next, from A to Z towards your self awareness from physical dominance, one-dimensional awareness, to three-dimensional awareness, and wholeness of spirit, mind, and body. Each chapter is designed to develop your ability to grow from backwards thinking to forward, introspective, reflective thinking from "within-without." By the time you progress through the various chapters, hopefully you will naturally think, reason, and introspect from "within-without" and do it so naturally that it will be as easy and normal as natural physical dominance and orientation formerly was.

Through the various, multiple foundational keys, the ultimate aim has been to provide a means to reshape and reform your perspective and awareness of the greatness of what lies within you when you realize you are a "SPIRIT with a mind and body," not just a physical body with a mind that has authority over all else. As you use these keys to reshape and reform your perspective and awareness of the wholeness of self, you will mature from adolescence towards adulthood. However, it is equally important that you realize that growth and development is just beginning. You must remember that self-awareness and self-actualization are the beginning of the

296

process of changing from physical orientation towards spiritual reorientation. The transition from childhood to puberty is a good comparison that is very appropriate to make my point clearly. As a child, you are not wholly aware of your sexuality or even concerned with the opposite sex. As you begin to enter the stages of puberty, you then begin to become aware of not only your own sexual maturation but also you become aware of your attraction for the opposite sex. That self-awareness is just the beginning point of how, as an adult, you must govern yourself in order to have a meaningful adult relationship with your eventual mate. There is still a great deal of knowledge, insight, and understanding you must obtain from your initial awareness as you mature through puberty. That knowledge, insight, and understanding is very much molded, shaped, and formed from your home environment, your day-to-day interactions with your peers, and the culture you live in that sets the governing morals and standards for how relationships are managed. This is also true for each and every essential key this book has provided to bring about your proper spiritual reorientation. Now that you are aware, know your full three-dimensional self and the proper order for your whole self, (spirit, mind, and body); the real work of transforming who you have to become to restore your full, three-dimensional completeness begins and will be ongoing for the rest of your life!

Along with serving as foundational and fundamental building keys for your self actualization to wholeness of spirit, mind, and body, this work has also been provided to help you do another very essential thing; focus on your own personal development wholly and fully. The easiest thing in the world to do is focus on, judge, and criticize others lives instead of dealing with your own strengths and weaknesses, pros and cons, assets and limitations, good and bad qualities, challenges, and opportunities. Yet, the world would be a far more compassionate place, a far more caring and loving place, a far more productive place, a far more positive place if we spend our energies on our own personal development. By focusing on our own personal development, we begin to get inside our hearts, minds, and spirits through "within-without" reasoning, and the proper counsel and conviction of the Holy Spirit, to realize we can have a positive influence upon others by properly dealing with our own life issues. We are far less critical of others when we displace that energy with the proper inner introspection, reflection, reasoning, and guidance because we realize our own vulnerabilities, limitations, challenges are shared by others; and more importantly, we find the proper solutions to have positive solutions to these vulnerabilities, limitations, challenges, and are thus not envious or threatened by the prospect that others are better off than us.

So it is most certainly my hope and prayer that each and every chapter has provided a variety of tools, keys, insights, perspectives, analogies, simple clear truths, and resources that will give you important knowledge, wisdom, and understanding to transform you in performing your own intimate personal self-focus and development.

Having properly provided the insights and clarity necessary to define why I have been led and used to provide the foundational, elementary keys of this book, it is time I finally tell you what the core purpose of this book is. The title I was led to name this book provides the answer. This book is about providing foundational, elementary keys but providing those keys is only to help get you to realize what and where the "Sacred Place" is. The "Sacred Place" is within you in your individual spirit. YES, YOU ARE THE "SACRED PLACE!" Of all of the aspects of your being that most intimately and closely connect to God, it is your spirit within that must be awakened, nurtured, matured, and developed to reconnect in order to have that special intimate relationship to God we originally lost through Adam and Eve's transgression. One of the great deceptions we are faced with is the realization I explained in the very first chapter. You are a spirit with a mind and a body, not a body with a mind and a spirit. While that seems like a fairly simple thing, it is not simple at all because without this important self awareness, you continue to view life from a physically dominant perspective. Because that physically dominant self was self-appointed, in our fall from grace, it separated our conscious awareness of the greatest identity within that connects us and identifies us to God, our spirits. Think of it this way. Our inner spiritual self is the best DNA marker of God within us because it is through that inner spiritual self that we reflect the very essence and identity of all that God stands for and means to all others we meet throughout our life's journey. From a physical standpoint, your physical mannerisms, features and characteristics are identifying features that tie you back to your Mother, Father, siblings, and other family members. Others can clearly see your physical connection to your family though these resemblances. How can they see God in you without seeing what your spiritual nature is? Does what you reflect even show an identifiable connection to your spiritual heritage?

Your inner spiritual connection to God also provides an intimate means of communication that was special and sacred to Adam and Eve before their fall from grace. Nothing else within our physical and mental capacity can replace that lost spiritual connection until we rediscover it. There are no physical wants, desires, and needs that can quench the inner thirst we possess to have an intimate communication and connection to God. A simple way to understand this is by realizing that physical nourishment is not filling to our mental needs for nourishment. We can eat until physically full but we will still require a totally different kind of nourishment for mental fulfillment. We may need to read a good book, play a stimulating mind game, relax in a cool, quiet, scenic place, have an intellectually stimulating conversation with a good friend, meditate on a positive, memorable experience, or solve a difficult problem at work to receive the mental nourishment we need. So, it is no mystery that neither physical sustenance, nor mental sustenance, can quench our inner thirst for spiritual sustenance. The greatest spiritual sustenance we seek, (just as Adam and Eve realized once they lost that intimate connection to God), is an intimate connection to God.

Let me share an amazing reality with you as it pertains to our intimate connection to God. God has never taken Himself away from us, and WAS, IS, and ALWAYS will be connected to us! It is not God that has severed His connection to us; it is us, through our physically dominant natures and lack of spiritual orientation and consciousness, which keeps the disconnection in place. God did not sever his connection to Adam and Eve. Adam and Eve severed their connection to Him. As we begin the process of spiritual reorientation, we begin to reconnect to His ever-present connection that has been there all the time. We now begin to hear that soft, quiet Holy Spirit voice that provides counsel, conviction, and perspective to our hearts, minds, and spirits, and the connection is clearly there. The only reason the connection goes in and out is we go in and out of physical dominance and focus, and in going in and out we fail to listen to, focus on, or hear His ever-present connection and voice. God is the ever present constant in this situation: we are the ever present changing ones that move towards Him and then away from Him as we continually grow from physical dominance to spiritual reorientation. One very important measure you can use to determine how well you are progressing in your spiritual reorientation is to gauge how often, well, and consistently you hear the quiet, inner voice of the Holy Spirit in your day-to-day life's choices, actions, and reactions.

I realize I cannot give you the core reason for this work, the reality that the "Sacred Place" is you and within you. without anticipating some further questions. I, myself, have many of the same questions I have posed in this book. I also realize that just as God filled me with the insights, perspectives, analogies, and keys for your benefit, He also gave me these questions so I can be as complete in my perspective as possible. Here is a question that comes to mind. Why is the world so filled with such an overwhelming amount of different sources of knowledge, perspectives, and confusion when it comes to rediscovering our spiritual connection to God? I'll stick with my customary habit of attempting to provide some insight and perspective.

There are a number of reasons that immediately come to mind on why there is such an overwhelming amount of knowledge, perspectives, and confusion in the world. I'd like to start where the confusion began, with Adam and Eve. Once Adam and Eve became physically dominant, their whole perspective changed. They were so overwhelmed with their new physical dominance that they began to get self-absorbed into all of their physical characteristics, feelings and emotions, and began to lose their once natural sensitivities to their spiritual nature and connection to God. While this transition may seem to be a fairly small thing, this transition into physical dominance was the most major thing they ever experienced. A large part of our wisdom, knowledge, and understanding is innate, intuitive, and within. A large part of our wisdom, knowledge, and understanding also comes through our actual experiences that give us the benefit of knowing from having experienced what we know. Up until that fateful fall from grace that Adam and Eve experienced, they were not even aware that they had such a physically dominant presence. Upon their initial creation they, (just like Christ), saw themselves as spirits with a body and mind. They were clearly spiritually dominant and thus their views, thoughts, wisdom, knowledge, and understanding were keenly tuned into spiritual things, spiritual views, spiritual connections, and spiritual communication with God. Before Adam and Eve became physically dominant, they had no need to focus on, react to, or concern themselves with their physical bodies. They could devote their entire efforts, energies, and focus on their spiritual interaction with God. After their fall from grace, they not only became fully aware of their physical bodies, they also experienced, for the first time, all of the wants, needs, and necessities their bodies craved to sustain physical existence. If you recall in Genesis, Chapter 1, verses 16 and 17, God told Adam and Eve they would now know about their physical necessities by telling Eve she would now know the suffering of pain through labor and He commanded Adam to work and toil for sustenance for physical nourishment. Let me see if I can provide an analogy to make my point more clear. Can you imagine what a modern day, wealthy American living in downtown Manhattan with all of today's technological advances, conveniences, and necessities would do if he were transported through time to the ice age during prehistoric times? How would his daily lifestyle change? How would his need to sustain the basic physical needs of food, clothing, and shelter change? Would the things he spent his thoughts, energies, efforts, and focus on change drastically? Would he even have time for any of the social, intellectual, or leisurely things he may have enjoyed in Manhattan? How extreme would the drastic change from wealthy, modern day Manhattan suburbanite to prehistoric ice age caveman existence be for him? Without any doubt, the differences in all of these things would be astronomical! I am sure the differences for Adam and Eve were even more astronomical than this comparison could ever be!

Adam and Eve also made another very critical mistake even before their fateful fall. They began to communicate with Satan, (represented in the form of the beguiling serpent), in Genesis Chapter 3. In beginning that communication in the Garden of Eden, they allowed an outside source to confuse the perfect, infinite knowledge, wisdom, and understanding they had access to through their communication with God. If you combine their new physically overwhelming dominance with this critical mistake, it is clear that our misinformation started at the very beginning of time. These same two key challenges, (our physical dominance and focus to understand life only through physical wants, desires, and needs), and (the confusion of God's Divine Truths); have continued to snow-ball ever since. Christ, and the perfect example He presented through His life, demonstrated clearly that we can find, hear, know, and understand God's Divine Truths in the midst of all of our physical dominance and all of the world's information and misinformation. It is my hope that the simple, fundamental keys and insights I have provided will assist you in duplicating Christ's model example!

SO NOW YOU KNOW. The most important message in this entire book is: YOU ARE THE SACRED PLACE! The question is: what will you do with this knowledge? Take from this humble book what you need to begin your journey of full self-actualization and proper orientation of spirit, mind, and body. Just remember that you are at a new and wondrous beginning. Take each life experience and each day as it comes and may your journey lead to the greater works Christ promised we are all capable of as we truly understand the fullness of spirit, mind, and body God made us to be!

With the conclusion of this book, several important final questions remain for your insights, perspectives, and reflections and I will close with these questions.

Final Question(s):

Now that you know – "YOU ARE THE SACRED PLACE" – and God has provided the tools, insights, perspectives, model example, and means to intimate access, interaction, communion, and relationship with Him, how will you apply, activate, and proactively develop your total spirit, mind, and body to become all that He created you and intended you to become? What will be your life's ministry and work and how will those works reflect HIM in YOU? How will you achieve the "greater works" for your life Christ spoke of?

Thoughts, Insights, and Reflections

Final Question(s) – Thoughts, Insights, and Reflections

Final Question(s) – Thoughts, Insights, and Reflections

Written, edited, and completed by J. Solomon Wise © July 23, 2006
Final editing on 12/12/07